A Journey of Ethnicity

A Journey of Ethnicity:

*In Search of the Cham
of Vietnam*

By

Rie Nakamura

Cambridge
Scholars
Publishing

A Journey of Ethnicity: In Search of the Cham of Vietnam

By Rie Nakamura

This book first published 2020

Cambridge Scholars Publishing

Lady Stephenson Library, Newcastle upon Tyne, NE6 2PA, UK

British Library Cataloguing in Publication Data
A catalogue record for this book is available from the British Library

Copyright © 2020 by Rie Nakamura

All rights for this book reserved. No part of this book may be reproduced, stored in a retrieval system, or transmitted, in any form or by any means, electronic, mechanical, photocopying, recording or otherwise, without the prior permission of the copyright owner.

ISBN (10): 1-5275-4309-9
ISBN (13): 978-1-5275-4309-6

TABLE OF CONTENTS

List of Illustrations viii

List of Tables xi

Acknowledgments xii

Introduction 1
  Why I Wrote this Book
    The Cham people in Vietnam
    Two groups of Cham
    The Cham ethnicity in Vietnam
    March 11, 2011

Chapter 1 14
  Champa
    Historical Champa
      Sa Hùynh culture and the emergence of Champa
      Mandala
      Hinduinization of Champa
      Riverine system
      Coming of Islam to Champa
      Vietnamese southern expansion (*nam tiến*)
      The end of Champa
      Cham outside of Champa
    Champa in Vietnamese national history
      Problems of the fall of Champa
      Being silent on the fall of Champa
      Class struggle
      Champa's own bad deeds
      Cultual exchange
  Conclusion

Chapter 2 44
Trouble in the Field
   The pre-reunification period (pre-1975)
      Front Unifie de Lutte des Races Opprimees (United Struggle Front
         for the Oppressed Races, FULRO)
      Ministry of Development of Ethnic Minroties (MDEM) (*Bộ Phát
         Triển Sắc Tộc*)
   The Communist period (post-1975)
   Troubles in the field
   Conclusion

Chapter 3 68
The Cham of the South-Central Coast Area
   Landscape of the Cham of Ninh Thuận Province
   The search for the pure culture of Cham
   Balamon and Bani
   Ahier and *awal* as a male and female dichotomy
   Awal, ahier and *akafir*
   Ahier and *awal* as the great tradition and the little tradition
   Cham traditional religion
   Orthodox Muslim Cham
   Conclusion

Chapter 4 106
The Cham of the Mekong Delta
   Landscape of the Cham of the Mekong Delta
   Champa or Angkor
   The Cham are Muslim
   Non-Islamic religious practice among the Cham in the Mekong Delta
   Hiệp hội Chàm Hồi giáo Việt Nam (The Association of Muslim Cham
      in Vietnam) and the awakening of Cham ethnicity
      Establishingment of *Hiệp hội Chàm*
      Hiệp hội Chàm's main activities
      Muda and *Tua* conflicts and *Hiệp hội Chàm*
      The meaning of *Hiệp hội Chàm*
   Conclusion

Chapter 5 136
Cham Ethnic Identity and *Dân Tộc* Cham
  Văn nghệ as a culture-manufacturing arena
  Cham fan dance
  The royal court dance: the Apsara dance
  The stereotype: ridicule as "the weapon of the weak"
  Conclusion

Chapter 6 153
The Cham Under *Đổi Mới*
  Mainstreaming Cham culture and alienation of the Cham people
  Portraits of ethnic minority people
    The Cham painted by Cao Thị Đư'ợ'c
    The works of Chế Thị Kim Trung
    The works of Đàng Năng Thọ'
  Conclusion

Conclusion 184
In the Name of Cham
  Cham as an interactional identity
  Cham as an invention
  Sacrifice for the state

Appendix 191
  Balamon funerals
    Ceremonies organized after the cremation
  Ceremonies during *Ramuwan*
  Ranks of priests
  Relationships of priests and other religious practitioners

Bibliography 198

Index 220

LIST OF ILLUSTRATIONS

Maps

1. Introduction: Location of Cham communities, Ninh Thuận and Binh Thuận provinces, An Giang Province
2. Chapter 1: Location of Sa Huynh, Tra Kieu Go Cam (archaeological map) (From William Southworth 2004, The Coastal States of Champa, Figure 9.1 in Ian Glover and Peter Bellwood (eds.) *Southeast Asia from Prehistory to History*. London & New York: RoutledgeCurzon, 2004, pp209-233)
3. Chapter 1: *mandala* and historical Viet-Champa borders (From the English version of Proceedings of the Seminar on Champa held at the University of Copenhagen on May 23, 1987, published by Southeast Asia Community Resource Center, Rancho Cordova, CA in 1994, p. iii)

Figures

1. Chapter 1: Bronson's riverine system
   A: the center at the river mouth; B & C: second and third order centers; D: the most distant upstream center to send the products to the A-based system; E & F: the ultimate producers of the trading items; X: an overseas center (Bronson 1977, 42-43)
2. Chapter 3: *hon kan*

Photographs

2-1: A textbook for learning the Cham scripts
3-1: Phu'óc Nho'n
3-2: Po Klong Garai
3-3: A group of Balamon priests outside of Hũ'u Dú'c
3-4: A group of Bani priests in Phu'óc Nho'n
3-5: Bani graves outside of Phu'óc Nho'n

3-6: Old *kut*
3-7: Balamon offerings at Po Klong Garai
3-8: Bani women wearing *khan djram*
3-9: Bani priests wearing *khan djram*
3-10: A Balamon priest wearing a *linga*-like white turban at Po Klong Garai
3-11: A Balamon priest's bags
3-12: A Bani priest's bags
3-13: A Bani priest carrying the three bags
3-14: Two *hala kapu* (*ahier* set) on the left and the two *hala tam tara* (*awal* set) on the right
3-15: A *rap* in Phu'ó'c Đồng
3-16: A torch-like object symbolizing Ja Tin
3-17: The priests' elevation ceremony at *kalaih Ramuwan* in Phu'óc Nho'n
3-18: Wives observing the priests' elevation ceremony in Phu'óc Nho'n
3-19: *Muh poh* in An Nho'n
3-20: A *chieu pang* in the position of *padang*
3-21: A *chieu pang* in the position of non-*padang*
3-22: A masjid in Văn Lâm 2010
4-1: The Cham village of Chau Giang
4-2: A pillar of a house
4-3: Mr. Dohamide
4-4: A cover of *Bangsa Champa*
5-1: A music band prior to 1975 (courtesy of Ustazah Hjh Basiroh Hj Aly)
5-2: The water fetching dance
5-3: The fan dance by Muslims
5-4: The Apsara dance (courtesy of Trần Kỳ Phu'o'ng)
5-5: The Apsara dance performed by the Cham students at HCM City University
6-1: Souvenirs made out of the Cham textile
6-2: The Apsara dance at the restaurant "Apsara" in Đà Nẵng
6-3: Lacquer paintings of ethnic minority people
6-4: An art gallery on the Đồng Khở'i street
6-5: A painting of Ding Ngoc Thang (courtesy of Ngueyn gallery)
6-6: A pastel painting by Cao Thị Đu'ọ'c (Picture taken at the gallery of Ho Chi Minh City Fine Arts University)
6-7: An oil painting by Cao Thị Đu'ọ'c (From Cao Thị Đu'ọ'c's postcards)
6-8: *Kate* festival by Chế Thị Kim Trung (Picture taken in the Ho Chi Minh City Museum of Fine Arts)

6-9: *Kate* festival by Nguyễn Công Văn (From Hội Văn Học Nghệ Thuật Ninh Thuận 2005. 74)
6-10: A terracotta sculpture by Đàng Năng Thọ' (courtesy of Trần Kỳ Phu'o'ng)
6-11: The original painting of "pray for rain" by Đàng Năng Thọ' (courtesy of Đàng Năng Thọ')
6-12: The revised painting of "pray for rain" by Đàng Năng Thọ' for his graduation (courtesy of Đàng Năng Thọ')
6-13: *Rija prong* by Chế Thị Kim Trung (From Chế Thị Kim Trung's gallery pamphlet)
6-14: *Rija prong* by Đàng Năng Thọ' (courtesy of Đàng Năng Thọ')
6-15: An old Balamon priest by Đàng Năng Thọ'

LIST OF TABLES

Table 1: Balamon and Bani
Table 2: *Ahier* and *awal*
Table 3: The Cham religion and the division of *ahier* and *awal*
Table 4: The concepts of *ahier* and *awal* among the Bani people
Table 5: Transformation of Balamon deities

Acknowledgments

I could not have carried out my studies without the help of various people. Unfortunately, it is impossible to name all the people that I am indebted to for my studies. However, I want to mention some who are representative of the body of people who assisted me so I can express my gratitude to all of you.

My utmost gratitude goes to the Cham people who kindly supported my studies and tolerated my presence in their daily lives. I especially thank the teachers and staff at the Office of Cham Language Editing Committee (*Ban Bien Soạn Sách Chữ' Chăm*) in Phan Rang city, which was not only my host institute but also the place I stayed and studied at during my field research. My special thanks go to Mr. Nguyễn Ngọc Đảo and Mr. Nguyễn Văn Tỷ. I would like to express my special admiration and gratitude to the Cham local scholars and their families for their assistance and guidance: Mr. Lâm Gia Tịnh, Mr. Quãng Văn Đại, Mr. Thành Phú Bá, Mr. Đàng Năng Qua, Mr. Tru'ợ'ng Tính, Mr. Inrasara, Mr. Musa Haji, and Mr. Muhammad Youssof. Mr. Đại and Mr. Bá were my teachers during my field research and they took me to various rituals and ceremonies, explaining to me the complicated concepts of *ahier* and *awal*. Without their help, I could not have conducted my studies in Ninh Thuận Province. I thank the Cham and the Vietnamese artists who helped my research on their works, especially Ms. Cao Thị Du'ợ'c, Ms. Chế Thị Kim Trung, and Mr. Đàng Năng Thọ'.

My appreciation goes to all the local government officials who permitted and assisted me to carry out my studies and took care of the many administrative procedures. I thank the Center for Southeast Asia and Vietnam Studies at the University of Ho Chi Minh City, which hosted me during my initial field studies. I especially thank Mr. Tru'o'ng Văn Mốn Sakaya, Professor Bùi Khánh Thế, and Professor Thành Phần for their kind assistance. Professor Thành Phần is a Cham from a Bani village in Ninh Thuận Province. He and his family introduced me to the Cham communities in the province and helped me by connecting with various local scholars and religious practitioners.

Researchers, officials, and friends at the Institute of Social Sciences in Ho Chi Minh City (currently Southern Institute of Sustainable Development) supported and assisted my field research. My special thanks go to Dr. Phan Văn Dốp, Mr. Phan Ngọc Chiến, and Dr. Lê Thanh Sang. I also thank my fellow Japanese researchers on the Cham and other ethnic minority groups in Vietnam who always provided significant information and insightful opinions: Dr. Toshihiko Shin-ne (新江利彦), Dr. Yasuko Yoshimoto (吉本康子), Dr. Mamoru Honda (本多守), Professor Mariko Yamagata (山形真理子), Professor Masako Ito (伊藤正子) and late Dr. Masanari Nishimura (西村昌也).

This book is based on my Ph.D. research at the University of Washington. I am deeply indebted to the Cham Refugee Students Association of the University of Washington whose members assisted and encouraged me to pursue the study of their people in Vietnam. My first field notebook was a gift from them. My academic progress at the University was slow and my poor English proficiency even further slowed down the process. I was fortunate to have very supportive and patient committee members. My special gratitude goes to Professor Steven Harrell and Professor Charles Keyes. It is my life's treasure to have had the opportunity to study under such renowned anthropologists.

My special thanks go to my friends who academically inspired me and emotionally supported me during my studies. Their friendships helped me to continue my studies and to publish this book: Mr. Trần Kỳ Phu'o'ng, Mr. Dohamide, Ms. Hajh Basiroh bin Haji Aly, and Mr. Sam Korsmoe. Sam shared my experiences in the field and provided me with emotional and financial support during the difficult times. He also took on the challenge of proofreading the manuscript of this book. His encouragement gave me the final push to publish this book.

Finally, my sincere gratitude goes to my parents who never once complained about my prolonged studies in the USA and Vietnam. The progressive thoughts of my father, who came from a conservative landholding family in northern Japan, never conflicted or opposed his daughter's desire to pursue her studies in a foreign land. Without my parents' understanding and emotional and financial support, I could not have become what I am now.

INTRODUCTION
WHY I WROTE THIS BOOK

My interest in Cham communities began with their refugee communities in Seattle, USA. I first became acquainted with these people when the Cham student organization held a festival called Cham Day at the University of Washington, where I was a graduate student. They invited the late Po Dharma, who was a Cham and a prominent scholar on Cham history and culture at the *École Française d'Extrême-Orient* in France. Po Dharma gave a lecture at this event and talked about the Cham people who were living in the central coast area of southern Vietnam. He characterized the Cham society as a matrilineal one consisting of two different religious groups. One group followed Hinduism and the other followed an indigenized form of Islam. He also talked about the upland Cham compared to the lowland Cham. The photos of the lowland Cham looked holy. They wore white robes and white turbans. The photos of the upland Cham looked like the highland minorities in Vietnam. In one, a man was carrying a big sword and a shield. They looked tough and war-like.

Later I became friends with the Cham students who organized the Cham Day event. These students came from An Giang Province in the Mekong Delta. They were quite different from the Cham whom Po Dharma talked about. They were all Sunni Muslims and were not followers of Hinduism nor of an indigenized Islam. The questions I had were: "Are these students also Cham? If so, then why are they Cham? Are the Cham that Po Dharma talked about the Cham from the past? Do Hindu Cham still exist in Vietnam?" I became curious about this group of people.

The Cham people in Vietnam

The Cham people are believed to be the descendants of the dominant group of the ancient kingdoms of Champa. They are considered to be a group of sea-oriented people from the past (Reid 1999; Momoki 2011). Cham people speak a language that belongs to the Malayo-Polynesian language family, a branch of Austronesiatic languages. It is argued to be the earliest Austronesiatic language. Coedès pointed out that the inscriptions found in Trà Kiệu, the capital of Champa, are three centuries older than those found in Srivijaya of southern Sumatra (Thurgood 1999: 3). Thurgood thinks that the Chamic language in Vietnam is one of "recently arrived, dialectically unified immigrant people" and suggests that pre-Chamic-speaking people arrived at the central coast city of Đà Nẵngin Vietnam (1999: 5, 251).

Champa developed at its current day location on the central coast of Vietnam around the 2nd century and accepted the Hindu culture around the 4th century. Champa enjoyed considerable prosperity from the 9th to the 15th centuries by providing significant relay ports along the maritime trade routes in the South China Sea. The vestiges of the wealth and power of Champa can still be seen along the coast of Central Vietnam (Shige-eda & Tran Ky Phu'o'ng 1997; Momoki 1999).

Approximately 132,000[1] Cham people lived in Vietnam in 1999 and their population is growing. Cham are also found in various parts of Southeast Asia, the largest community being in Cambodia, where the population is estimated at several hundred thousand. After the reunification of Vietnam in 1975, a number of Cham people left Vietnam for Australia, Canada, France, USA, and other parts of the world.

There are two distinct groups of Cham people in Vietnam if we consider their place of residence, their historical background, and their religion. One group lives in the south-central coast region, particularly Ninh Thuận and Bình Thuận Provinces (Map 1). These two provinces used to be one large province called Thuận Hải, which covered about the same area as a part of Champa called Panduranga, and they are where the largest concentrations of Cham people in Vietnam can be found. About 86,000[2] Cham people lived in these two provinces in 1999. The Cham who live in this region practice their traditional religion, which can be divided into two different groups. One group practices the religion of Balamon, which is an indigenized form of Hinduism, and the other group practices Bani, which is an indigenized form of Islam.[3]

---

[1] The National Census of 1999.
[2] The National Census of 1999.
[3] Toshihiko Shin-e argues that the group which call themselves Cham or *ahier* are not really the adherents of the Balamon religion but also believe in Allah. This is the result of a misunderstanding by French scholars on the Cham religion during the French colonial period. Though both Cham (Balamon) and Bani are adherents of Islam, only Bani practice ceremonies for Allah, while Cham (Balamon) practice ceremonies for gods known to the people prior to Allah (Shin-e 2001b: 243, n8, n9). In this book I have adopted the conventional understanding of the differences between Balamon and Bani based on local informants' explanations.

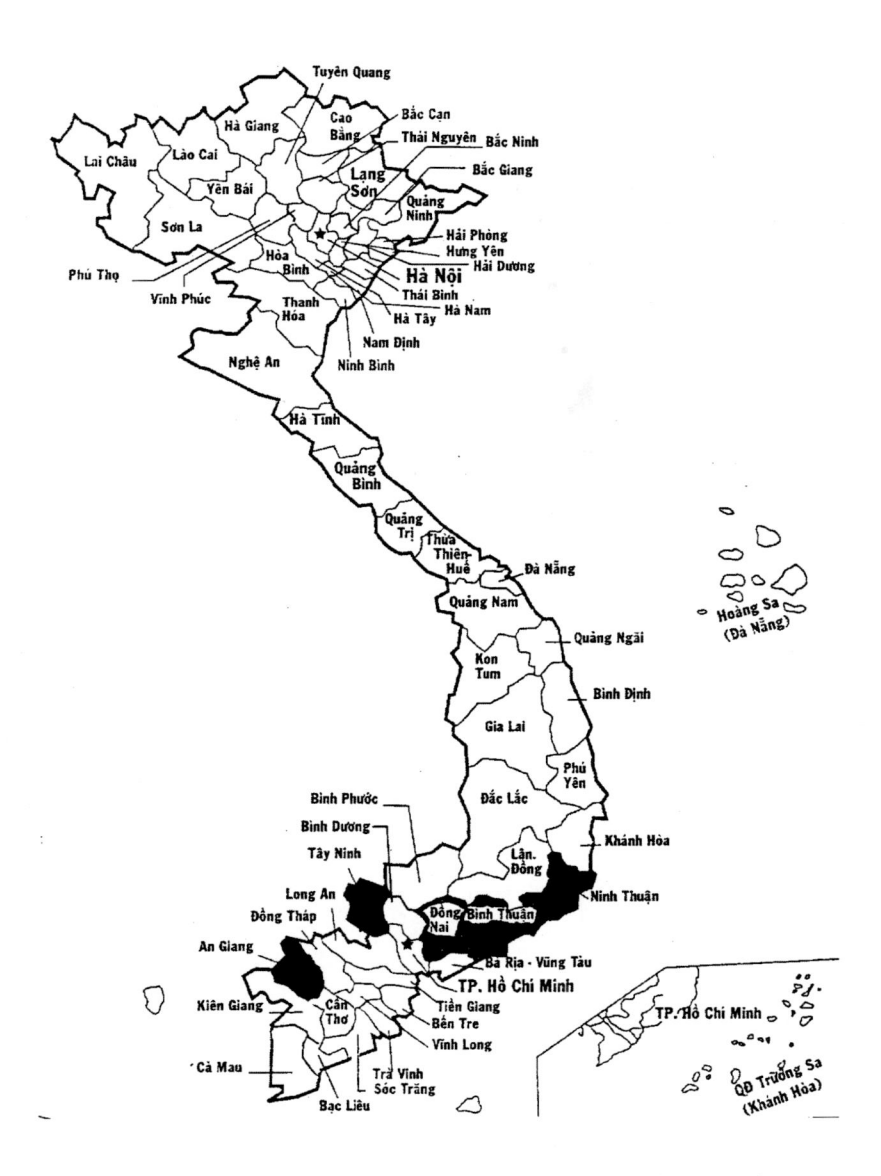

Map 1. Location of Cham communities, Ninh Thuận and Bình Thuận provinces, An Giang Province

The second group lives in the Mekong Delta, mainly around Châu Đốc city in An Giang Province, which is near the border with Cambodia. About 12,000[4] Cham people lived in this region in 1999 and they are almost all Sunni Muslims. The Mekong Delta Cham also live in Ho Chi Minh City and its surrounding provinces such as Đồng Nai and Tây Ninh (Phan Văn Dốp & Nguyễn Thị Nhung 2006: 25).

There is also a small group of people called Cham Hroi who are classified as one of the sub-groups of the Cham ethnic group. They live in an area north of Ninh Thuận called Phú Yên Province. The Cham Hroi appear to be a part of the population of Champa who remained where they were after most of the Cham had moved to the south. They have been left alone without any contact with other Cham communities, and have gone through acculturation with neighboring ethnic groups such as the Bahnar and Ede (Khong Dien 2002: 19, 24).

Two groups of Cham

I went to Vietnam for the first time in 1993. I mainly stayed in Ho Chi Minh City where about 5,000 Muslim people, most of them Cham from An Giang Province, were living then. I visited the Islamic Center for Ho Chi Minh City at a *masjid* (mosque) in the Phú Nhuận district. I was struggling to communicate with an official in both Vietnamese and English when a lady passed by us. As soon as she recognized me as a foreigner, she came up to me and asked in English where I came from. Since she had better English proficiency than him, the official ordered her to answer my questions and left us alone.

This woman, who I will call Aisah in this book, was a quite charming individual. She had a nice warm smile, which made me relax. Aisah was born in a village near Châu Đốc city in An Giang Province, and she had been living in Ho Chi Minh City for over 20 years. She was the daughter of a very well-respected *Hakim*, a Muslim religious leader, who had unfortunately passed away several years before. In his life, he made the *hadji*, a pilgrimage to Mecca, twice. He also won several Qur'an reading competitions in Malaysia. Aisah was also well known for reading the Qur'an and had won the first prize in many reading competitions too. We continued to have a discussion on her classes and her teaching of the Qur'an. However, when we talked about her family background, the smile on her face faded away and her eyes became watery. I was afraid of having said

---

[4] The National Census of 1999.

something wrong to make her upset. I did not know what to say to carry on our conversation. Suddenly, she started to talk about her marriage.

According to their custom, the Muslim Cham in An Giang Province get engaged when they are still very young. Engagements are made between two families and they prefer marriages between cousins (both cross and parallel cousins). Aisah had a fiancé by such an arrangement at a very young age. However, she did not marry the man who had waited almost 10 years for her to be his wife. Instead, she married a Cham man from the vicinity of Phan Rang city, the capital of the Ninh Thuận Province. Many of her relatives were against her decision to marry this man[5] who was not born a Muslim but became a Muslim later on. They told her the Cham from Phan Rang were different from the Cham in Châu Đốc and that the Cham from two different regions would not make a good couple. Despite all these warnings, she married him, partially because of love and also because of her concerns about Cham society. She said:

> The Cham from Châu Đốc and the Cham from Phan Rang have been separated. They do not even like each other. I wanted all the Cham to be together and to rise up. I wanted to make the two Cham groups shake hands. It is why I married my husband.

However, when I met Aisah, somehow their four-year marriage had started to fall apart. She attributed her marriage failure to the differences between the Cham from Phan Rang and Châu Đốc.

The story of her broken marriage was the starting point of my research and the point I always come back to when I think of these two groups of Cham people living in Vietnam. The Cham communities in the different localities officially belong to the same ethnic group, but they do not want to be identified with each other. Yet, sometimes they show unity as one Cham community. It was just like Aisah's marriage. In her married life, she experienced a constant cycle of separation from her husband and reunion with him. They were not sure if they could be a couple or should remain as two individuals.

---

[5] The Muslim Cham people from Mekong Delta often refer to the Cham from the south-central coast area as Cham Phan Rang, while the Cham from the south-central coast area refer to the Muslim Cham in Mekong Delta as Cham Châu Đốc.

The Cham ethnicity in Vietnam

Despite their differences, the Cham agree that they all belong to the one same ethnic group. But at the same time, they do not want to be seen as the same Cham. What it means to be "Cham" is different among the Cham in different localities. Tu Wei-Ming describes the changes in meaning of being "Chinese" during the course of history, and China's relationship to the Chinese diaspora including Hong Kong, Taiwan, and Singapore (1994: 12). Considering Tu's argument, being Cham might have been different in the course of their history and geographical context. It will also perhaps appear differently in the future. Thus, their ethnicity requires an ongoing articulation of who they are.

Contrary to the dynamism of ethnic identity, the official Vietnamese definition of an ethnic group is somewhat static. The Vietnamese government has adopted Stalin's definition of the nation to classify its population into *dân tộc*, equivalent to nationalities, and ethnic groups. In his book *Marxism and the National Question* published in 1913, Stalin defines a nation as "a historically constituted stable community of people, formed on the basis of a common language, territory, economic life, and psychological make-up manifested in a common culture" (Marxists Internet Archive 1913). This definition is not suitable to classify actual ethnic groups since they do not necessarily share a common language, territory, economic life, or culture, as many researchers including Edmund Leach (1964) and Michael Moerman (1965) have argued. Some Vietnamese ethnologists have pointed out the significance of people's self-identity to a certain group (Phan Ngoc Chien 1993: 48), but the ethnic classification has more to do with external labeling in Vietnam. Vietnamese ethnologists depend heavily on language for ethnic classification, and the population of Vietnam is divided up into the three major language groups: Austroasiatic, Sino-Tibetan, and Austronesiatic. The 54 officially recognized *dân tộc* are classified under these linguistic categories (Yoshizawa 1982; Khong Dien 2002). The people of Vietnam must choose only one *dân tộc* to belong to and changing one's ethnic identity is not permitted without the state's approval (Phan Ngoc Chien 1997: 5).[6]

In this book, I examine how the various Cham groups negotiated their ethnic identities in different situations. The fluidity, malleability, and negotiated nature of ethnic identity have been discussed in numerous studies

---

[6] Ito's (2008) work on ethnic classification in Vietnam discusses this problem and how people negotiate with the state-given static ethnic classification.

and it seems pointless to repeat these same arguments here. However, I believe my study can remind scholars that the Vietnamese official ethnic classification is far from the "ethnic reality." Yet, it is the "living reality" of the ethnic minority people. It further demonstrates how the classification of *dân tộc* is actually generating ethnic identity. As Brakette Williams argues, the clue to understanding ethnic groups and ethnicity can be found in the context of the nation-state since one's ethnic identity becomes salient when the people are placed in the framework of a nation-state (1989).

Introducing the variety of Cham, or the meaning of being Cham, is my attempt to challenge a competitive discussion among researchers in the search for the "pure and true Cham." Searching for "original," "true," or "pure" Cham culture differentiates cultural diversities as derivative or corrupted and makes Cham society and its culture monolithic and static. Questioning such a static understanding of the Cham ethnic group is also another challenge to the conventional image of the Cham people. Cham people are often discussed within the framework of Champa. In recent years, there has been increasing interest in Champa. *École Française d'Extrême-Orient*, led by the late Po Dharma, successfully established a Champa studies program at the University of Malaya in Kuala Lumpur, Malaysia. New books on the history and archaeology of Champa have been published, and seminars and conferences on historical studies of Champa have been organized in Asia and Europe. In Vietnam, the many vestiges of ancient Champa, including the UNESCO-recognized historical heritage site of Mỹ So'n, are featured in tourist guidebooks, brochures, and posters. The rise of Champa studies and the increasing promotion of Champa heritage in the Vietnamese tourist industry has made the Cham a somewhat historical people. This book is an endeavor to assert that, despite the image of Champa as ancient and historical, the Cham are contemporary people who live in the same world and share the same concerns as their contemporaries, and they will continue to develop their communities in the future.

March 11, 2011

The information and data I used in this book mainly come from the field research that I conducted between 1995 and 1996 for my Ph.D. dissertation. For quite some time, I could not bring myself to publish my dissertation as a book. It was because I realized that it was not a perfectly formed analysis and the argument hadn't been developed as much as I would have wished, which made me hesitate to publish it. However, I have now decided to publish my thesis despite such shortcomings.

This is due to the events of March 11, 2011, in my home country of Japan. On that day, a giant tsunami swept cities, towns, and people's livelihoods away on the Pacific side of the northeastern region of Japan. The tsunami was triggered by an earthquake of extraordinary scale, with a magnitude of 9.0 at the epicenter.[7] On March 11, I was away from Japan, having a late lunch while watching a Japanese program broadcast by satellite TV. Suddenly, the announcer reported a jolt that was felt at the studio. The screen changed to show a large tsunami invading the Sendai plain where well-attended farming lands were being inundated by waves of black water. The TV announcer was speechless. There was no sound and an eerie silence dominated. I could not do anything but just stare at the TV screen. However, at that time, I had no idea that Japan would face an even more horrifying disaster: the meltdown of the Fukushima (福島) nuclear reactors.

Until the Fukushima disaster, I did not realize that Japan had constructed as many as 54 nuclear reactors since 1966. The Fukushima disaster was thought to be inadvertent since no one could have predicted that such a large-scale earthquake and tsunami would hit the nuclear reactors. The Tokyo Electric Power Company (TEPCO), which is responsible for the Fukushima nuclear plant, emphasized the unprecedented scale of the earthquake and tsunami so that the people of Japan would be convinced that it could not do much to prevent the accident. However, later, we began to understand what really happened and learned that the accident was caused by the company's policy that prioritized profitability over safety.

In 1997 Professor Ishibashi of Kobe University warned about the danger of a huge earthquake impacting the nuclear reactors. He said that a large-scale earthquake could cause a combination of various problems such as the loss of the external electricity supply and failure of the diesel generators. Without electricity, the cooling water cannot be supplied for the nuclear fuel, which could possibly lead to a steam and hydrogen explosion of the reactors. He repeated the same warning at a hearing of the Lower Diet in 2005. A local representative asked TEPCO to review and revise its safety measurements of the Fukushima nuclear plant: "in the current situation, Fukushima nuclear plant cannot deal with the scale of tsunami equivalent to the one caused by the Chile earthquake (magnitude 9.5)" (Fukushima Project 2012: 191-192). These alerts and this request were ignored.

TEPCO's inadequate crisis management is contrasted with the Onagawa nuclear plant of the Tohoku Electric Power Company. The Onagawa nuclear plant is also located on the shore of the Pacific coast and was also

---

[7] Press release of the Japanese Meteorology Agency, March 13, 2011.

hit by the tsunami on March 11. However, it survived without having a major crisis like the Fukushima plant. Before constructing the Onagawa nuclear plant, the Tohoku Electric Power Company did historical research to examine the major earthquakes and tsunamis that had occurred in the region from the 9th century onwards and they also completed geological studies. As a result, the Onagawa nuclear plant was built 14.8 meters above sea level, while the Fukushima nuclear plant was built just 10 meters above sea level. The earthquake triggered land subsidence of 1 meter at the Onagawa nuclear plant and it was hit by a 13-meter high tsunami. The Onagawa nuclear plant was saved by a height of 0.8 meters and this was a significant difference between Onagawa and Fukushima nuclear plants in terms of safety (Fukushima Project 2012: 192-193).

The meltdown of the Fukushima nuclear reactors could have been prevented if the company had better safety policies, systems, and training to deal with emergency situations (Asahi Shinbun Tokubetsu hodobu 2012: 188-259; Fukushima Project 2012: 11-224; Yoshioka 2011: 382-389). The government propagated the safety of nuclear reactors and the necessity of this energy source for the resource-poor country of Japan. But the fact that Fukushima became one of the world's worst nuclear accidents made us realize that the idea that 'nuclear power is a perfectly safe and clean energy source' is a mere myth.

Various studies have pointed out that nuclear energy is not actually a cost-effective energy source as the Japanese government has propagated. There has been a hidden agenda to keep nuclear power in Japan and this agenda is closely related to the issue of national security. After World War II, Japan's nuclear program was started with the support of the USA in the midst of the Cold War. The USA expected Japan to be like a fort, protecting the region from spreading communism, and for that reason it wanted Japan to have nuclear technology (Arima 2008; Yoshioka 2011).

Japan does not have nuclear weapons. As the first nation to be exposed to nuclear weapons, Japan has kept three non-nuclear principles of "not possessing, not producing, and not permitting" the introduction of nuclear weapons, which is in line with Japan's Peace Constitution. There is a report that Japan is the only country without nuclear weapons, yet it has obtained "sensitive nuclear technology" including enriched uranium, chemical reprocessing of spent nuclear fuel, and fast-breeder reactors which can be applied to develop nuclear weapons (Fukushima Project 2012: 232). Not only that, but by insisting on reprocessing spent nuclear fuel despite its high cost, Japan has accumulated large amounts of plutonium with which a few thousand nuclear bombs could be built (Fukushima Project 2012: 232-239).

It can be said that Japan is keeping nuclear power for the purpose of national security.

Vietnamese interest in nuclear power goes back to the pre-reunification of North and South Vietnam. The Institute of Nuclear Research in Đà Lạt was established in 1958 with the support of the USA. This is in the Central Highlands and is about 100 km from the city of Phan Rang of Ninh Thuận Province. After 1975, the USSR became a new partner and Vietnam continued to develop its nuclear program. The Russian Federation succeeded the partnership and it has since made an agreement to build the first nuclear reactor in Ninh Thuận Province in 2010.[8]

Then Japan came in as a new partner. During a summit meeting between Japan and Vietnam in October 2010, Japanese Prime Minister Naoto Kan received an order from Vietnam to build a nuclear plant. However, the Fukushima meltdown put a halt to Japanese exports of nuclear plants to Vietnam. Prime Minister Kan changed his energy policy to a renouncement of nuclear energy as a power source after March 11 and he refused to write a letter to the Vietnamese Prime Minister Nguyễn Tấn Dũng to confirm the Japanese export of its nuclear plant. However, Prime Minister Kan resigned and his successor, Yasuhiko Noda, reconfirmed to Prime Minister Nguyễn Tấn Dũng, who visited Japan in October 2011, that Japan would not terminate its original plan, and would export a nuclear plant to Vietnam (Ito 2011).

The Japanese agreement to export a nuclear power plant to Vietnam has since been reassured after a landslide victory of the Liberal Democratic Party (LDP) in the election of the Lower Diet at the end of 2012, which brought the LDP back to power. The new prime minister, Shinzo Abe who took office for a second time, has emphasized the importance of the economic recovery of Japan. His new economic policies are coined Abenomics. He has chosen ASEAN countries for his diplomatic debut as the prime minister and he has visited Vietnam. Abe and the Vietnamese prime minister agreed to Japanese economic assistance to the amount of 500 million USD, to cooperation in the trade of rare earth minerals, and to develop Vietnamese infrastructure including the construction of a nuclear reactor (Tokyo Shinbun 2013).

The *Asahi* newspaper's editorials have published strong opposition to Japan's export of a nuclear reactor to Vietnam. It criticized that the government has a double standard. While it reduces dependency on nuclear

---

[8] A personal communication with Shin-e Toshihiko (新江利彦) on February 1, 2012.

energy in Japan, it is exporting the very same nuclear reactors to foreign countries. The editorials have also pointed out the possibly enormous risk that Japan may have to bear due to its deep involvement with the Vietnamese nuclear project. The assessment research of the nuclear reactor site will be conducted by the Japanese government. Japan will loan money at a low interest rate to cover the construction expenses of the reactor and it will provide training for nuclear engineers. Japan will be asked to provide support for the disposal of nuclear waste, and so on. If an accident occurs, who will take responsibility? There is no clear agreement between the two sides on these issues (Asahi Shinbun 2012).

There is deep skepticism among Japanese citizens about their country's nuclear technology and this has developed into a persistent movement against nuclear power. Since March 2012, individual citizens have gathered in front of the parliament and the official residence of the prime minister every Friday afternoon. They are demonstrating for the abolishment of nuclear plants in Japan. It started as a small crowd of just 300 people, but the number of demonstrators has been increasing and in July 2012, approximately 20,000 citizens gathered. The organization called 'Metropolitan Coalition against Nukes' (首都圏反原発連合) is orchestrating the demonstrations and they managed to have a face-to-face meeting with Prime Minister Noda in August 2012 (Shutoken Hangenpatu Rengo).

With the decreasing popularity of nuclear power, the people's demand for utilizing more clean energy, and an anticipated population decline as one of the world's most rapidly aging societies, Japan's demand for electricity will most likely be reduced in future. Facing limits in the domestic market, Japanese nuclear businesses which have invested large amounts of capital will need to look for new markets outside of Japan. The newly developing countries in Asia are its potential business partners. In fact, besides Vietnam, within Southeast Asia, Indonesia, Malaysia, Thailand, and the Philippines have plans to establish nuclear energy plants (Fukushima Project 2012: 459). While having people's distrust of nuclear power in Japan, it is a double standard to keep exporting the nuclear plants as a safe, clean technology. Ito, from Kyoto University, argued that Japan should support Vietnam, which produces oil and has abandoned water resources, to provide technology to establish renewable energy, and thermal and hydroelectric power generation (2011).

Despite a growing movement to abolish nuclear power in Japan, only a handful of scholars and researchers in Vietnam openly oppose the Japanese government's move to export nuclear power plants to Vietnam. Nguyễn Xuân Diện, who is a scholar at the Han Nom Institute in Hanoi and a popular blogger, published an appeal to the Japanese House of Councillors and House of Representatives to cancel the nuclear power plant program in Vietnam. A total of 626 people inside and outside of Vietnam have signed the petition and their names have also been published on his blog (*"Bảovệtôquốc"*). However, a few days after posting the appeal, his blog was shut down and he was summoned by the authorities, forced to pay a penalty, and received psychological and physical threats (BBC 2012).

Japan has a considerable number of researchers and scholars who have made Vietnam their field of study. Many of them, including myself, are not sure how to position themselves between politics and academic work. I have discussed the issue of Japan's export of nuclear power plants to Vietnam with several colleagues. Most of us are opposed to, or have negative opinions about, the export of nuclear power, yet we remain silent. We are afraid that saying something in opposition to the decision made by the Vietnamese Communist regime may jeopardize our research there.[9]

Our silence made me remember the question that I had when I was in graduate school about the relationship between people who study and people who are studied. A field study is only possible after establishing a rapport with local people and gaining trust among them. Researchers must behave in response to this trust and must protect their subjects' privacy, their interests, and their welfare, even at the price of their own studies. With this book to introduce the Cham people of Vietnam and their rich culture, I would like to appeal to protect their livelihood and society. If there is a nuclear power plant located in Ninh Thuận Province, which is a former territory of Champa, it will place in danger one of the most important historical sites of Vietnam and also the Cham ethnic minority people, who have played a significant role in the enrichment of Vietnamese history and culture. Vietnam should not sacrifice its ethnic minority people for national

---

[9] Masako Ito of Kyoto University is one of the most outspoken scholars openly opposing the Japanese government's decision to export nuclear power plants to Vietnam. Her argument was published in the opinion column *"Watashi no shiten"* (私の視点) (my view) of the *Asahi* newspaper on October 7, 2011, and also as an article in *Asahi Shinbun Weekly* AERA June 4, 2012 (p. 45). Recently she has published a book, *Genpatsuyushustu no Giman* (原発輸出の欺瞞) (*The deceit of Japan's export of nuclear program*), together with other Japanese scholars and Vietnamese intellectuals. The book was based on the panel presentation organized at the conference of Southeast Asian Studies at Kagoshima University in 2013. It provides a critical voice opposing Japan's export of its nuclear program to Vietnam. (Ito & Yoshi-i 2015).

interests or so-called public welfare. One overseas Cham shared his concerns with me about the nuclear plant. He believed the construction of a nuclear plant in Ninh Thuận Province is the Kinh people's "final solution" to wipe out all the Cham people from Vietnam. I could not laugh at his opinion as a delusion of persecution since I felt that the nuclear plant would enforce the Cham's identity of "suffering minority people" and deepen the divide between the Cham and the majority Kinh people.

This book consists of six chapters and a conclusion. Chapter One discusses the historical background and characteristics of the historical polity of Champa. This historical polity provides a significant foundation for the establishment of Cham ethnic identity, especially of the Cham who are living in the south-central coast area. Chapter Two examines the development of Vietnamese minority policies. The consistent attitude of the Kinh majority people toward the ethnic minority people throughout history is discussed. Chapter Three examines the formation of the ethnic identity of the Cham living in Ninh Thuận Province. It discusses how their ethnicity has been developed by the connection to Champa. The dualism of *ahier* and *awal* are explored. In Chapter Four, the discussion is moved to the ethnicity of Muslim Cham living in the Mekong Delta. Different from the Champa-oriented ethnic identity, the Muslim Cham in the Mekong Delta developed their ethnic identity based on their religion of Islam. The little-studied Cham-initiated organization called *Hiệp hội Chàm Hồi giáo Việt Nam* (The Association of Muslim Cham in Vietnam) established in South Vietnam is also examined in this chapter. Implications of the establishment and the social impact of *Hiệp hội Chàm* are explored. Chapter Five examines negotiation processes between the ethnic identities of Cham in the south-central coast area and Cham in the Mekong Delta. It also examines the state-given identity of *dân tộc* Cham through studying the Cham's adaptation of Kinh discourse on ethnic minority groups and their new invented traditions, such as a dance by the Muslim Cham. The Cham people's ethnicity in the context of the nation-state is the main concern in this chapter. Chapter Six deals with the new position of ethnic minority people under the renovation policies of *đổi mới*. The mainstreaming of the ethnic minority culture as Vietnamese national heritage and tradition alongside the alienation of ethnic minority people from their own culture is discussed. Artworks by Cham artists are examined in this chapter to demonstrate a possibility for the Cham to express their own identity by using their own symbolic vocabularies. In conclusion, the survival of the Cham's identity is forecasted.

CHAPTER 1

CHAMPA

Before discussing the Cham communities in Vietnam, historical Champa needs to be understood since it is a significant foundation for the Cham people to establish their ethnic identity. In this chapter, the first half of the discussion is on historical and political characteristics of Champa, while the latter half of the chapter is an examination of the integration of Champa into Vietnam's national history. Champa no longer exists on maps and its former territories now belong to the Socialist Republic of Vietnam. Since Champa was absorbed into Đại Việt in the course of the Vietnamese southward expansion (*nam tiến*), Champa holds a problematic position in the national history of Vietnam.

Historical Champa

Sa Hùynh culture and the emergence of Champa

Around 1000 BCE, a civilization with technologies of rice cultivation and metal tools had developed in the central part of Vietnam. This civilization was named after the village called Sa Hùynh in the northeast region of Bình Định Province, where the first archaeological site of this civilization was discovered. Archaeological findings similar to Sa Hùynh, such as earrings with three lugs named Lingling-o as well as urns, have also been discovered in the Philippines [10] and Taiwan. This indicates that elements of the Sa Hùynh civilization were spread across the South China Sea and were likely established by sea-oriented people (Momoki 1997: 4; Wade 1993: 83).

---

[10] Geoff Wade argues that cultural affinities of the Sa Hùynh with the Philippines were inherited by Champa, and it was Cham script that the Philippine script was derived from between the 10th and the 14th centuries (1993: 83-87).

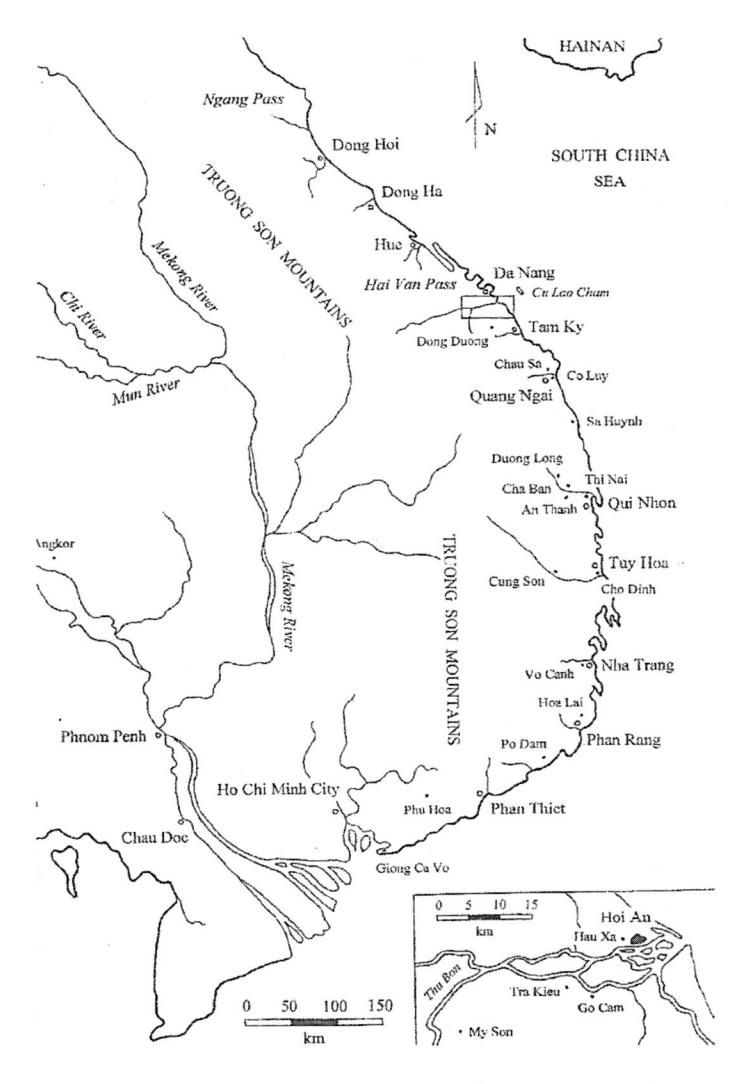

Map 2. Location of Sa Hùynh, Trà Kiệu Gò Cầm (archaeological map) (From William Southworth 2004, The Coastal States of Champa, Figure 9.1 in Ian Glover and Peter Bellwood (eds.) *Southeast Asia from Prehistory to History.* London & New York: RoutledgeCurzon, 2004, pp209-233).

The Sa Hùynh civilization is now seen as a proto-Cham society. Sakurai argues that Champa was established on the basis of the Sa Hùynh culture by adapting Indian culture (1993: 52). The large numbers of glass, carnelian, and agate beads found in the Sa Hùynh culture region indicate that they were manufactured in India or reproduced in Southeast Asia with Indian techniques and the materials were brought over from India (Glover & Kim Dung 2011: 59). However, Momoki mentions it was China rather than India that had the first influence on the emergence of Champa (1997: 5). Yamagata's extensive archaeological works on Trà Kiệ which was known as the capital of Champa and also known as Linyi (林邑) by the Chinese, reveal significant Chinese cultural influences between the 2nd and the 3rd centuries when Champa emerged as an independent polity (Yamagata 2011: 88-98). Glover and Kim Dung's studies on the Gò Cẩm archaeological site near Trà Kiệu support significant Han Chinese cultural influence in the early stages of Champa (2011: 54-78) (Map 2).

Yokokura examined the relationship between the Đông So'n culture of northern Vietnam, which is known for its bronze drums, and the Sa Hùynh culture, and argued that the Đông So'n drums found throughout mainland Southeast Asia and the Southeast Asian archipelago were brought over by people from the Sa Hùynh culture. The Đông So'n culture established inland river transportation networks connected with Sa Hùynh maritime culture and also established an infrastructure for the eventual emergence of port-city nations in Southeast Asia. Yokokura argues that the birth of Champa was the result of connections between the Sa Hùynh culture's sea networks, which were linking the eastern shore of the Indochinese Peninsula and the Philippines to Chinese economic zones (1993: 152-167).

Mandala

According to Chinese documents, Champa was established around 192 CE as a result of a rebellion led by a person named Ou Lien (区連)[11] who was one of the sons of a local official under Chinese control at Xiang Li (象林 *Tu'ọ'ng Lâm*) in the county of Rih Nan (日南 *Nhật Nam*) under the Eastern Han (後漢). This location is said to be in the vicinity of modern day

---

[11] Maspero identifies Ou Lien (区連) with King Sri Mara, whose name appears on the Võ Cạnh inscription found in Khánh Hòa Province of southern Vietnam. The Võ Cạnh inscription is dated approximately to the 3rd century and is known as the oldest Sanskrit inscription in Champa and also in Indochina (Sugimoto 1956: 146; Yao 1995: 3-4).

Huế in Thừa Thiên Huế Province. The Chinese called this new independent country Linyi (林邑) (Sugimoto 1956: 95; Coedès 1968; Hickey 1982a: 69-71; Taylor 1983: 60; Majumdar 1985: 18; Momoki 1994a, 1994b; Maspero 2002). The name Champa (Zhancheng 占城) first appears in Chinese texts in the late 9th century, and the earliest Cham inscriptions which contain the name of Champa are dated to approximately the late 6th century to the early 7th century (Sugimoto 1956: 99, 114, 25).

Champa has been mentioned as a kingdom in historical literature, but the word kingdom may mislead people to think that Champa was one unified kingdom with a strong centralized political system. Po Dharma, who points out the information in the Royal Chronicles of Champa written in the modern Cham scripts, argues that "Champa was not a unitary state but a kind of confederation of principalities" (1994: 55). Endo attributes the image of a unified Kingdom of Champa, which had clear territorial boundaries and people of the kingdom, to the Western view of a "nation-state" (1996: 73-91).

Champa was divided into different geographical areas by branches of the Tru'ò'ng So'n mountain range, which generally runs from north to south in Central Vietnam. There were five areas divided by the mountain range, which correspond to the coastal plains. These were called, ranging from the north to the south, Indrapura (current day Quảng Bình, Quảng Trị, and Thừa Thiên Huế Provinces), Amaravati (current day Quảng Nam-Đà Nẵng and Quảng Ngãi Provinces), Vijaya (current day Bình Định Province), Kauthara (current day Khánh Hòa Province), and Panduranga (current day Ninh Thuận and Bình Thuận Provinces) (Po Dharma 1994: 55; Quach-Langlet 1994: 21-32; Shige-eda 1994: 9) (Map 3). Each of these five regions (*pura*) of Champa had its own political, economic, and religious center and they existed more or less independently (Hardy 2009: 108). Vickery noted that it is not certain that envoys sent to China from Champa during the 11th century were all from the same region. The different regions in Champa may have established different relationships with China separately (Vickery 2009: 52).

Champa's political system is often referred to as *mandala* (Trần Kỳ Phu'o'ng 1994; Trần Quốc Vu'o'ng 1995; Momoki 1994a, 1994b; Shige-eda 1994). The word *mandala*, or "circles of kings," was adapted by Wolters to describe characteristics of socio-political systems which are commonly found in ancient Southeast Asia. In each *mandala*, there was one *mandala* overlord who claimed "hegemony over other rulers in his *mandala* who in theory were his obedient allies and vassals" (Wolters 1999: 27).

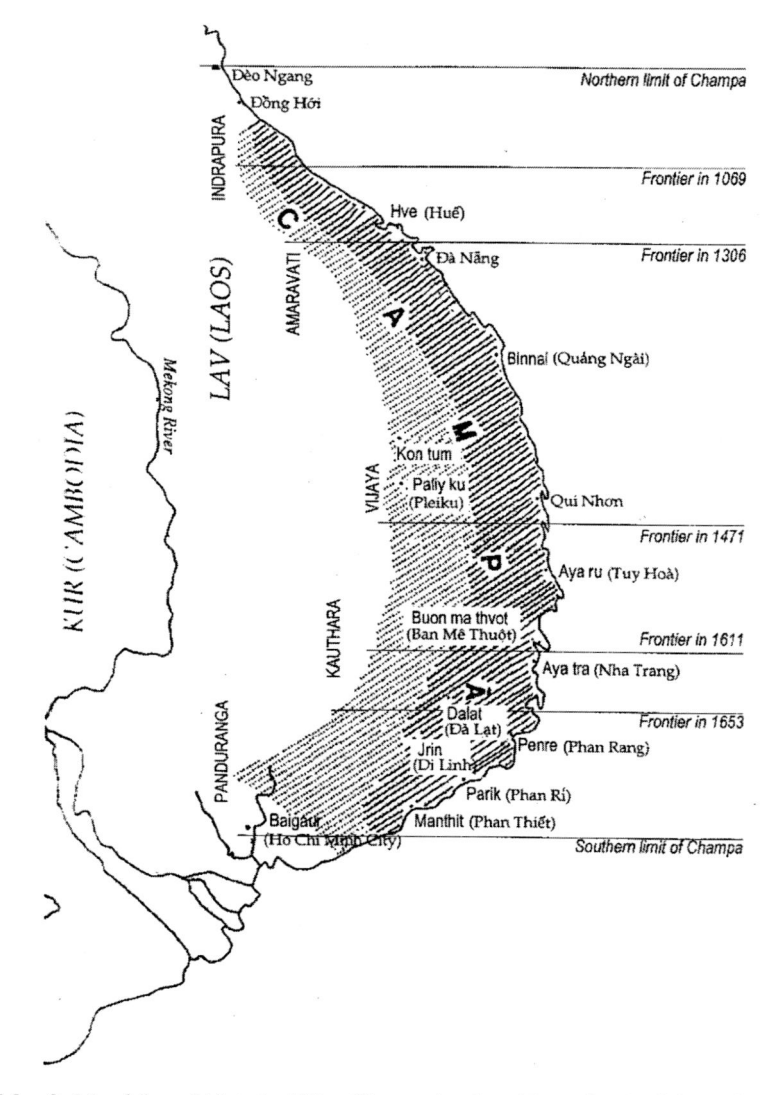

Map 3. *Mandala* and historical Viet-Champa borders (From the English version of Proceedings of the Seminar on Champa held at the University of Copenhagen on May 23, 1987, published by Southeast Asia Community Resource Center, Rancho Cordova, CA in 1994, p. iii)

A *mandala* was not a territory-based polity. It depended on the personal influence of the *mandala* overlord who identified themselves with divine authority. The connections between the different centers and peripheries of each *mandala* were built on patronage and personal magnetism, which Wolters called "patrimonial bureaucracy" in contrast to institutionalized bureaucracy. For the vassal states, they constantly looked for the most influential center which could provide security and spiritual authority, and at the same time, they would also seek opportunities to build up their own vassal relationships with others. The center of political power kept shifting in a *mandala* and it had a short life-span and was an unstable political system (Wolters 1999: 27-31).

Hinduinization[12] of Champa

In the past, there was an argument that the formation of early Southeast Asian polities was attributed to Indian migrants. Majumdar assumed that Champa was established by migrated Indians, and thanks to "Indian colonists," Champa had the strength to expel Han domination in the 2nd century. He illustrated Champa as a colony of India (Majumdar1985: xx-xxiii). Sugimoto pointed out an inscription which contains a story about a king whose name was Ganga Raja. He was intelligent and brave and was expected to ascend to the throne of Champa. But he declined the throne and went to Jahnavi (the Ganges region). With this story, and the possibility of early trade relationships between the Ganges region and Indochina, Sugimoto hypothesized that the Indian immigrants from the Bengal region existed in Champa and they named the country after their home in India because of the similarities between the two places. Both regions produced precious woods, many elephants were living in both places, and their landscapes were similar (Sugimoto 1956: 143-169).

However, the idea of the formation of early Southeast Asian polities as Indian colonies has been discredited nowadays (Smith 1999: 1). Majumdar's rather ethnocentric analysis of Champa's early history echoes the French colonial Orientalists' view of Champa which became worthy for their study only after its adaptation of "superior" Indian civilization (Lockhart 2011: 5). Coedès rejected the view of Indianized countries of Southeast Asia as Indian colonies populated by Indian immigrants. He

---

[12] Wolters prefers the term Hinduinization over Indianzation since he considered that the influence from India to Southeast Asia was only the Hindu religion (1999: 110).

explained that the influx of Indian traders and immigrants, including religious leaders and scholars, into Southeast Asia through trade routes between India and China had become a steady flow during the 2nd and 3rd centuries. However, the traders might not have stayed in Champa long enough to influence the local communities. He argued that the Indianized countries of Southeast Asia were the countries of "Indianized native societies" (Coedès 1968: 14-27).

Many historians who have studied inscriptions of Champa argue that Indian culture which had influenced Champa was of southern Indian origin. Sugimoto's detailed analysis of the almanac system used in Champa determines that it was the same as the southern Indian calendrical system called *amanta* (1956: 143-169). By examining Indian sources of navigation, the Chinese and Mediterranean travelers' accounts, and archaeological findings, Coedès argued that in the region of Kanchi (or Kanchipuram) of the southern Indian state, Tamil Nadu played a major role in introducing Indian civilization to Indochina. However, Coedès criticizes that Indian influence on Indochina being exclusively from southern India is "an oversimplified view" and points out that other regions such as the Dekkan, the Ganges valley, northwest India, and the Iranian frontier have also contributed to the introduction of Indian civilization to Southeast Asia (1966: 52-53).

Smith, who studied Indian history, has adapted Mabbett's argument of two waves of Indianizing phenomenon in Southeast Asia. She attributes the Indian influence in Southeast Asia to the Gupta dynasty (Smith 1999: 3, 11-15) of northern India. She states that it was after the 4th century when the Gupta dynasty of India was established that Southeast Asia adapted Indian influences. Coedès negates any Indian influence in Champa prior to the 4th century (1966: 64), and archaeological studies indicate that Champa was under Chinese cultural influence until the 3rd century (Yamagata 2011). The Gupta dynasty was, according to Smith, the first long-lived and steady political organization which provided a coherent socio-political structure. Under the Gupta dynasty, the Vedic Hindu tradition was revived, yet it did not mean the elimination of Buddhist practices, and some Buddhist temples received financial support from the court (Smith 1999: 3-13). The practice of blending Hinduism and Buddhism found in Champa and in early Southeast Asia reflects the religious practice of the Gupta dynasty.

I believe newly emerged polities in Southeast Asia like Champa preferred to adapt Indian political techniques over Chinese influence which was often accompanied by military intervention. Smith introduced Champa (she called it "Lin-i") as "a good example" (Smith 1999: 18) of Southeast Asian polities' position between Indian and Chinese influences. While Champa grew stronger to counter Chinese influence, its strength was demonstrated by its adaptation of Indian culture. Adaptation of a Chinese socio-cultural and political model had a danger of inviting Chinese political control, while an Indian model did not have such a potential threat. Like other Southeast Asian polities, Champa chose the Indian model over the Chinese model (Smith 1999: 18-19).

Mus argued that the religion of Hinduism was probably accepted by the population of Champa without any resistance because of their cultural predisposition. He explained that an area from the Bay of Bengal of India through Indochina, Southern China, Indonesia, and other Pacific islands used to belong to one cultural area called the Monsoon culture. In the Monsoon culture, people believed in animism [13] which is a belief that spirits are dwelling in every kind of thing in the world. Among these spirits, the spirit of the earth was one of the most important. In order to worship the earth spirit, which was an abstract being, people erected stones at holy places. The erected stones were not yet personified, and heads of communities played a significant role as a link between the earth spirit and the person conducting the ceremony. Sometimes, the community leader personified the earth spirit. Having such a religious environment, the people of the Monsoon culture did not perceive the newly introduced Hindu religion as a totally foreign practice, but rather as something familiar. Thus, Hinduism could penetrate into Champa which belonged to the Monsoon cultural area without any major resistance, and it spread widely. Further, Mus argues that such a local religious background was the cause of the localization or indigenization of the Hindu religion later on (1975).

Hinduism was adapted by the newly emerged polity of Champa in order to strengthen its influence on the neighboring polities. By adapting Hinduism, *mandala* overlords succeeded in impressing their vassal states and gaining their loyalty through spiritual superiority. This religious

---

[13] According to the Cham local scholars in Ninh Thuận Province, there are villages where people still practice a pre-Hindu religion or animism. They are the villages of Palei Rio and Palei Bingu, located next to each other at the east end of a large Bani village called Văn Lâm. The village of Palei Rio was originally located about 2 km away from Văn Lâm village, but the French, who were afraid of the Viet Minh influence in the village, relocated it closer to the other Cham village during the First Indochina War. The Cham from Palei Rio practice wedding ceremonies according to the religion of Balamon and marry the Cham people in other Balamon villages. However, unlike other Cham following the Balamon religion, the Cham in Palei Rio are not cremated when they die.

superiority attracted their vassals and Wolters argued that Indian cultural influence, especially Hinduism, made such overlords' spiritual superiority possible. The adaptation of Hinduism was a prerequisite for the *mandala* system (Wolters 1999: 22).

Riverine system

Kenneth Hall explained the political and economic networks of the Champa by applying Bronson's riverine exchange network model. According to this model, the exchange network system has a coastal-based trade center which is usually located at the mouth of a river. There are also distant upstream centers that are the initial concentration points for products originating in more remote parts of the river watershed. These products were produced by the non-market-oriented people living in upland or upriver villages (Bronson 1977; Hall 1985) (Figure 1). Similarly, by examining archaeological findings from the central coast of Vietnam, Southworth argued that Bronson's model is quite useful to reconstruct the historical development of the Champa polity. He also suggested that local people's rebellion against Chinese control, which is considered to be the emergence of Champa, could have been caused by China's attempt to directly control upstream trade centers bypassing the downstream trade centers. China's ambition to control riverine trade systems resulted in the resistance of an alliance of upstream and downstream trade centers (Southworth 2011). Champa's prosperity was mostly developed through upstream–downstream riverine trade exchange[14] (Guy 2009: 128) and each *pura* or region of Champa was based on such a riverine exchange network.

Champa can characteristically be seen as a loose, marginally interdependent alliance network among a series of river-mouth urban centers whose very nature was politically and economically unstable. Champa's political authority was concentrated in coastal and riverine centers near the coast.[15] The Champa royal center shifted among several of these river-mouth urban centers over time. This has been explained as indicative of the corresponding shifts from one dynasty's rule to that of another. It was actually a reflection of the transfer of authority from the elite of one Champa riverine system to that of another (Hall 1985). In Chinese

---

[14] Guy mentions that the Cham also engaged in sea raiding and piracy to supplement their income (2009: 129).
[15] Southworth mentions that many of Champa's political centers moved inland later on due to potential naval attacks (2011: 111).

historical documents, Champa, which China had tributary relationships with, appeared in different names such as Linyi (林邑) until the mid-8th century, then Huanwang (環王) until the late 9th century, and then Zhancheng (占城 *Chiêm Thành*) until the 19th century. The changes of its name may also reflect shifts of dominant *pura* within a particular riverine system over the course of history (Momoki 2011).

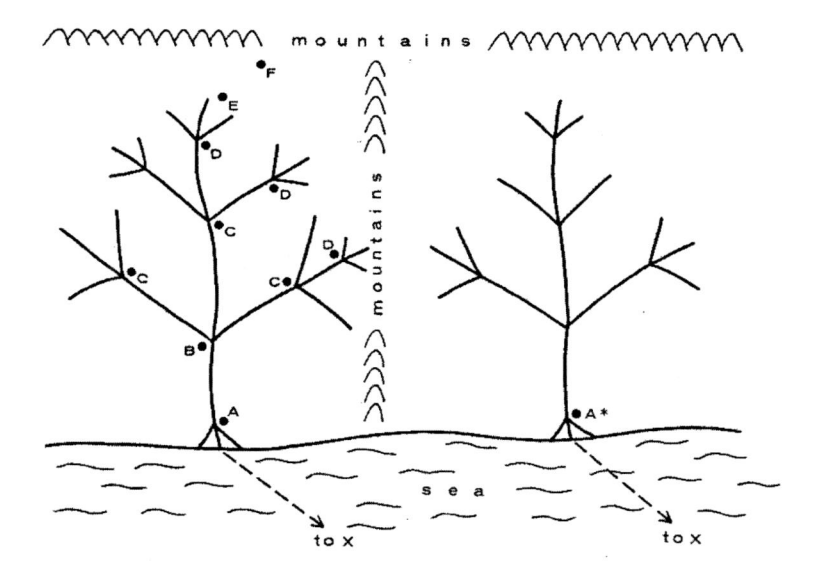

Figure 1. Bronson's riverine system. A: the center at the river mouth; B & C: second and third order centers; D: the most distant upstream center to send the products to the A-based system; E & F: the ultimate producers of the trading items; X: an overseas center (From Benneth Bronson 1977, 42-43)

Wolters states that *mandalas* were lowland political systems and the highlands were out of reach of the *mandala* kings' influence (1999: 39). There is some archaeological and historical evidence that *mandala* Champa had some influence in the highlands. Cham vestiges sites such as the Yang Prong temple-tower in Đắk Lắk Province have been found in the highland regions (Hickey 1982a: 91-105). Yet it is understood that it is unlikely to find evidence of Champa's direct control over the highland population through "taxation, corvée and military service" (Hardy 2009: 115).

Shin-e's detailed analysis of local Cham and Vietnamese documents on relationships between the Cham and the highland ethnic groups reveals that the Cham had a more dominant presence in the highlands. A king's lineage that had survived until recently used to own a large rice field in Kalon (current day Kalon-Sông Mao nature reservation area) in Bình Thuận Province from the mid-19th century until 1963. The royal family's rice field was attended by the highland ethnic minority people (Shin-e 2007: 150-155). Shin-e also pointed out that the Cham used force to control highland ethnic groups and collected capitation and requested corvée labor from them. However, most of the historical information relating to the Cham's direct control over the highland ethnic groups is dated after the 17th century when Champa was subordinated to Vietnamese domination. As Shin-e argues, the Cham's control over the ethnic groups in the Central Highlands was the result of the expansion of Vietnamese political dominance into the area. The Cham took an administrative role to collect tax, precious highland products, and corvée labor. At the same time, Shin-e suggests that the Cham became bureaucrats to control the Central Highlands under Vietnamese regulation because of their prior domination over the Central Highland ethnic groups (2007: 115-161).

The nature of Champa's influences on the Central Highlands needs to be further explored, but many scholars have agreed that having steady relationships with the highlands was essential to Champa's economic activities. In the 17th century, the aromatic wood known as eaglewood or aloeswood was recorded to be sold for gold at the same weight (Hardy 2009: 117). Champa depended on the precious rare items like eaglewood for its maritime trade, which was collected from upstream areas by the highland ethnic groups.

Cham legends indicate that the highland ethnic groups were loyal and they protected Cham wealth. The legend of King Po Rame, who himself was of highland origin, tells the story of his Ede (Rhade) wife. King Po Rame had a Cham wife but they did not have a child, so he married a second wife from the Ede ethnic group of the highlands. They had a daughter, but Po Rame still married a third wife, who was a Vietnamese princess from the Nugyễn court. The Vietnamese princess was actually sent by her father to lay a plot on Po Rame. She pretended to be sick and told the king that the *Krek* tree[16] was the cause of her illness. But the *Krek* tree was the source of

---

[16] William Collins collected the story about the *Krek* tree from the Cham in Cambodia. He mentions that this legend is widely known among the Cham in Cambodia. In the Cambodian Cham version of the legend, the king who falls into

the king's power. Because of the magnificent power of this tree, Nguyễn Vietnam could not defeat Champa. However, Po Rame completely trusted his beautiful young wife and cut down the *Krek* tree. When the *Krek* tree fell down, red blood-like sap gushed out. The Vietnamese forces entered the capital of Champa and occupied it. King Po Rame was captured and sent to Huế where he was prosecuted. When he was cremated, his first Cham wife refused to throw herself into the king's cremation fire according to the tradition; instead, his second Ede wife jumped into the fire to follow the king's destiny. In this legend, the second wife who came from the highlands gave King Po Rame a child and remained loyal to him during the time of his wretched defeat (Aymonier 1890: 173; N. Taylor 1989).

The Highlanders were guardians of the Cham royal treasure. When the *École Française d'Extrême-Orient* created an inventory for the Cham royal treasure, they found out that various highland groups had taken responsibility for safekeeping the treasures. Aymonier mentions that the group of Chu Ru and Koho people served as honest and faithful guardians of the Cham royal treasure (1890: 182; Hickey 1982a: 106; Collins 1996: 41).

All the Cham royal treasure seems to have been lost, but the Raglay[17] people still symbolically maintain the role of the guardian of the treasure through a ceremonial relationship with the Cham people. A day before the ceremony called *Kate* among the Cham of the south-central coast of Vietnam, a group of Raglay people bring down ceremonial clothes for the goddess of Po Inu Nugar in the village of Hũ'u Dú'c near Phan Rang. One of the Raglay who brought down the clothes for the goddess told me that the Cham and Raglay were just like brothers and sisters.[18]

---

the trap is Po Gelong Gahoul, and the tree is called the *Kerik* tree (Collins 1996: 26-27).
[17] Both the Cham language and the Raglay language belong to the Malayo-Polynesian family and they are mutually comprehensible.
[18] The Cham people tend to focus on mutual interdependency and peaceful relationships between the Highlanders and the lowland Cham. However, in the newsletters and information published by former FULRO members in North Carolina, the Cham were depicted as invaders who stole the coastlands where the Highlanders claimed to live 2,000 years ago (Montagnard Foundation Inc. 1998: 5).

Coming of Islam to Champa[19]

Three major religions have been practiced in old Champa: Hinduism, Buddhism, and Islam. During the 9th and 10th centuries, Champa adapted Mahayana Buddhism. The Buddhist sanctuary called Đông Du'o'ng[20] was established. The Mahayana Buddhism introduced to Champa was called Vajrayana, a branch of esoteric Buddhism that spread to Nepal, Tibet, and East Asia from northeast India (Chaturachinda et al. 2000: 132). It was mixed with the Hindu religion and ancestral worship after the Gupta dynasty. An inscription found in Đông Du'o'ng suggested that Champa practiced both Buddhism and Hinduism which were fused to each other (Shige-eda & Trần Kỳ Phuong 1997: 90). However, unlike Islam, Buddhism did not survive over the course of the history of Champa, and one can only find the remnants of Buddhist influence in the ornaments of contemporary Cham ceremonies.

Islam has now become the dominant religion among the entire Cham population. The question as to when Islam was introduced to Champa has been debated among historians. Cabaton (1965: 1209; see also Manguin 1985: 1) introduces two hypotheses for the date of the coming of Islam to Champa:

1. Islam could have been brought to Champa by Arab, Persian, or Indian merchants from the 10th to the 14th centuries.
2. Islam might have been introduced later by Malay immigration.

Champa has been known by the Arab people for many centuries. The region of the Southeast Asian and South China Sea was called the Cham Sea by the Arab geographers during the 10th century (Andaya 2010: 18-19). Middle Eastern sources indicate that Muslim people existed in Champa earlier than the 10th century. Fatimi, whose argument was introduced by Scupin, dates the existence of Muslim communities in Champa based on the Persian and Arab sources as being in the 8th century (Scupin 1995: 304).

---

[19] This section was originally published as "Coming of Islam to Champa" in *Journal of Malay Branch of the Royal Asiatic Society*, Vol. 73 pt. 1 (June 2000).

[20] Đông Du'o'ng is located 65 km south of the port city of Đà Nẵngin Central Vietnam. It was the largest religious sanctuary of Champa which stretched 1.3 km from east to west. French scholar Henri Parmentier studied Đông Du'o'ng in the early 20th century. Unfortunately, Đông Du'o'ng was completely destroyed during the First Indochina War (1946–1954) (Shige-eda & Tran Ky Phu'o'ng 1997: 90 & 98).

Chinese sources mention Cham ambassadors to China between the 10th and 11th centuries, and some of them had the name of *Pu* which was said to represent the Arabic *Abu*, indicating that the person was Muslim (Manguin 1985: 3).

Tasaka discusses Ferrand's collection of stories in which the Arab geographer Al-Dimashqi, around the mid-14th century, reported that the country of Champa was populated by Muslims, Christians, and idolaters, and that the Muslim religion came there in the time of Caliph Usman III around the mid-7th century. Later, a group of followers of Ali were expelled from the Umayyads and came across the Poix Sea and found refuge in Champa. Al-Dimashqi's report indicates that the first form of Islam introduced to Champa was Shi'ia Islam. Several local Cham scholars indicate that the Shi'ia influence was found among Bani Islam[21] (Manguin 1985: 2; Tasaka 1952: 53).

Although Tasaka saw Al-Dimashqi's report as not being sufficient to determine the time of Islam's arrival in Champa, he argued that Islam was introduced by the Muslim merchants who came through Champa on the way to China. The first known ambassador from the Islamic country to Tang (唐) dynasty China was in 651, which matches the time of the coming of Islam to Champa given by Al-Dimashqi (Tasaka 1952: 53-54).

Archaeological findings suggest a later date for the existence of Islam in Champa than the dates that historical materials indicate. A group of Japanese archaeologists found Islamic ceramics as well as Chinese ceramics in Cù lao Chàm (Cham Island), which is located about 100 km off the shore of Hội An, and in Trà Kiệu, the former capital of Champa known as Sinhapura, which suggests a trade relationship between Champa and Islamic countries in the 9th century (Yamamoto et al. 1993: 165).

Two Arabic inscriptions which were deciphered by Ravaisse indicate the existence of a Muslim community in Panduranga, in the modern Phan Rang and Phan Rí area, around the latter half of the 10th century to the 11th

---

[21] Shi'ia Islam might have a significant influence on Islam introduced to mainland Southeast Asia. Scupin discusses the significant role in politics and commerce played by Persian Muslims during the Ayutthaya period in Thailand, and mentions that one of the important Shi'ia rituals to honor Ali, the son-in-law of the Prophet, was organized regularly in Ayutthaya (1980: 62-67). An anthropologist, Emiko Stock, reported the popular ritual to celebrate the birthday of Ali practiced among a group of Cham called Jveas (traditionalists; they have a practice similar to the Bani in Vietnam) in Cambodia at the International Seminar on Historical Relations between Indochina and the Malay world at the University of Malaya between October 20 and 21, 2009.

century (Manguin 1985: 1; Tasaka 1952: 54). Ravaisse argued that there must have been a city-like settlement around the place where the Arabic inscriptions were found and inhabited by foreigners who had different customs and religion. Under the protection of the kings of Champa, they probably enjoyed autonomy in the city (Ravaisse 1922; Tasaka 1952: 54). Chinese records indicate many Muslim people, perhaps Muslim merchants, were sent to the Chinese court as tributary envoys by the Champa court during the Northern Sung dynasty from the 10th to the 12th centuries (Chang Hsiang-Yi 1974: 285).

Champa probably experienced two different kinds of contact with the Muslim people in different time periods. The beginning of the first wave might be as early as the 9th century. They were mainly Persian, Arab, Indian, and Chinese Muslims. By the 11th century, the Muslim community had established a prominent presence in Champa. Maspero's and Ravaisse's translations of Cham documents suggest the firm foundation of the foreign Muslim community in Champa. The community consisted of not only Muslim merchants, but also artisans, scholars, religious leaders, and other craftsmen, and it had elaborated political, legal, and judicial instructions to serve the needs of its community. Maspero indicates that the Muslim community had a representative called *Seih es-Sug* (Syndic of the market place) who represented them to the Cham leader (Scupin 1995: 304). With the evidence of Islamic tomb stones, chronicles of later dates, coins, and the reports of external visitors, Reid speculates that there was a substantial group of Malay/Javanese-speaking Muslims in the port cities on the major trade routes in Southeast Asia (1993: 155-156).

Yet, conversion to Islam might not have become a pervasive phenomenon among the native population during the first wave of contact with the Muslim people into Champa. Daniel Hall argues that Arab and Persian merchants came to Southeast Asia at an earlier time, but local people's conversion to Islam did not happen prior to the 13th century. He suggests the role of Sufi mystics from India in introducing Islam and attributes Sufism's tolerance of non-Islamic local traditions to the popularization of Islam in Southeast Asia (Hall 1960: 249). Reid recognizes the difficulties in estimating how deeply Islam penetrated society before the 16th century (1995). There must have been individual Cham conversions to Islam, but these would have been rather isolated phenomena, limited to commercial circles and the court having relationships with the foreign communities (Manguin 1985: 3-8).

Collins points out Moura's statement that the Cham people were newly converted to Islam around the time of the fall of Vijaya in 1471 (Moura

1883: 485) and suggests regional differences in spreading Islam in Champa by introducing Leclère's argument. According to Leclère, "Islam gained followers among the Cham of the north in the process of mobilizing resistance to Vietnamese pressure from the north," while in the south, the region of Panduranga was still populated by Hinduist Cham. Compared to the Muslim Cham of the north who had borders with Vietnam, the Vietnamese were rather tolerant of the Hinduist Cham in the south and were not much interested in conquering them (Collins 1996: 29).

Collins' argument is interesting, but the fact that the oldest Arabic inscriptions were found in the southern part of Champa and also that the Cham kings remained Hinduist until very late indicate that differences in conversion to Islam among the native population were not because of their regional differences, but because of their differences in socio-economic status. According to most historians, we have to wait until the fall of Vijaya in 1471 to find a significant number of the indigenous Cham converting to Islam. The intensity of commercial activities in Southeast Asia during the period of 1550–1650 created intense contact with Middle Eastern and local Muslim people. Also, there were trade routes which made the Malay world directly accessible from the Middle East. Muslim apostles and scholars accompanied the merchants from Arabia, and local Muslims were able to make the pilgrimage to Mecca (Coedès 1968: 238-239; Robson 1981: 276; Manguin 1985: 5-6; Scupin 1995: 304-305; Maspero 2002: 4-5).

The further arrival of the Portuguese Christians at the beginning of the 16th century provoked the political associations among the Muslims in Southeast Asia. They grouped themselves around explicitly Islamic centers and prepared to counterattack the Portuguese (Reid 1993: 163-164). It was probably during this time when the conversion to Islam by the Cham people became pervasive. Reid points out the historical incidents of Muslim Cham participation in battles against the Portuguese and Demak's War in Java, and also their close alliance with Malay Muslims during the Cambodian turmoil, and he states that it was around the 16th and 17th centuries when the Cham diaspora of traders, warriors, and refugees throughout Southeast Asia was Muslim or in the process of becoming Muslim (1995: 316-317). Chambert-Loir provides a date around the end of the 17th century for the Islamization of part of the Cham population and the Cham court (1994: 96).

The story of King Po Rame during the mid-17th century provides records of the conversion to Islam by the Cham people in his kingdom. King Po Rame is one of the deified kings who is still well respected and worshipped among the Cham people in the south-central coast area of Vietnam. He is known for solving a dispute between Muslim Cham and Hindu Cham. He made both groups respect each other's customs and made religious leaders from both sides attend each other's religious ceremonies (Manguin 1985: 10).

Hainques and Mahot in the Paris Foreign Missions Society (*Missions Etrangeres de Paris*) who traveled to Champa give us information about the state of the religion of Champa during the 17th century. In 1665 Hainques wrote, "The greater part of the native subjects of the country is infected with the errors of the Sarazins," and he wrote in 1675 that almost all committed to the Islamic faith (Manguin 1985: 9). Mahot reported in 1678:

> As for the state of religion in this Kingdom, the Malay, who are Mahometans have been much more vigilant than we; they immigrated and settled in great number, they attracted the King and his whole Court to their accursed religion. The Cham of whom more than half are Moors with the King. (quoted by Manguin 1985: 9)

Manguin attributes the cause of Islamization of the Cham people to their active participation in the maritime trade networks of Southeast Asia, and also considers Malays as the people who propagated Islam among the Cham. Thus, he agrees with Cabaton's second hypothesis as the explanation of the coming of Islam to Champa. Manguin gives the state of Malacca credit for the conversion to Islam of the people of Champa. He argues that not only the state of Malacca but also the Malay colonies in Cambodia that had been in contact with Cham refugee communities played a significant role in their conversion to Islam (Manguin 1985: 13).

Vietnamese southern expansion (*nam tiến*)

While Champa was establishing a significant position in the South China Sea's maritime trade, Vietnam gained its independence from China in the 10th century. By the latter half of the 10th century, Vietnam had begun its southern expansion. A series of territorial concessions of Champa's territory to the Vietnamese occurred, e.g. the region of Indrapura (modern day Quảng Bình and Quảng Trị Provinces) in 1069, and Thừa Thiên Huế Province as the bride price of a Vietnamese princess to the Cham King Chế Mân in 1306. By the first half of the 14th century, the Vietnamese had gained control as far north as Hải Vân Pass.

However, *nam tiến* was not a steady linear progression toward the south by the Vietnamese and Momoki criticizes such a picture of *nam tiến* as a "Kinh-centric historical view" (1999: 65). In fact, Champa counterattacked and recovered almost all the above-mentioned territories lost to Vietnam during the latter half of the 14th century. A Cham king known by the Vietnamese as Chế Bồng Nga (制蓬莪) attacked the capital of Đại Việt, Thăng Long, three times and even occupied the city for six months (Li 1998: 20-21). Li Tana describes that "Vietnamese expeditions to Champa might have happened again and again" (1998: 19).

Li's study of the southern part of Vietnam under the Nguyễn lord (阮氏) reveals rather peaceful co-existence of Kinh (Vietnamese), Cham, and other highland ethnic groups. The Vietnamese settlements between the 12th and the 15th centuries in former Champa territories were scattered and not very systematically controlled. The Vietnamese migrants adapted Cham culture, especially religious practices. Many Buddhist sites in Central Vietnam are the former religious sites of Champa (Li 1998: 24, 101-155). The war captives brought back from Champa to Vietnam formed a community that lived near the Vietnamese capital (Momoki 2001: 72-73). Trần Quốc Vượng discusses strong Cham influences found in Vietnamese culture such as music, dance, architecture, and sculpture, and mentions that its cultural influences are found even in northern Vietnam, which was beyond Champa territories (2011).

Vietnamese *nam tiến* was not motivated by the search for agricultural lands which were scarce in the Red River delta of the north due to population increases, as previously thought. Yao argues that it was the Vietnamese ambition to control the international entrepôt cities for maritime trade in the South China Sea where many trade products were concentrated rather than to control the lands.[22] The maritime trade between Southeast Asia and China used to take a route in which ships coming from the south first dropped by the central coast of Vietnam, then ports in the Bay of Tonkin and Hainan Island, before finally going to Guangzhou. However, toward the end of the Tang dynasty (618–906), the route had shifted so that trading ships went directly to Guangzhou from the ports in Central Vietnam without stopping in northern Vietnam. In order to control trade with China, Vietnam, which had newly gained its independence from China, needed to

---

[22] O'Connor sees the conflicts between Vietnam and Champa as monoculture, wet-rice cultivators versus multi-cropping garden farmers. The differences in production between these two societies had created a village- or community-oriented society in Vietnam, and a household-lineage-oriented society in Champa. He attributes the Vietnamese victory over Champa to the superior status of rice in the market economy, "as the market blindly rewarded whoever had the most rice, what counted now was mono-cropping, where wet-rice specialists gained a new advantage" (O'Connor 1995: 984).

take over as many entrepôts in Central Vietnam as possible (Momoki 1990: 229; Yao 1995: 19).

Li reports that the name of Champa had disappeared from the list of trading ports of Japanese red seal ships, *shuinsen* (朱印船), after 1609; instead the Vietnamese name, Hội An, appeared as the major trading port. The foreign trade of the Nguyễn lords'-controlled region increased up until the 1740s and its economy relied on maritime trade. However, foreign trade with China and Japan declined in the mid-18th century and changes to the physiognomy of the Hội An port made it no longer a suitable entrepôt for foreign trade. It was the rice production of the Mekong Delta that became a stable commodity for foreign trade after the 18th century, which gave another incentive for *nam tiến* (Li 1998: 24, 59-65, 119, 156-158). During this new type of *nam tiến*, Champa ceased to exist on the political map.

The end of Champa

Until recently most historians considered the end of Champa as the fall of Vijaya in 1471, when the army of the Lê dynasty (黎朝 1428–1789) marched into the capital city of Vijaya. Around 60,000 Cham were killed and 30,000 were taken prisoner. The king was arrested and died in captivity. "His body was cremated" and "his head was stuck upon the bow of the imperial ship" (Maspero 2002: 118). A Cham general, Bo Tri-tri, led the remaining Cham people and took refuge in Panduranga. Champa returned the territories north of Cù Mông Pass (a provincial border between current day Bình Định Province and Phú Yên Province). By the end of the 15th century, the territories that remained to Champa were only Kauthara and Panduranga (current day Phú Yên Province, Khánh Hòa Province, Ninh Thuận Province, and Bình Thuận Province). Vietnamese Emperor Lê Thánh Tông (黎聖宗) transformed the annexed territory of Champa into the Quảng Ngãi administrative unit. "Here ends the history of the Kingdom of Champa" (Maspero 2002: 118).

However, Aoyagi, who studied so-called Champa ceramics,[23] proposes to re-examine the commonly accepted year of the end of Champa as 1471. Champa ceramics were distributed widely and have been reported to be found in Egypt, the United Arab Emirates, Malaysia, and the Philippines. Aoyagi examined kilns found in Bình Định Province, a former region of

---

[23] Champa ceramics have been mistaken as Chinese ceramics. A joint Vietnamese-Japanese research team identified them as locally produced ceramics, most likely by foreign (possibly Chinese) craftsmen who stayed in the region (Aoyagi 1999: 92).

Vijaya which produced the Champa ceramics. According to him, the production of Champa ceramics lasted from the 14th century until the latter half of the 17th century. The peak of Champa ceramic production was between the 15th and the 16th centuries (Aoyagi 1999: 95-96).

Po Dharma points out inconsistencies in the Vietnamese Annals. They recorded the disappearance of Champa in 1471, but also recorded Champa attacking Vietnam in 1611, 1653, and 1692 (Po Dharma 1994: 57). Shin-e discusses seven different opinions about the year of the fall of Champa: 1195–1201, 1471, 1693, 1695, 1822, 1830, and 1834. He argues that these various years indicate that the fall did not happen in a short period of time but rather was a long process and that Champa gradually disappeared. He examines the different nature of the relationship between Vietnam and Champa before and after the fall of Vijaya in 1471, and argues that Vietnam had shifted its policy on the Cham people from self-governing to assimilation. He concludes that the Vietnamese assimilation policy had an aim to destroy Cham culture, and the history of Champa from 1471 to the 1830s was that of its slow downfall (Shin-e 1991).

Momoki examines Champa's history in the context of maritime trade. He states that when we reconsider the role which the Cham people played in the maritime trade in Southeast Asia, we understand that although previously historians had considered the 15th to 17th centuries as an epoch of decay, Champa was not losing its power (Momoki 1994a; 1994b). In the account of Dampier, who traveled in Asia in the 17th century, the name of Champa appears several times (1697: I-400-401, II-2-3). He describes the Cham traders whom he met in the Gulf of Siam in 1687:

> They were of the idolaters, natives of Champa, and some of the briskest, most sociable, without fearfulness or shyness, and the most neat and dexterous about their shipping, of any such I have met with in all my travels.
> (Dampier 1697: I-400)

Momoki raises several points to support his argument. In the 16th century, a king of Champa dispatched an army to help the kingdom of Johor of Malacca fight against Portugal. In Cambodia, the Cham people allied with the Malay people to defeat the Spanish navy. In Thailand, the Cham rebelled against King Narai with the Malays and the Makassar people (Momoki 1994b: 25-27, 1999: 70-71). Momoki argues that Champa ended its history when the maritime trade carried out by local Southeast Asian people or Musim merchants from Arabia and India ended and the colonization by Europe began (Momoki 1994a: 70, 1994b: 27). This date matches around the time Po Dharma defines the absorption of Champa by Vietnam in 1832 when the region lost its autonomy (Po Dharma 1994: 68-61).

Wanting to affirm its sovereignty over the Vietnamese immigrants who had moved into the reduced territory of Cham people, the Court of Huế adapted a system called Thuận Thành (順城鎮 1692–1832), in which the Vietnamese people who were living in Panduranga were subjected to the authority of the Huế Court, while the Cham people were subjected to the authority of the Panduranga royal family (Momoki 1999: 67). Since the Vietnamese immigrants living in Panduranga were not concentrated but rather scattered around, Panduranga lost its geographical unity. However, the Court of Huế allowed the Cham in Panduranga to continue to preserve a kind of autonomy among themselves. The Thuận Thành system continued intermittently until 1832 (Hickey 1982a: 91; Weber 2012: 162).

During the Tây So'n rebellion (1771-1802), Cham people were divided into followers of Tây So'n and followers of the Nguyễn lord (Chúa Nguyễn), Nguyễn Phúc Ánh, and Panduranga became a battlefield (Momoki 1999: 72). After Nguyễn Phúc Ánh's victory, followed by his enthronement as Emperor Gia Long, the first emperor of a unified Vietnam, the Panduranga principality was restored. Having loyal Cham alliances during the battle against Tây So'n, Gia Long respected Cham traditions and customs and did not try to suppress them. However, the situation drastically changed during the reign of Emperor Minh Mạng (1791–1841) (Weber 2012: 164). In 1832, the governor of Panduranga was arrested for allegedly supporting the rebellion led by the Vietnamese mandarin Lê Văn Khôi with Cham people against Emperor Minh Mạng. The governor was sent to Huế and prosecuted. Weber points out that historical Cham documents do not corroborate the Cham's participation in the rebellion (2012: 164; Hickey 1982a: 91); however, this put an end to the Thuận Thành system which technically was the end of the Champa (Momoki 1997: 8). Historical Vietnamese and Cham documents also indicate the end of the Thuận Thành system in 1832 as the end of Champa (Shin-e 2007: 172-173).

After the abolishment of the Thuận Thành system, there were anti-Vietnamese revolts among the Cham between 1833 and 1835 (Momoki 1999: 73; Weber 2012: 164). But the Cham people were still placed under the direct control of the Nguyễn dynasty. The new administration system destroyed the Cham's traditional social hierarchy and its economic system. The Cham also suffered from severe assimilation policies under Minh Mạng, which destroyed Cham economic systems, traditions, religion, and culture (Weber 2012: 166-180).

Cham outside of Champa

The Cham people have migrated to various parts of Southeast Asia and beyond. Thurgood argues that the proto-Chamic-speaking people who stayed in the north first encountered the Vietnamese southward movement and then left the mainland peninsula. They moved to northern Sumatra and became Acehnese-speaking people (Thurgood 1999: 252).

The Musim people living on Hainan Island of China call themselves Utsat. By examining Chinese documents, some historians argue that these people are the descendants of Champa who escaped the turmoil caused by wars in their mother country (Tasaka 1952: 57-58). Paul Benedict, a linguist, points out the similarity between the Utsat people's language and the Cham's, and alludes that the Utsat people of Hainan originated in Champa (1941). Thurgood similarly argues that the Utsat are a Cham refugee community after the fall of Indrapura, the northern capital of Champa, after 1000 CE (1999: 252). Pang, an anthropologist, conducted field research among the Utsat people and notes that they now accept Champa as their land of origin. One Utsat man even told her that he wanted to go to Vietnam to learn the Cham language and understand the "pure" version of their culture (Pang 1996: 199-200).

The Cham people found Cambodia as a refuge from Vietnamese pressure. Mak Phoen counts three major influxes of Cham refugees from Champa to Cambodia. The earliest influx of the Cham population to Cambodia was after the fall of the Champa capital of Vijaya in 1471 due to the Vietnamese invasion. The second one took place after the Vietnamese takeover of Phan Rang, the capital of Panduranga, in 1692. The last major Cham migration to Cambodia took place around 1835 during the Nguyễn dynasty (Mak Phoen 1988: 77).

Some Cham who initially migrated to Cambodia further migrated into Thailand. Scupin, who studied a resurgence of the Cham ethnic identity among the Muslim community in an area called Ban Krua in the city of Bangkok, gives a historical account of the development of the Cham community in Thailand. According to him, the first known Muslim Cham migration from Cambodia to Thailand was during the Ayutthaya period (1351–1767). The Cham in Thailand were involved in the military, especially in its naval section. The Cham defended the capital against the Burmese, but the Ayutthaya kingdom was eventually destroyed by the Burmese in 1767, and King Taksin (1767–1782) moved the capital from Ayutthaya to the Bangkok area, and many Cham followed him. As a result of their loyalty in serving the Thai military, the royal family gave the Cham an area in Bangkok known as Ban Krua. After 1782, as a result of both internal and external political activities of Thailand and Cambodia, other Cham came to settle in Bangkok. In the early 1990s, about 6,000 Muslim people were living in Ban Krua (Scupin 2000).

Between 1975 and 1982, as a part of approximately 250,000 refugees from Indochina, the Cham immigrated to Malaysia (Wong 2013: 151-154, 165) due to the ethnic cleansing policy of Pol Pot's ultra-communist Khmer Rouge regime (1975–1979) (Kiernan 1988; Ysa 2002). It is believed that more than 50,000 Cham are now living in Malaysia and their number is increasing (Wong 2013: 151-154, 165). Farouk reports that Cham refugees from Cambodia are also found among the small Muslim communities in Laos (Farouk 2008: 81).

A Japanese photo journalist, Higuchi, traced Cham communities in Cambodia, People's Republic of China (PRC), Japan (though it is only one family), Malaysia, and Thailand. His accounts, accompanied by the photos that he took, tell us about the Cham people's struggle to retain their Cham identity in different socio-political contexts (Higuchi 1995, 1999).

Champa in Vietnamese national history

Problems of the fall of Champa

Today, the Cham are one of the 54 officially recognized ethnic groups in Vietnam. While the government stresses the unity among these ethnic groups and considers them as brothers and sisters, how to incorporate the history of Champa into the nation of Vietnam has become a tricky task because of the historical rivalries between the Cham people and the Kinh people. Lockhart's studies on the historiography of Champa explain the different treatments of the history of Champa in Vietnamese national history by Vietnamese scholars since 1959. He points out that in the studies published between 1959 and 1960, they mention Vietnamese aggressiveness toward Champa, and the studies have a rather sympathetic view of Champa's loss of its territories. In the studies published between 1960 and 1970, Vietnamese military campaigns against Champa are often omitted or reference to them is kept to a minimum. The studies published in the 1980s mention the Vietnamese southern expansion and annexation of Champa territories, yet occupation of Champa land is described as the result of self-defense or peaceful extensions of Vietnamese national territory. Recently, studies have discussed the absorption of Champa by the Vietnamese more openly, yet they put an emphasis on the cultural exchange between two ethnic groups and the Kinh-Cham hybrid culture of Central Vietnam (Lockhart 2011: 16-22).

Since the historical incident of the fall of Champa contains a seed of rivalry and antagonism between the Kinh and the Cham, explaining this fall is one of the most sensitive issues in Vietnamese national history. Borrowing ideas from Lockhart's discussion, I classify four different national narratives explaining the fall of Champa. The first explanation is to be silent on the fall of Champa. The second is to explain the fall of Champa as a class struggle. The third is to blame the Cham people's own drawbacks for destroying their country. The final explanation is to stress the cultural exchange that took place between the Kinh and Cham.

Being silent on the fall of Champa

Marr mentions that Hồ Chí Minh created the standard communist historiography of Vietnam by "selectively combining anti-traditionalism with nationalistic appreciation of Vietnam's past" and that the Vietnamese history written by the Viet Minh was "selective redemption of the past" (1981: 284-285). He says that the Viet Minh praised the Vietnamese resistance to foreign intervention as glorious, but there was little mention of the internal wars and "the near annihilation of the Cham" (Marr 1981: 284-285). Lockhart points out Champa's minor role in Vietnamese national history published in the 1970s. There is no detailed analysis of the absorption of Champa and its territories into Vietnam and no discussion of Vietnamese "expansionism" (Lockhart 2011: 17-18).

The History of Vietnam written by Nguyễn Khắc Viện mentions Champa in the section on the Mongol invasion of the 13th century and Cham influence on Vietnamese music during the Lý (李朝) and the Trần dynasties (陳朝), from the 11th to the 14th centuries (Nguyễn Khắc Viện 1987: 43-50, 63). However, there is no mention of Champa in the following Lê dynasty (後黎朝). It talks about the frequent revolts among the ethnic minorities living in the highlands, but it does not mention the military clash between Lê and Champa or the fall of Vijaya in 1471 (Nguyễn Khắc Viện 1987: 68-92).

A colorful picture book introducing the national ethnic groups published in 1991 includes a brief history of Champa. But it does not explain the fall of Champa and in fact there is no hint of Vietnamese involvement in the fall of Champa. It simply mentions that "the kingdom of Champa was disintegrating" and "the ancient kingdom of Champa has disappeared" as if it was a natural process (Chu Thái So'n & Đào Hùng 1991, see section on the south-central coast region).

The General History of Vietnam published in 2002 mentions the fall of Vijaya of 1471 in just a few sentences: "In April 1471, the capital of Chà Bàn (Trà Bàn) was occupied; Cham King Trà Toàn was arrested. Vietnamese Emperor Lê Thánh Tông left some lands of Champa locating south of Cù Mông Pass to Cham people. Since then Champa has declined" (Tru'o'ng Hũ'u Quýnh et al. 2002: 324). From these passages, we do not clearly see who occupied Champa's capital, who arrested the Cham king, or what the actual reasons are for Champa's decline.

There is a slightly different explanation of Champa's loss of its territories. Lockhart points out that a history of Kinh migration published in the early 1990s argues that there was a gradual withdrawal of Champa toward the south between the 11th and 15th centuries. Thus, the Vietnamese entered abandoned and vacant land (Lockhart 2011: 20-21). I heard a similar explanation from a high school English teacher I was acquainted with in Phan Rang city during my field research. According to his explanation, when the Nguyễn army entered the capital of Champa, the soldiers found an empty city. No Cham were found. Some Vietnamese historians explain the deserted capital as the result of a natural disaster such as an earthquake and flood or the spread of an epidemic disease. The point of these arguments is that it was not the Kinh who caused the disappearance of Cham people.

Class struggle

A book on ethnic minority people in Vietnam published in 1984 explains the Vietnamese southern expansion as "the process of national unification of Vietnam" and attributes the end of Champa to the death of the last king of Champa: "Late in the 18th century, Po Klong Khuan, the last king of Champa died at Phan Ri, putting an end to the dynasties of the Cham aristocracy" (Đặng Nghiêm Vạn et al. 1984: 234). One of the first comprehensive books on the Cham people published by the Institute of Social Sciences in Ho Chi Minh City in 1989 states, "The feudal Nguyễn dynasty replaced the Cham feudal class and controlled the Cham area of Thuận Hải for a long period of time" (Phan An 1989: 349).

When the fall of Champa needs to be addressed, it has been often described in the context of a class struggle. By adapting "Marxist terms," conflicts are explained as being between the feudal or serfdom ruling class and the working class which is united against its common class enemy (Lockhart 2011: 19). Therefore, Cham peasants and Vietnamese peasants were not only united with each other in the matter of chasing off the foreign invaders, but they also strongly resisted the oppression of the feudal class. The best example is the Cham response in the battles under the Tây So'n peasant movement against the Nguyễn feudal lords at the end of the 18th century (Nguyễn Tuấn Triết 1989: 326).

Prior to the absorption into Vietnamese territory, the Cham society was portrayed as a feudal one where the people were divided into four castes according to their Hindu influence and "marked by vestiges of the matriarchal system" (Đặng Nghiêm Vạn et al. 1993: 187). The Cham kinship is based on matrilineal principles and it practices matrilocal residence patterns. In Morgan's family evolution, which was adapted into the Marxist theory by Engels, matrilineal systems were said to be pervasive among people in the period of savagery or in the lower stages of barbarism. Engels set four evolutionary stages of family organization based on marriage systems. It evolved from group marriage to monogamous marriage by the creation of incest taboos in the course of socio-economic progress. In any form of group marriage, the identity of the father of a child is not certain, while that of its mother is. Therefore, "so far as group marriage prevails, the descent can only be proved on the mother's side" and "only the female line is recognized" (Engels 1985: 71).

In the past, the matrilineal system of Cham society has been mistaken by some French colonialists and Vietnamese scholars as a sign of a matriarchal society.[24] Baudesson, who lived among the Cham communities in the south-central coast region, explains the Cham society as "man belongs to an inferior order of creation," and "all political and social authority is exercised by women" (1919: 177). He further exaggerates Cham women's role in society in his description of polyandrous practice (Baudesson 1919: 177). The combination of a matriarchal society with the practice of polyandry placed Cham society far away from being "civilized" in the eyes of French people and also of many others.

By combining a feudal system and a matriarchal system, Champa is depicted as backward and less civilized. Such descriptions of Champa provide the legitimacy for the Kinh absorption of Champa. The fall of Champa marks the emancipation of the Cham people from the old oppressive feudal regime and backward social practices. The people of

---

[24] Phan Xuân Biên opposes the argument by many scholars who attribute the Cham's backwardness to its matrilineal system and that it should be changed into a patrilineal system (1989: 199).

Champa were freed from a stagnant situation and set up to move forward to progress with the solidarity of the Kinh people.

Such legitimization of Vietnamese advancement toward Champa is often found in officials' talk. A Cham person, who had served in the provincial People's Committee for years, explained to me that Champa was a feudal kingdom, and the feudal lords of Champa were defeated. The Cham people were liberated by the Nguyễn dynasty, and they were given land in the Mekong Delta. In his talk, the Nguyễn dynasty's advancement toward Champa was legitimized as rescuing the Cham people from their "backward and oppressive" feudal regime.

Champa's own bad deeds

Similar to the class struggle explanation, sometimes the fall of Champa has been attributed to the area's own bad deeds. Champa was the one who threatened the national borders with Vietnam (Lockhart 2011: 17-18). *The History of International Relations of Vietnam and Southeast Asia* written by Phan Lạc Tuyên attributes the loss of the country of the Cham to their warlike national characteristics. He argues that it was Champa that had territorial ambitions: "Many times Champa showed clearly its intention to occupy the Ma Delta (Thanh Hóa) and the Red River" (Phan Lạc Tuyên 1993: 61). He then explains the Vietnamese expansion toward the south as self-defense: Vietnam had no choice but to fight back to destroy Champa for its own survival and progress (Phan Lạc Tuyên 1993: 61).

The storyline goes on that Champa's defeat was simply due to the fact that they were not as good as the Vietnamese. Nguyễn Khắc Viện attributes the decline of Champa to its failure to develop a strong political system and internal dissension among the aristocratic Cham clans, while Vietnam could establish a strong centralized government with the Mandarin system which was formed in the Confucian school and recruited through examination (Nguyễn Khắc Viện 1987: 121-127).

Champa's domestic problems are often used to explain its decline. One of the staffs at the UNICEF office in Phan Rang city, who had numerous experiences working with minority people including the Cham, argued that Champa collapsed because of its lack of unity and solidarity. The Cham could not sustain their own country because of their internal fights and were thus destined to be governed by the superior political organization of the Kinh people. He did not go into the historical details but shared his observation of the Cham people, that the Cham were competitive among themselves and always failed to organize things by cooperating.

Cultural exchange

The fourth type of explanation of the fall of Champa is to highlight the cultural exchanges of the two societies. Lockhart notes that cultural exchange is the most frequently applied and significant perspective in discussing the consequences of Vietnamese southward movement (Lockhart 2011: 20). In this type of narrative, the role of Vietnamese dynasties in the establishment of Champa is stressed. Ongoing Vietnamese struggles with the powerful northern country, China, which historically always had an intention to expand its power toward the south, had provided a buffer state for other Southeast Asian people on the Indochinese Peninsula who could establish their own polities. Champa is often depicted as a beneficiary of the Vietnamese buffer[25] (Cao Xuan Pho 1988: 188).

The Champa and Vietnamese union and solidarity against the Chinese oppressor is most highlighted during the Mongol invasion. Nguyễn Khắc Viện argues that in Vietnam, the different nationalities historically had a tendency to unite progressively into a single nation because they needed each other economically and were closely bound by the necessity of common defense against foreign aggressors. The incident of the Mongol invasion gave an opportunity for the natural tendency for national unity to become a reality (Nguyễn Khắc Viện 1987: 41, 50).

The two Indochinese wars are very good recent subjects to describe so-called intimate and beautiful images of the joint struggles of the Kinh and the Cham peoples. Descriptions usually include a reminder of the historical national unity and solidarity among the different peoples in Vietnam who have stood shoulder to shoulder in the struggles against their foreign oppressors. Such solidarity and union between the Kinh and the Cham promoted friendly cultural exchanges which were said to be historically inevitable.

The cultural exchanges of Cham and Kinh peoples are claimed to be observed in a wider range of Vietnamese society, from agricultural techniques to religious beliefs, and resulted in a Kinh-Cham hybrid culture peculiar to the central coastal region of Vietnam (Lockhart 2011: 20).

The interactions between Vietnamese dynasties and Champa are illustrated as a metaphorical union of "marriage" which indicates a voluntary union of two cultures and the peaceful exchange of cultural elements, almost like a

---

[25] Yamamoto argues that due to its conflicts with Champa, the Tang dynasty had difficulties in expanding its power toward Vietnam (1975: 3).

reciprocating gift exchange. Yet there is no explanation of how the cultural exchange actually happened.

Dohamide and Dorohiem, Cham brothers from the Mekong Delta, published the history of the Cham people in 1965 in Saigon. Originally, the text was 165 pages long. After a censorship inspection, they were ordered to remove about six pages. These six pages contained the information about the Nguyễn dynasty's assimilation policy and the process of the Kinh people's migration into Cham lands. The South Vietnamese government, which was dealing with ethnic minority movements resisting its assimilation policy, perhaps could not allow publications which might provoke the sentiment of antagonism against the majority Kinh. The scarceness of historical writings on the Cham under the Nguyễn dynasty might have a similar explanation. The words "cultural exchange" or "marriage of cultures" seem to camouflage the Kinh domination and occupation of the Cham land which resulted in cultural assimilation.

Finally, we can also speculate that explaining the relationship of two groups of people as "friendly cultural exchanges" or a "marriage of two cultures" can serve another purpose: preventing the Cham from claiming autonomy. The Central Highland minority people's demand for autonomy was denied because of their lack of above-village-level political organization (Evans 1985). But for the Cham, who once had a national political organization, their claim for autonomy could be justified. In order to keep them intact in the nation of Vietnam, the state can use the historical peaceful co-existence of the Cham and the Kinh to argue that since Cham have been well integrated into Vietnamese society through cultural exchanges, there is no need for them to have their own separate political entity.

Conclusion

We know that historical Champa is characterized by *mandala* polities which correspond with maritime trade ports. The powerful *mandala* lord who won submission of other neighboring *mandalas* was considered as a deified king based on Hindu tradition. Champa's prosperity was based on its involvement in maritime trade and its precious trade items were brought from the highlands by various highland ethnic groups. Foreign traders were present in Champa and through them, new religions such as Islam were introduced. Champa benefited from the maritime trade but at the same time, it attracted Vietnamese dynasties who wanted to take control over the trade. Their takeover of the Champa's international ports put an end to its political independence.

However, our understanding of historical Champa needs further study. The history of Champa has many unsolved puzzles to be investigated. In 1996 I joined Nishimura Masanari, a late Japanese archaeologist and friend, to see Champa archaeological sites in the Bình Định Province. There are three Champa walled cities established around the 9th to the 11th centuries. We visited one of them called Thành Cha. It was a large sugar cane field and many old bricks and roof tiles were scattered around the area. We even found a long sandstone which was most likely used to hold doors to a temple. We were astonished by the size of the site. I was excited to think about the possible findings from this enormous site of Champa people's dwellings if systematic archaeological research could be carried out: the city plan and structure, people's daily activities, and so on. Suddenly, historical Champa became so real. Yet, Nishimura said that there would be little possibility of archaeological research on this site. It was due to the fact that such a large-scale site needs a long-term (at least 10 years) systematic investigation. It would be like the excavation of Pompeii and the government of Vietnam would not have the capability to support such an archaeological investigation.

It is also due to the questionable position that Champa holds in the national history of Vietnam. Is Champa included in or excluded from the national history of Vietnam? If it is included, how should it be told? Vietnam has not yet determined an agreeable view on Champa. Nagai, who studied Vietnamese national identity through policies of preservation of cultural heritage, notes that Champa's cultural and historical heritage will not be protected unless its history in a true sense is recognized as a part of Vietnamese national history (2009: 211).

CHAPTER 2

TROUBLE IN THE FIELD

In this chapter, I discuss the troubles and difficulties that I faced during my field research. These reflect the problems of Vietnam's ethnic minority policies, the characteristics of which are the country's prolonged engagement with wars and its socialist ideology. Vietnam's minority policies reflect the phases of progress in the two Indochina wars and are tightly connected with the development of socialism after reunification in 1975.

In an overview, I first explain the modern Vietnamese policies toward minorities. This is divided into two periods: the pre-reunification period (pre-1975) and the communist period (post-1975). In the pre-reunification period, I discuss the movement called *Front Unifie de Lutte des Races Opprimees* (United Struggle Front for the Oppressed Races, FULRO) because the Cham people's involvement in it makes them "a problematic ethnic minority group" in the eyes of the authorities. Such a view might have contributed to some of the difficulties that I faced during my field research, which I discuss in the latter part of this chapter.

The pre-reunification period (pre-1975)

Before the reunification of the North and the South, the two Vietnamese governments took contrasting approaches toward their minorities. The North Vietnamese minority policy was based on self-determination, aimed at integrating ethnic minorities into the nation of Vietnam by protecting their political and economic rights as well as their right to maintain their cultural heritage. South Vietnam, on the contrary, took an assimilation policy. It forced minorities to become Vietnamese by making them give up their cultural heritage and by removing them from their means of subsistence (Hickey 1982b; Jackson 1969).

In South Vietnam, the minorities living in the Central Highlands played a dominant role in minority affairs. West of the central coastal plain is an area called *cao nguyên* (highland) and it is inhabited by about 20 different ethnic groups who belong to two major language families: the Mon-Khmer and the Malayo-Polynesian. Most of the highland people practice semi-nomadic slash-and-burn dry-rice horticulture, while some groups like the Chu Ru and the Sre (*Xrê*) have long been practicing wet-rice agriculture which was probably introduced by the Cham people. The highland people have remained rather distant from the Kinh culture (Hickey 1993: xiii, xxviii).

During the French colonial period, highland people received different treatment than the Kinh majority by the colonial administration. The Catholic missionaries were the first French to enter the minority communities in the Central Highlands. The French became interested in the Central Highlands primarily for reasons of border security. They were concerned about Siam's eastward expansion as a sign of increasing English influence in the region. There was an incident where the Vietnamese Emperor Hàm Nghi (reign 1884–1885), who resisted the French through guerila activities in the Central Highlands, took refuge among the Siamese. The other reason for French interest in the Central Highlands was the possibility of finding useful minerals in the region (Hickey 1982a: 199-224).

In 1895, the highlands nominally came under the authority of the French colonial administration. Under French control, the Highlanders, who had previously been taxed by the Vietnamese court, were now taxed by the French, and even the highland villagers in the more remote interior were also subject to taxation. Previously, under Vietnamese control, the taxes imposed on the Highlanders had been paid in kind, while under French control they were required to be paid in currency and incorporated into a cash-based market economy. Male Highlanders aged between 16 and 60 were also subjected to corvée labor for road construction and other public works, or occasionally for the privately owned French plantations (Hickey 1982a: 273, 291).

In 1913, Leopold Sabatier became the head of the autonomous district of Darlac, and during his term (1913–1926) the political and strategic colonial administration was established. Sabatier became fascinated with Ede, (Rhade) culture and carried out field studies among these people. Because of his knowledge of highland customs and traditions, he was able to create an administrative and geographical infrastructure within Darlac. During his term, Sabatier established the Franc-Rhade school in Buôn Ma Thuột, an indigenous law court, and medical facilities. He organized the military consisting of Highlander militiamen, which was called the *Garde Indigene Moi*. He transformed an old ritual among the Highlanders to a new one, *palabre du serment*, in which the Highlanders swore an oath of allegiance to France. Most importantly, the rights to the land among the Highlanders, who practiced shifting cultivation, were protected under his administration (Hickey 1982a: 297-308; Salemink 1991: 248-255). His image of the highland people, as naive, credulous, fierce, and loyal, legitimized the necessity of French protection and the guidance of the Highlanders. In order to protect the Highlanders, he kept out Kinh and Chinese traders, and also French missionaries and businessmen as well (Salemink 1991: 254-260).

While the French colonial administration set up a different administrative system for the highland minority people in the South, they seemed to leave the administration of the Cham communities in the hands of the Kinh. Leuba (1915: 401) notes that after the fall of Champa the social organization of the Cham lost its characteristics and became nothing more than a reflection of the Kinh organization. Therefore, similar to Kinh villages, a Cham village consisted of a couple of hamlets and was administered by a group of notables who were elected by the inhabitants. Eight to ten villages made up a unit called a *canton* which was under the direct order of the *Chef de Canton*, and three or four *cantons* then made up a *huyen*. Under this system, the Cham seemed to have relative autonomy to elect their own officials (Leuba 1915: 401).

A rubber boom after World War I (1914–1919) created pressure to change the colonial administration of the highlands, which had suitable soil for cultivating rubber. Sabatier was forced to leave his office in 1926, and his successor, Giran, opened up the highlands for colonialists, investors, and businessmen from France. The Highlanders' rights to their lands were disregarded and almost the entire province of Darlac fell to a handful of French colonialists. The Highlanders' resentment against French control was expressed in a form of a millenarian movement called the Python God movement [26] which emerged around 1937 throughout the Central Highlands (Hickey 1982a: 309-320; Salemink 1991: 255-260).

During the First Indochina War (1945–1954), the highlands became a strategic asset for the French. They tried to keep it a separate domain from lowland Vietnam. In 1950, the highlands became Emperor Bảo Đại's domain, *Domaine de la Couronnedu Pays*, which generally is referred to as *Pays Montagnard du Sud*, but it actually continued to be administered by

---

[26] According to their beliefs, a Jarai (*Gia rai*) woman gave birth to a python that could talk like man. This was the god Dam Klan, who told the people that during the seventh month in a future year there would be a great calamity. On that day a fierce typhoon would come and all foreigners in the highlands, French, Vietnamese, and Lao, would be killed. The surviving Highlanders would divide the wealth of the foreigners, and from that day on they would be free from corvée labor and taxes (Hickey 1982a: 321-322, 352-358; Salemink 1991: 261).

the French (Hickey 1982a: 406; Salemink 1991: 264). While they remained under direct French colonial administration, highland ethnic minorities were always kept separate from the rest of the Vietnamese population. Consequently, this policy allowed a certain degree of autonomy in the highlands, and the solidarity and ethnic consciousness among the Highlanders was nurtured. This later provided a base for a series of ethno-nationalist movements during the Second Indochina War (1955–1975) (Hickey 1982a; Volk 1979).

After the Geneva Agreements in 1954, Vietnam was temporarily divided into North and South Vietnam at the 17th parallel. In the south, the Republic of Vietnam was established in 1955. The new government was headed by President Ngô Đình Diệm who took on an assimilation policy toward the minorities. The Central Highlands population was put under his direct administration and the government tried to expel French influence from the highlands and plant a Kinh majority culture among them. An anthropologist, Condominas, who stayed among the Mnong Gar people from 1948 to 1950, revisited one of the villages in 1958 and was deeply disturbed by the drastic change in the inhabitants' lives in the village. He criticized the Diệm government's minority policy as ethnocide (Condominas 1977: xiv). The Highlanders were forced to take Vietnamese names and forbidden to wear their traditional clothes. Their Highlander law courts were abolished and only the Vietnamese language was allowed in the schools. The Diệm regime's assimilation policy was also applied to the lowland minorities such as the Cham, the Khmer, and the Chinese (Hickey 1982b: 47-60; Mạc Đư'ò'ng 1978; Volk 1979; Jackson 1969).

In 1957, the General Commissariat for Land Development was created. This body established the Land Development Program (LDP) whose goals were twofold: economic development in the Central Highlands by transforming slash-and-burn horticulture to agriculture and modernization of the Highlanders by resettling massive numbers of Kinh people into the highlands (Hickey 1982b: xviii; Volk 1979). The Saigon government also had the problem of a vast influx of refugees from the North after the Geneva Agreements. By 1963, about 40% of the total population of the Central Highland provinces was estimated to be Kinh majority people (Hickey 1982b: 62).

A few Central Highland minority people had joined the Viet Minh and later the National Liberation Front (NLF). Labrie reports that by 1959, the Communist Party of North Vietnam was sending back to the Central Highland cadres who had been trained in the North after 1954 to form the nucleus of the new communist political infrastructure (1971: 116). In order to prevent communist infiltration, in 1959 the South Vietnamese government promoted a policy of resettling Highlanders from "unprotected" areas to the fortified settlements protected by locally recruited self-defense groups. The new settlements were known at different times as the Agrovilles, New Life Hamlets, and Strategic Hamlets. Most of the Highlanders were forced to move into the new settlements. At least 65% of highland villages have been relocated since 1945 (Hickey 1982b: 228).

The resettlement projects had the most negative effect on the minority people in the Central Highlands. The projects were generally ill-prepared and badly carried out. The resettlement locations were chosen solely based on security purposes, without consideration of the minority people's livelihoods. Sometimes, relocation was done without prior notice to the people and the government did not provide sufficient aid for them to start a new life in their new settlements (Osnos 1971: A1, A3; Volk 1979: 80). The highland minority people suffered from inadequate housing, lack of sufficient water resources, and delayed food rations in their new resettlements (Hickey 1982b: 166). Considerable numbers of Highlanders died in their new settlements from malaria, dysentery, and salmonella (Osnos 1971: A1-A3). There was growing anger among highland leaders about this relocation program.

Front Unifie de Lutte des Races Opprimees (United Struggle Front for the Oppressed Races, FULRO)

The Diệm government's strong assimilation policy and mismanagement of the Central Highlands' affairs provoked various anti-government movements among the ethnic minority people. This included: (1) the Bajaraka movement in the Central Highlands, whose name was derived from the key letters of the ethnic groups that joined the resistance—Bahnar, Jarai (Gia rai), Rhade (Ede), and Koho; (2) the Can Sen So (White Scarves), or later known as the Struggle Front of the Khmer of Kampuchea Krom (KKK) among the Khmer people living in the Mekong Delta provinces in Vietnam; and (3) the Front for the Liberation of Champa among the Cham people in the central coastal provinces, Tây Ninh Province, and the provinces in the Mekong Delta (Hickey 1982b: 47-60).

After the coup d'etat which overthrew the Ngô Đình Diệm government in 1963, more Bajaraka leaders were freed from jail and they contacted the Front for the Liberation of Northern Cambodia[27] and the Front for the

---

[27] It seems that this organization was the same as the Struggle Front of the Khmer of Kampuchea Krom, or had some relationship with it.

Liberation of Champa. Both organizations were initiated by a Muslim Cham named Les Kosem[28] (Hickey 1982b: 60). The Front for the Liberation of Northern Cambodia and the Front for the Liberation of Champa were fused into one organization called the Front for the Struggle of the Cham, which was renamed as the Front for the Liberation of the South Vietnamese Highlands or also known as the Front for the Liberation of the Champa Highlands (Hickey 1982b: 60-62).

Les Kosem had a vision to merge three groups—the Cham, the Khmer, and the highland minority people—into one group. He was particularly close to Khmer Krom leaders and Lon Non, who was a brother of General Lon Nol in Cambodia. All of them studied at the same *lycée* in Phnom Penh. They had a similar anti-Vietnamese sentiment and they came to share the similar goal of the re-establishment of the Cham and the Khmer kingdoms (Hickey 1982b: 92).

Les Kosem's vision materialized in 1964 as a movement called the *Front Unifie de Lutte des Races Opprimees* (United Struggle Front for the Oppressed Races, FULRO) . In 1964, FULRO members[29] revolted and delivered a statement that said the aim of the revolt was to regain the territory that the Vietnamese had taken from the Highlanders and the Cham (Hickey 1982b: 100).

In the same year, another coup d'etat made Nguyễn Khánh the new president of South Vietnam. He created a new policy for the minorities and published a booklet called *The Highlander Issue in Vietnam*, which provided the basis for the new highland minority policy. The Bureau of Highland Affairs was upgraded to the Directorate of Highland Affairs under the Ministry of Defense and moved its headquarters from Huế to Saigon (Hickey 1982b: 93-94). The new government held a conference with FULRO leaders in 1964 at the highland city of Pleiku. FULRO outlined their needs, such as an increase in ethnic minority officers in the provincial and district administrations, the right of land ownership for highland minorities, the right to have their own law courts, indigenous language education, and the right to receive foreign aid outside the channel of the

---

[28] Les Kosem, who was a Lieutenant Colonel in the Royal Khmer Army, is generally known as a Muslim Cham from Cambodia (Hickey 1982b: 62). However, Dohamide argues in his email correspondence that he was actually a Cham from Vietnam who originally came from a Cham village named Phum Soai in Châu Đốc.
[29] Hickey reports that by around 1965, FULRO had 5,000 to 6,000 troops in Cambodia, mostly either Ede or Mnong (*Mnông*) ethnic groups, and around 15,000 dependents (1982b: 117).

Saigon government. The government promised that it would act on most of the requests made by the FULRO leaders (Hickey 1982b: 111-113).

In 1966, the Ministry of Development of Ethnic Minorities (MDEM) (*Bộ Phát Triển Sắc Tộc*) was created with Paul Nur of the Bahnar ethnic group as the minister in order to implement the promises made to the ethnic minority people at the Pleiku Conference. The Ministry represented the Central Highlanders, northern highland ethnic minority refugees, and the Cham, but the Khmer Krom were not included (Hickey 1982b: xix, 164). Hickey mentions that the MDEM had a vague responsibility in general (1982b: xix). It appears that this ministry was created for the government as a gesture to tackle the concerns of the ethnic minority people, whose homeland became a significant strategic area in the progress of the war. It can be also seen as the government's attempt to create schisms among the FULRO members. There were some internal conflicts between the FULRO leaders who became the MDEM officials and those who did not.

There are ambiguities about the objectives, organization, and association of the FULRO movement. A book published by the MDEM in South Vietnam in 1969 claims that FULRO was a resistance against the inadequate policies of the South Vietnamese government, especially the Ngô Đình Điệm regime which enforced assimilation policies among the ethnic minority people. FULRO is depicted as a movement to protect customs, religions, and traditions of the ethnic minority people and to make progress among them, finally, to promote solidarity between the ethnic minority and the majority Kinh to work for the improvement of their livelihoods (Nguyễn Trắc Dĩ 1969).

Another book published by the People's Police in 1982[30] perceives FULRO as an anti-Kinh movement which could be a potential threat to national unity. It describes FULRO as having sought alliances with neither the South Vietnamese government nor the Communist Party, but almost consistently finding support from foreign countries. Therefore, FULRO was used as a means to manipulate the minority population of South Vietnam by French and Americans who were fighting against the communists (Ngôn Vĩnh 1982).

---

[30] The book, written by Ngôn Vĩnh, has a detailed description of foreigners who were suspected of being involved in the movement, such as a French missionary, Father Gérard Moussay, who had established a Cham cultural center in Phan Rang city, and a young American named Jay Scarborough, who joined the International Voluntary Service after graduating from Cornell University and taught English in the high school for the Cham people in Phan Rang.

Some French as well as American researchers saw FULRO as an organization supported/operated by the Central Intelligence Agency (CIA). Salemink argues that there was no evidence that FULRO was actually organized by the CIA, but that there was a distinction between FULRO and Civil Irregular Defense Groups (CIDG) which was initiated by the Central Intelligence Agency (CIA) as part of a village defense program in 1962 (1991: 270, 276). Labrie argues that the US involvement was passive and the US did not want to commit to involvement in the highland minorities' movement beyond their cooperation to prevent communist infiltration into the highlands. Furthermore, he comments that the US soldiers' tendency to trust highland minorities over Kinh soldiers caused the impression in the South Vietnamese regime that the US was supporting their struggle for autonomy in the highlands (Labrie 1971: 121-124).

Jaspan sees FULRO as a revival of Champa (1970), but Hickey criticizes Jaspan for exaggerating the role of the Cham in the FULRO movement. He sees more equal participation of the Cham, highland minorities, and the Khmer Krom, and solidarity among them. For Hickey, FULRO was the expression of the culmination of Highlanders' ethno-nationalism (1982b: 111-113). Labrie sees the FULRO movement as the successor to the Bajaraka movement, but he also pays attention to the Cham initiative within the movement and gives this as the reason why the predominantly highland minorities' united front consistently used such designations as DEGA-Cham or Champa-Highlands Liberation Front, and also why it insisted on special rights and privileges for the Cham people whose population was considerably smaller than that of the highland minorities (1971: 113).

The reason for the ambiguity of the objectives and the nature of the FULRO organization is probably due to the fact that there were various factions in the group. According to a former member, FULRO consisted of three liberation fronts: Kampuchea Krom (the area from Saigon to Trà Vinh), Kampuchea Nord (Champasak in Laos), and Champa. FULRO often changed its name, probably due to shifts in leadership and in external associations. The frequent name changes are also due to the fact that FULRO tried to use any support it could obtain regardless of political principles. Hickey mentions that FULRO held ongoing negotiations with the South Vietnamese government at the same time that it was also contacted by the Vietnamese Communist Party, which proposed the creation of autonomous zones in the highland (1982b). Salemink mentions that pro-American Highlanders, who were mainly associated with the MDEM, made a deal at the American Embassy in April 1975 to continue fighting in exchange for American support after the communist takeover. They kept fighting under the banner of FULRO (Salemink 1991: 273).

There is information available about the continuation of the FULRO movement in the Central Highland region after the reunification of Vietnam (Butterfield 1979). Ieng Sary, Deputy Prime Minister of Khmer Rouge, indicated in an interview that FULRO was the most serious resistance to Hanoi in Indochina other than the Khmer Rouge. FULRO approached the Khmer Rouge to exchange intelligence and military experience, and to receive guerrilla warfare training (Chanda 1979: 11).[31] There was a strong possibility of FULRO obtaining arms from PRC through the Khmer Rouge, and Chanda mentions that FULRO had a representative based in Beijing (1981: 10).

Quinn-Judge comments that the alliance between the Khmer Rouge and FULRO could have been a serious concern for both Hanoi and Phnom Penh; however, because they lacked arms, food supplies, and personnel, FULRO was inactive after 1980. Contrary to the declining FULRO movement, Quinn-Judge points out an article in the Vietnamese daily newspaper *Sài Gòn Giải Phóng* announcing a partial success of pacifying FULRO in 1982 and stating that FULRO had always had the capability of being a source of apprehension for the Vietnamese government (Quinn-Judge 1982: 14). In 1992, there was a report that a 400-strong "Vietnamese" force from FULRO, allied to the Khmer Rouge, was seeking to surrender to the United Nations (UN) (Far Eastern Economic Review 1992: 7). Many former FULRO members and their families have migrated to the USA. They founded the Montagnard Foundation, Inc[32] in North Carolina in 1990.

FULRO still causes anxiety among the Vietnamese government. One of the well-known Cham scholars at the *École Française d'Extrême-Orient*,

---

[31] Kiernan reports in his article "Orphans of Genocide" (1988) that about 90,000 Cham, one-third of their population in Cambodia, perished during the Khmer Rouge's ethnic cleansing campaign. Collins mentions Serge Thion's argument that the killing of the Cham people carried out by the Pol Pot regime was not because of their ethnicity, Cham, but because of their religion, and he concluded that the Cham were victims of an attempt to eradicate religion (1996: 56-57). To consider the fact that nearly the entire population of Cham in Cambodia are Muslim, Thion's argument does not make much sense. His argument is something like saying that Hitler did not persecute the Jews for their ethnic background but for their religion.

[32] They periodically publish their newsletters and have their own website, http://www.montagnard-foundation.org. They organized a festival on September 20, 1998, in Charlotte, North Carolina, to commemorate the first military uprising of FULRO.

Po Dharma, who participated in FULRO in his youth, was not allowed to go back to his home town in Ninh Thuận Province for decades. Even after he was finally allowed to visit his family in his native village, he was under tight surveillance during the visit and his movements were strictly controlled by the police.

The Cham people's involvement in FULRO always provokes Vietnamese government suspicion about foreign researchers working among the Cham people. Shin-e believes that because of the continuation of FULRO resistance against the Communist Party with foreign support, the Vietnamese government does not want any foreign researchers or scholars to have contact with the Cham or the ethnic minority people in the Central Highlands. Studying the Cham and other highland ethnic minority people is like an act declaring that "I am a suspicious person" to the central and local governments in Vietnam (Shin-e 2007: 5). In 2001, the Central Highlands minority people's revolts shocked the Vietnamese government. Immediately after the incident, my friend living in Ho Chi Minh City received a phone call from the city police who asked about my whereabouts. Though I rarely went to the Central Highlands for my study of the Cham people, the Vietnamese authorities were suspicious of my connection with the highland ethnic minority people.

Ministry of Development of Ethnic Minorities (MDEM) (*Bộ Phát Triển Sắc Tộc*)

The Ministry of Development of Ethnic Minorities (MDEM) did make some achievements to improve ethnic minority people's lives. In 1971, a Jarai person, Nay Luett,[33] was appointed a minister for the MDEM. He gathered ethnic minority leaders from the Central Highlands who participated in planning various programs. During his era, the schools for minorities were established. Phan Rang city of Ninh Thuận Province had a high school called Po Klong whose students were all Cham.

However, toward the end of the war as it was intensifying, the South Vietnamese government neglected its ethnic minority policies. The communists launched more destructive offensives while the US military was withdrawing from Vietnam. The defense of the highlands was left to the inadequate and badly trained South Vietnamese soldiers, and this left the highland people in a vulnerable situation (Hickey 1982b: 231). In March 1975, the highland city of Buôn Ma Thuột fell to the communists. President Nguyễn Văn Thiệu declared that he was going to give up defense of all areas

---

[33] Nay Luett was a FULRO member.

north of Buôn Ma Thuột. An estimated 200,000 to 250,000 people tried to flee from the highlands, but only about one third made it to the lowlands. This news shocked the MDEM. It immediately called a conference and demanded autonomy for the highlands and the right to form its own military force. The Saigon government rejected this proposal (Hickey 1982b: 281-282).

On April 30, the communist forces entered Saigon. They allowed the MDEM to continue to function until the end of May, but it was abolished in June. The leaders among the highland minorities were arrested and sent to re-education camps. There was a report of executions of some high-ranking officers in the MDEM (Hickey 1982b: 284).

The MDEM had many positive plans for the ethnic minorities but Labrie points out that in practice, there were many problems in the MDEM's projects. First of all, they had little freedom for independent action. Most of the programs and projects were coordinated with other ministries such as the Ministry of Defense, the Ministry of Interior, the Ministry of Open Arms and Revolutionary Development, and so on. Secondly, the MDEM's ethnic minority officials found themselves in between the ministry and their Vietnamese superiors. They suffered trying to satisfy the needs of each side (Labrie 1971: 128-129).

South Vietnam's minority policy was influenced by two factors. The first was to isolate minorities from communist propaganda and influence in order to prevent them from supporting the communists. The second factor was to pacify a series of ethno-nationalist movements which had been continually bothering the government. The minority policy actually had nothing to do with the lives of the minorities but rather it was a strategy to defeat the government's enemy.

The Communist period (post-1975)

After defeating the French in 1954, the newly established Democratic Republic of Vietnam created three autonomous zones for its ethnic minorities one after another between 1955 and 1957. The common characteristics of these three autonomous zones were that all consisted of not only one but various ethnic groups and they were located in strategically significant areas. All three autonomous zones, however, disappeared sometime during 1959 without any clear explanation (Connor 1984). In the 1960 Constitution, minority areas became inseparably integrated parts of the nation which denied the right of secession of the minority regions. The rapid establishment of autonomous zones, then the disappearance of them without clear explanation, and, later, the denial of the right of secession of the minority autonomous regions reflect that the promises to minorities made by the communists were created strategically to gain their support during the two Indochina wars (Connor 1984).

After reunification in 1975, Hanoi's concerns regarding minorities shifted from mobilizing minorities in order to win the wars to one of integrating them into the new framework of a unified socialist nation of Vietnam. The government created economic development policies within the framework of socialism by emphasizing equality, collective ownership, and the development of a new socialist era (Gammelgaard 1990).

There were similarities between the general highland minority policies of the former Saigon government and the Socialist Republic of Vietnam. Both emphasized the decentralization of Highlanders and the protection of forest resources. They recognized the importance of developing natural resources in the area and encouraged large numbers of Kinh to settle in the highlands. Volk argues that the Vietnamese government tried to bring "development" to the Highlanders simply by transporting the Kinh people from overly crowded lowlands to the highlands. Development seemed to indicate that the Highlanders should become like the Kinh people (Volk 1979).

The minority policies by socialist Vietnam can be called "the Communist civilizing project" as discussed by Harrell, who examined the minority policies of PRC. Harrell explains that a civilizing project is "a kind of interaction between two actors, the civilizing center and the peripheral peoples, in terms of a particular kind of inequality" (1995: 4) and discusses three different civilizing projects in the PRC: the Confucian civilizing project, the Christian civilizing project, and the Communist civilizing project. The first requirement for the civilizing center is to define and objectify the subjects of the civilizing project as inferior, and thus in need of civilization and suitable for the improvement of the civilization. Unlike the Confucian and the Christian civilizing projects, the Communist civilizing project does not, in theory, have a prior assumption that the center consists of a particular group of people who are superior to the rest of the population. The goal of the Communist project is:

> not to make the peripheral peoples more like those of the center, but rather to bring them to a universal standard of progress or modernity that exists independent of where the center might be on the historical scale at any given moment. (Harrell 1995: 23)

However, despite the ideology of the Communist civilizing project, the Han inherited an innate sense of superiority to the minority people due to their prior civilizing projects. Harrell mentions that as long as such an innate sense of Han superiority remains, the actual program of the Communist project will be based on the unconscious assumption that Han ways are better, more modern ways (1995: 26). Similarly, in Vietnam, "becoming 'socialist' looked a lot like becoming Kinh" (McElwee 2011: 196).

The Communist Party denied their intention to assimilate the ethnic minorities, yet after 1975 the Vietnamese government did not adapt to the multinational model and did not foster the cultural distinctiveness of the different minority groups (Keyes 1987: 23). After 1975, special minority education disappeared. The minority high school for Cham students, Tru'ò'ng Po Klong in Ninh Thuận Province, was opened to non-ethnic minority students. Religious activities among the ethnic minority people were restricted. The schools that taught the Qur'an among the Muslim Cham in Ho Chi Minh City were closed and the Cham children had to learn the Qur'an secretly at home. The religious pilgrimages to Mecca and proselytization were prohibited. Collectivization of agricultural lands prevented the Cham people from practicing their rituals concerning their rice fields. Directive 214 of the Communist Party Central Committee Secretariat regulated various customary practices such as marriages, burials, and death anniversaries to "check backward practices" among the ethnic minority people (McElwee 2011: 197). The Cham people's various traditional practices and rituals such as funerals, buffalo sacrifices, and harvest feasts were considered to be primitive, superstitious, and too wasteful, and thus they were banned.

After 1985, the state of Vietnam made a shift in its minority policies. This occurred in the period when the whole nation of Vietnam went through significant economic change called *đổi mó'i* (renovation), in which the state switched from a controlled economy to a free market economy to increase the nation's productivity. The state's examination of prior minority policies resulted in self-criticism. The failure to promote economic development among minorities was attributed to the fact that since minority policies had been considered in the framework of national economic development, the state had been ignoring the significance of minority culture (Gammelgaard 1990; Mạc Đu'ò'ng 1991; Lục Văn Pao 1992). Đang Quang Trung mentions that the shortcoming in the implementation of the nationalities policy was that the state never paid attention to the interests, socio-economic characteristics, psychological composition, or customs of the minorities (1989).

The reformed minority policy first appeared in the 6th Congress of the Vietnamese Communist Party in 1986, and in the 7th Congress, a clearer presentation and implementation of a new minority policy appeared. The 7th Party Congress stated:

> To achieve equality, solidarity, and mutual assistance among the people of various nationalities; create conditions for the people of all ethnic groups to advance on the path of civilization and progress in close relation to the common development of the community of all Vietnamese nationalities; respect the interests, traditions, culture, dialects, customs, and faiths of all ethnic groups; and oppose big-nation chauvinism and racial discrimination and division. Socioeconomic policies must suit the characteristics of various regions and ethnic groups, especially ethnic minority people. (Nông Đú'c Mạnh 1992: 41)

The significant point of the minority policy that appeared in the 7th Congress was that the Communist Party admitted that there was a multilateral path toward socialism. In order to achieve socialism and socialist culture, which is the "harmonious combination of the very best of the unique cultures of the fraternal ethnic groups within the great family of ethnic groups of Vietnam" (Ngo Duc Thinh 1987), people are not required to follow a single path of advancement. Instead, they can follow different paths appropriate to their ethnic backgrounds.

The state now tolerates religious practice among the minority people. Cham Muslims in Ho Chi Minh City have been allowed to teach the Qur'an at school since 1988, and the Muslim community has sent a group of pilgrims to Mecca each year since 1995. In Ninh Thuận Province, sacrifices of water buffalo in the ceremony called *Klang Kôi Kubao* were held during my field research. This ceremony had not been held since 1975 due to its extravagant expense. The revival of *Klang Kôi Kubao* is due to the softening of state control over religious practices. The Office of Culture and Information in Ninh Thuận Province provided financial support for organizing the *Klang Kôi Kubao*, and it recorded the entire ceremony.

In 1991, there were ethnic policies specifically made for the Cham people, such as Notice No. 3 of the Communist Party Central Committee Secretariat on Policies toward the Cham community (*Thông tri của Ban Bí thu' về công tác đối vó'i đồng bào Chăm*).[34] In these policies, protection and preservation

---

[34] Ito suspects that Notice No. 3 of the Communist Party Central Committee Secretariat on Policies toward the Cham community and also Directive 68 of the Communist Party Central Committee Secretariat on Policies toward the Khmer area

of cultural heritage and development of the Cham culture were mentioned. Continuation of the teaching of the traditional Cham writing system and publishing textbooks for language education were highlighted and, furthermore, it was stated that the system will provide special care for the bilingual Cham language teachers (Shin-e 2001b: 244-245). The Cham writing system has been taught in primary schools in Cham villages, and the Cham Language Editing Committee (*Ban Biên Soạn Sách Chữ' Chăm*, BBSSCC) is campaigning to eliminate illiteracy among the Cham people in Ninh Thuận Province (Photo 2-1). The Institute of Social Science in Hanoi compiled several translations of folk tales from each minority group in Vietnam and published them in four volumes in 1992. There are publications written in minority languages and also TV and radio programs broadcast in minority languages in various regions.

Photo 2-1. A textbook for learning the Cham scripts

---

were released in 1991 because the Vietnamese Communist Party was cautious about the resurgence of FULRO which was once allied with the Khmer Rouge after Vietnam's withdrawal from Cambodia upon the Paris peace treaty (2009b: 52).

One of the shortcomings of the previous minority policies was an institutional weakness. Notice No. 3 of the Communist Party Central Committee Secretariat on Policies toward the Cham community states the significance of increasing numbers of Cham communist members who understand the political, economic, and cultural situation of the Cham people (Shin-e 2001b: 246). In both provinces where I conducted field research, I rarely met Cham officials. At the time of my field research, there were only two Cham officials working in the office of minorities. There were no Cham people working for the Office of Culture and Information. At the Cham cultural center in Phan Rang, there were a few Cham researchers and staff, but the center was headed by a Kinh official and the majority of the staff were Kinh. Đặng Nghiêm Vạn points out that the position of responsibility, who is in charge, is not clear at either the central or the local level of administration in the matter of minorities. This is due to the shortage of personnel who have knowledge of minorities and who have been trained to carry out work among the minorities (Đặng Nghiêm Vạn 1990).

The changes in the minority policies were welcomed. However, at the same time, the government emphasized the necessity of eliminating harmful customs and non-scientific superstition. But there was no clear guideline to define what superstitions and harmful customs were, and this provided the possibility for the state to legitimize its control over the minority culture and traditions. How the state balances its actions of protecting minority cultures and eliminating certain traditions among the minorities is quite vague.

Since 1993, Vietnam has been contemplating the idea of having a Law of Ethnic Groups. Ito (2009b: 62-63) lists four reasons for drafting the law. First, the collapse of the USSR by ethnic conflicts in 1990 made the Vietnamese Communist Party re-aware of the significance of ethnic groups in the nation. Second, during this time, in order to appear as a law-governed country, Vietnam was drafting various laws with financial and technical support from the outside. The Committee for Ethnic Minorities and Mountainous Areas tried to draft the new laws just like other ministries. Third, there was a concern about ethnic conflicts caused by land disputes in the Central Highlands among the Communist Party cadres who wished to solve the problems by the law. Fourth, the Communist Party had made several laws for ethnic minorities but they turned out to be less than effective to balance the interests of different ethnic groups.

The Law of Ethnic Groups was first drafted in 1993 by the committee responsible, which consisted of 25 members. Ten of those 25 were members of the National Assembly who were at the same time members of the Ethnic

Council. The rest were from the Committee for Ethnic Minorities and Mountainous Areas, Ministry of Health, Ministry of Interior, Ministry of Culture, Sports and Tourism, Ho Chi Minh National Academy of Politics, and the Association of Ethnologists. At that time, the Standing Committee of the National Assembly anticipated having the bill of the Law of Ethnic Groups passed in 1995. However, there were disputes over the areas that the law covered. Some argued that the law should be comprehensive by covering political, economic, social, and cultural aspects of ethnic groups. Others argued the law should only cover social and economic aspects, while some further narrowed down the areas of concern to language, writing system, customs, and traditions (Ito 2009b: 47-48). Consequently, the committee redrafted the law 13 times and the final draft was presented to the Politburo of the Communist Party in 1997. With a lot of disappointment, the draft law was rejected. It was said that drafting the Law of Ethnic Groups should be based on careful analysis of social and economic aspects of the national ethnic groups. It needs continuous study and cautious preparation (Ito 2009b: 53).

Drafting the Law of Ethnic Groups was restarted in March 1999. The Ethnic Council drafted the law with the Committee for Ethnic Minorities and Mountainous Areas, the Ministry of Justice, the Ministry of Interior, and the Vietnamese Fatherland Front. As Ito points out, previous drafting committee members such as the Association of Ethnologists, Ministry of Culture, Sports and Tourism, and Ministry of Education were not included this time. After 1999, six drafts were made of the Law of Ethnic Groups and previously praised ideas, such as protection of traditional culture and respect of the cultural diversity of ethnic minority people, were completely omitted from the draft. The changes of objectives in drafting the Law of Ethnic Groups must be due to the aftershock of the uprisings in the Central Highlands in 2001. At this current time, the Law of Ethnic Groups has not yet been issued (Ito 2009b: 55).

The state's endeavor to create the Law of Ethnic Groups demonstrates the fundamental principle of the state toward the ethnic minority people: the state must control them. There are no official regulations for minority people to form organizations which advocate their opinions. The minority people are always the subjects to be taught, guided, and instructed by the state to make rational choices which lead them toward assumed progress.

Troubles in the field

When I tried to start my field research in Vietnam, I was never clear about the necessary procedures. Difficulties in obtaining permission for field research depend on various things such as the person's nationality, the topic of field research, and the area of studies, but the most crucial thing for getting permission is to find a good host institute. I had an affiliation with the Center for Vietnamese and Southeast Asian Studies at the University of Ho Chi Minh City (current day University of Social Sciences and Humanities of Ho Chi Minh City) where I was a language student. I had to study the Vietnamese language for a certain amount of time per week to maintain my student status. When I told the Center that I wanted to quit my Vietnamese language class and start my field research, they told me that it would not be any problem to go off into the field without changing my visa status from a student visa to a research visa. One of the Vietnamese linguists at the Center became my research advisor since he had a connection with the Cham communities in Ninh Thuận Province. With his arrangement, I was introduced to the Cham Language Editing Committee (*Ban Biên Soạn Sách Chữ' Chăm*, BBSSCC) in Ninh Thuận Province and, under the guidance of the Language Center and the Office of Education in the province, I could start my research among the Cham communities in Ninh Thuận.

I spent the first month visiting different offices and officials in the field. First, I went to the provincial People's Committee in Ninh Thuận Province. An official at the office of public relations showed great understanding and support for my research and wrote me several recommendation letters to the different lower-level offices. I felt that things were going well, and I started to have an optimistic feeling about my research. However, the letters of recommendation from the provincial government did not work like a magic wand at the lower-level offices. I had to go through another negotiation process with them and the negotiations were also ongoing because they seemed to change their policies over the course of my field research.

After six months, I left Ninh Thuận Province for Ho Chi Minh City to prepare for my second field research among the Cham people in the Mekong Delta. Meanwhile, I went back to Ninh Thuận Province to observe one of the biggest Cham festivals. While I was staying at Phan Rang city, I received a fax from the Center for Vietnamese and Southeast Asian Studies at the university requesting my immediate return back to Ho Chi Minh City. I rang the Center but the person who answered the phone knew nothing about the fax I received. I decided not to go back immediately and observed the festival until the end before going back to Ho Chi Minh City.

In Ho Chi Minh City, I was told by the Center that no researchers would be allowed to conduct any field research for a while, but they did not give me any specific reasons for it. One of my Japanese friends, who was also affiliated with the Center and had just come back from her one-month field research among the Catholic communities in a province near Ho Chi Minh City, was also told that it would be difficult to go back to her field for a while. I talked to various people to find out the real reason behind this sudden restriction on our field research. One of the Vietnamese teachers at the Center told me that "Hanoi" had decided not to permit any further fieldwork by foreign researchers because they had loosened up their regulation so much that they became alarmed by the increasing number of foreign scholars in the field. This made them subsequently tighten up the regulation.

Most of my foreign friends in Vietnam suggested that I remain quiet and wait until people forgot about the matter of field research. So, I went back to Japan to visit my family for a while. When I came back to Ho Chi Minh City, however, the situation was the same. Finally, through my friend's connection, I received an explanation from a person working at the Ministry of Foreign Affairs about me being banned from field research. I was on a cruise boat for my friends' wedding anniversary party. The hired band was playing music and people started to dance to it. The person from the Ministry of Foreign Affairs was also invited and he asked me for a dance. While we were dancing, he whispered to me what had happened in the field.

What he told me concerned a conflict between two offices in Ninh Thuận Province. I was under the care of the Office of Education, which made the Office of Culture and Information in the province annoyed because they thought they were the ones who should take care of a foreign researcher working on the Cham ethnic minority group. The rivalry between these two offices had created a problem for me. The Office of Culture and Information reported me as a suspicious person to the Ministry of Interior in Hanoi. They claimed that a few pictures I took in Ninh Thuận Province contained the scenery of restricted areas. After they filed the report in Hanoi, the information was sent to the Ministry of Interior in Ho Chi Minh City, and the Center for Vietnamese and Southeast Asian Studies at the university was warned by them. The Center did not want to go through any hassles due to foreign researchers, so they just stopped all foreign students affiliated with the Center from going into their fields.

This reminded me of an incident with the Cham cultural center under the Office of Culture and Information. At the beginning of my field research, I frequented the Center hoping to work with their researchers. However, the

Center told me to seek research support from the Office of Education and in the end, one sympathetic researcher at the Center advised me not to visit so often since the officials there saw me as an annoyance. I also remembered that the director of the BBSSCC, with which I had a direct association, did not have a good relationship with the Office of Culture and Information. The workers at the Cham cultural center under the Office of Culture and Information were mostly Kinh people, while those working at the BBSSCC were entirely Cham. The situation indicated the Kinh control of Cham culture. In order to gather information about the Cham, I should have affiliated with those who controlled the cultural information rather than those who practiced it.

When I received this information, almost four months had passed. I started to seek a way to carry out other field research I had originally planned in a province of the Mekong Delta by hoping that enough time had passed so that the authorities would pay less attention to me. Since the Center for Vietnamese and Southeast Asian Studies at the University of Ho Chi Minh City did not actively support my field research because of their fear of getting into trouble with the Ministry of Interior or other ministries, I had to appeal to a different office at the university which might push the Center to help me start my second field research. I consulted with a director at the Office for Scientific Research and International Cooperation who was of a higher rank than the director of the Center for Vietnamese and Southeast Asian Studies at the university. This director, who had gone overseas for his study, had the courage to pressure the Center and promised to process my paperwork for obtaining a new visa which would allow me to carry out my field research.

Finally, my visa was issued. I asked my advisor to accompany me to An Giang Province to introduce me to the local officials. Since I had decided to live in the village where Aisah came from, she also joined our trip. Her skill of "talking sweetly" made the negotiation process a whole lot different. In An Giang Province, we first consulted a Cham man who had recently retired from the People's Committee in the province. With his advice, we first contacted the head of the ward who was a Cham man. He contacted the village officials and we went to the People's Committee in the village. The officials told me that they could allow me to stay in the village if I requested, but for the research I had to talk to the provincial People's Committee in Long Xuyên, the capital city of An Giang Province.

We spent three hours on a rough road and arrived at the People's Committee in Long Xuyên where an official listened to my advisor's explanation for about five minutes and then gave us a piece of paper. It appeared to be an introductory letter to the Office of Culture and Information in the province. We went to the Office of Culture and Information with the piece of paper and talked to a very young director there. He had a very friendly manner and immediately created several introductory letters to the Office of Culture and Information in the different districts and promised to call them up to tell them about my visit in advance. That was the end of the official business. In Ninh Thuận Province, I was prohibited to stay in a Cham village, but in An Giang Province, I could stay in a Cham village for over three months and conduct field research as I planned.

There are various possible reasons to explain the relative success in conducting field research in An Giang Province compared to Ninh Thuận Province. First, I did not stir administrative autonomy in An Giang Province, while I became a disturbing element to lower-level administration in Ninh Thuận Province. In Ninh Thuận, I approached the higher administration office with an assumption that if the higher office agreed with my research and released an order to the lower office, the lower office would follow its order. However, the lower offices resisted the order. They seemed to be annoyed by me coming to their office with the order of a higher administrative unit without any prior notice or negotiation. In An Giang, I made contacts with the lower administrative units. The officers at the local level were the ones I had to deal with frequently and they were the ones who kept a close eye on me. Once they had agreed to have me as a researcher in their ward, they directed me to contact certain upper administrative units and to whom I should talk. Automatically, I could see a pathway through the administrative maze that I needed to follow.

Second, the relationships between the Cham community and the Kinh majority community were different in these two provinces. In Ninh Thuận Province, the Kinh people were seen as intruders of the Cham land by the Cham people, and the Kinh people were also aware of this historical consequence. The Cham villages were mostly physically isolated so that entering a Cham village gave an impression of going to a Cham domain. The BBSSCC, which hosted me in Ninh Thuận Province under the Office of Education, was a Cham domain. The office was headed by a Cham person and all the teachers and workers were Cham. While the Center of Cham Cultural Studies under the Office of Culture and Information was the Kinh domain, most of the people at the Center including the director were Kinh. These two offices had not had any collaborations or corporations. In An Giang Province, however, the Cham people and the Kinh people both settled in former Khmer land, and the Cham villages and the Kinh villages were next to each other along canals or rivers. The numerous contacts between

Cham and Kinh in daily life facilitated a familiarity between the different ethnic groups.

Third, the degree of commoditization of Cham cultural information between the two provinces was different. In Ninh Thuận Province, the Cham cultural information was commoditized by the Office of Culture and Information, while in An Giang Province, such a matter was unknown. In Ninh Thuận Province, the Office of Culture and Information was keen on gathering information on Cham people's customs and traditions. They received funding to rebuild the Cham cultural center with a museum attached to it. The officials at the Office of Culture and Information were proud of the amount of Cham cultural information they had collected and how many foreign scholars had visited them to seek assistance and cooperation. The office monopolized Cham cultural information and gained some material benefit as well. During my field research, I had to pay a certain fee to the office every month for taking pictures in the Cham villages. They warned me that I had to pay more if I videotaped any activities in the villages. A Cham scholar from Ho Chi Minh City who was born in one of the Cham villages in the province was charged by the office when he videotaped a ceremony at his own parents' house. At the end of the field research, I had to send all my notes together with photographs to the Office of Culture and Information for inspection. They kept my research data for about one month and called me in. They warned me concerning some information about my data for inaccuracy. In An Giang Province, on the other hand, I was never charged for gathering cultural information nor asked to present my research data to the local authority for inspection.

The monopoly of cultural information by the Office of Culture and Information also reflects the state's authority over the culture of its own ethnic minority group. The "ethnic information" of the Cham people collected by the Office of Culture and Information stored in the form of photographs, videos, and tapes has become part of Vietnamese national heritage. Regardless of the credibility of the materials, in the view of the Office of Culture and Information, I should have retrieved the "ethnic information" from the office's storage instead of going around the Cham communities by myself. Since I insisted on gathering information by myself, I became a nuisance to the Office of Culture and Information. As a result, I was denied access to the official "ethnic information" and my non-official ethnic information had to be examined by the state authority.

Conclusion

Thinking back to my field research in Vietnam, the first things that come to my mind are bitter feelings of frustration, confusion, disillusion, and loneliness. My confusion and frustration in the field are rooted in the ambiguity of Vietnamese minority policies. Since there is no office which deals with both policy-making and implementation, a researcher has to travel around to various ministries and offices in order to obtain various topics of information regarding ethnic minorities. It is an introduction to the bureaucratic maze of Vietnam, and it is a maze that the ethnic minority people have to go through in order to solve their various problems.

Compared to the mid-1990s when I was conducting my field research, Vietnam is now much more tolerant to the researchers. Many people are conducting field research in Vietnam and my own recent experiences of this among the Cham were less tense and less stressful. However, there was an incident that brought back my old memories. I was working with a Vietnamese researcher from Ho Chi Minh City to conduct research on the spread of Orthodox Islam among the Bani people. The People's Committee of Ninh Thuận Province permitted our research and the Office of Culture and Information supported it, yet they told us to obtain permission from the Office of Religion since our research dealt with religion. We tried to negotiate with the Office of Religion for two days. But the officer in charge was never in his office and never answered our phone calls. No other officers replaced him to help us. In the end, we could not carry out our research. This experience reminded me that the information concerning ethnic minority people is still tightly controlled. The authorities still decide what the researchers can see and hear.

McElwee calls ethnic minority policies in Southeast Asia in general "schizophrenic" (2011: 189). While they call for the respect for historical and cultural differences among the ethnic groups, they are "pursuing policies of forced assimilation" (McElwee 2011: 204). It can be summarized that there have not been any ethnic minority policies for these people per se in Vietnam. The country's ethnic minority policies are strategies to achieve other historical objectives: to win wars, to unify the nation, to achieve socio-economic developments, and to maintain the authority of the Communist Party. They are not solely concerned for the welfare of ethnic minority people. Since they are a means to an end, ethnic minority policies have suffered from the uncertain administrative structure, ill-planned and fragmented projects, a lack of capable personnel to deal with ethnic minority problems, and little participation of ethnic minority people in the bureaucratic system.[35]

Evans argues that the Vietnamese minority people's situation is no better than that of the other ethnic minority people living elsewhere. Actually, the Vietnamese minority people's situation is worse because they do not have the freedom to organize among themselves or with other minority people for solidarity (Evans 1985: 301). There is no possibility for forming ethnic minority people's grassroots organizations in Vietnam (McElwee 2011: 189). Despite various laws and regulations to protect minorities' rights, there is no system for ethnic minorities to advocate their voices. They are mere recipients of the state's policies. The people remain voiceless and deprived of being a master of their own life.

---

[35] Chuengsatiansup argues that exclusion of the ethnic minority people from bureaucracy was to impose the state's official structural order as the only legitimate political order placed upon the local community's organization (1998).

CHAPTER 3

THE CHAM OF THE SOUTH-CENTRAL COAST AREA

In this chapter, I discuss how the Cham people of the south-central coast area, particularly in the province of Ninh Thuận, define themselves as Cham. A dual structural principle in Cham cosmology called *ahier* and *awal* is examined extensively. This is because I believe that the *ahier* and *awal* principle represents a unique world view of the Cham people and holds the key to understanding the way their ethnicity is constructed.

Landscape of the Cham of Ninh Thuận Province

The Cham people were once known as skillful seamen. The oldest cemeteries of a group of Cham people in the Ninh Thuận Province are located right on the seashore and this indicates their close affinity to the sea. Now, however, the Cham people in the Ninh Thuận Province live away from the sea and they engage in wet-rice cultivation (Photo 3-1).

The Cham people in Ninh Thuận Province prefer to live away from Kinh communities. They usually form their villages a short distance away from the markets and major roads where the Kinh population usually concentrates. When some Kinh people migrated close to their village, some Cham people in An Nho'n moved out of their village and established a new one nearby. The Cham villages are surrounded by their rice fields and vineyards,[36] and often one has to cross a small stream before entering the village.

Almost all the Cham houses are surrounded by a fence and have some kind of gate at the entrance. Inside the villages, there is usually an open space where various religious ceremonies and rituals are performed. The Cham people in the south-central coast area keep rich ritual traditions. According to the local scholar Nguyễn Vân Đài, approximately 150 different religious ceremonies are known.

---

[36] Ninh Thuận Province is one of the few places where grapes can be grown in Vietnam, and it is quite profitable.

Photo 3-1. Phu'óc Nho'n

Cham society is known for its matrilineal and matrilocal system. When Cham people marry, the husband goes to his wife's house to live with her family. The Cham were made to adopt Vietnamese names, and nowadays their children take their father's family name. However, it does not mean that the children belong to their father's lineage. They still belong to the mother's lineage and property is passed down through the female line. Usually, the youngest daughter gets a larger portion of the parents' property because she and her husband are the ones who will take care of their aging parents. When the husband dies, his body is sent back to his natal village and he is buried in the graveyard there. There are a few exceptions, but generally, a husband and a wife are never buried side by side.

During my six months of field research among the Cham communities in Ninh Thuận Province in 1995, the Vietnamese local authorities did not permit me to stay in Cham villages. I stayed in the BBSSCC in Phan Rang city and I made day-trips to the Cham villages from there. The Cham people in the south-central coast area keep the traditional writing of Champa called *akhar thrah (akhar sarak)*. The *akhar thrah* script has evolved from Sanskrit and all the religious texts, legends, and poems were written in *akhar thrah*. Traditionally, the people who could read *akhar thrah* were limited. Now, *akhar thrah* is taught in the public schools in Cham villages. The BBSSCC is the office responsible for publishing textbooks used in the Cham writing classes and for training teachers to teach *akhar thrah*.

The people working in the BBSSCC were all Cham and the head of the office at that time was Mr. Ty who was educated at a *lycée* in Đà Lạt, spoke fluent French, and was quite keen about the development of education among the Cham people. The education level of the south-central coast Cham people is rather high. There are many Cham school teachers. One Cham village has so many school teachers that some of them have to go to teach in the Kinh villages. The provincial hospital is crowded with Cham doctors, nurses, and pharmacists. There are Cham lawyers and scholars working in Ho Chi Minh City.

The search for the pure culture of Cham

The Cham people in Ninh Thuận Province are very interested in their own culture and the origins of the Cham people. There are a considerable number of local scholars who told me that they were "*say mê*"—infatuated with Cham culture. Those local scholars are the people who have a very good command of reading Cham scripts, *akhar thrah*. In the field, my Japanese-made pens were very popular among the local scholars. They were looking for a quality pen with which to copy old Cham books. Literacy in the Cham language means access to cultural knowledge, and the local intellectuals collect and copy old books written in the Cham scripts.[37]

Many south-central Cham think that without the knowledge of *akhar thrah*, one cannot understand the culture (*ilimo*). The Cham people would always tell me by pointing at their books that these were the *ilimo* of the Cham people, and if I wanted to learn their *ilimo*, then I had to study their *akhar thrah*. Doris Blood, an anthropologist, who lived among the Cham people for several years before 1975 notes that the Cham value literature more highly than oral tradition (1981: 6). In answer to my questions, elderly Cham people often read and translated their books for me. Such things happened so often that I came to suspect that Cham intellectuals believe that the Cham culture only exists in written form. Culture is not something acted out, not something that one can observe.

This reliance on texts is peculiarly similar to the 19th-century Orientalists' attitude to their studies, described by Edward Said. The knowledge that the

---

[37] The Cham people carefully keep their books private and dislike loaning them to others. A Cham scholar, Thành Phần, managed to identify and compile a catalog of Cham books owned by individuals in Ninh Thuận Province (see Thành Phần 2007).

Orientalists possessed about the Orient came from books. The "classical Orient"—found only in texts—was considered to be the real Orient, while the modern Orient was seen in terms of problems to be solved (Said 1978: 94, 204-207). In the Cham case, their intellectuals' textual orientation can be understood as a denial of Cham modern cultural practices. This is because Vietnamese government minority policies have resulted in the loss of many Cham religious ceremonies and the modification of their rituals. The Cham intellectuals probably see their contemporary cultural practices as impure by comparison with the culture formerly practiced in Champa, which they deem genuine and truly original. For them, real original Cham culture may thus be found only in the texts, and if one is seeking "correct" cultural information about the Cham, one should learn to read *akhar thrah*.

The Cham intellectuals often complained about the Kinh researchers' lack of a scientific approach to studying their culture in comparison with the French scholars to whom they gave credit for genuinely understanding the Cham culture. As far as I know, none of the Kinh scholars have studied the Cham language in order to speak Cham or to read Cham scripts, while French scholars—as a matter of fact, French Orientalists—are the ones who have collected and deciphered old Cham inscriptions. The Cham dictionary written by Aymonier and Cabaton in 1906 holds the ultimate authority in the usage of Cham language among the Cham intellectuals. Many of my Cham teachers had a photocopy of the dictionary, and often they looked things up in it to teach me "correct" words with correct spellings. By contrast, Cham-Viet dictionaries published by the university in Ho Chi Minh City were thoroughly examined by these Cham local scholars, and many mistakes and inappropriate translations were pointed out and criticized.

The Cham local scholars were usually very eager to show me their collections of books and to explain aspects of their culture. Since they all tried to give me "pure" or "correct" information on Cham culture, they often fought among themselves to find the one correct answer to my question. Many times, I also saw a small group of elderly Cham men arguing about things like correct spelling or pronunciation of a Cham word at ceremonial gatherings. Cham books written by a Cham scholar were ripped apart by these local Cham scholars' criticisms. Each of them had their own explanation and interpretation of Cham words and they believed their ideas to be the "truth," and the true form should be only one, original, and pure, not contaminated by the Vietnamese culture.

The Cham intellectuals are competing to grasp this most authentic form of Cham culture, and it can be said it is their obsession. Their abilities to access and possess "genuine" knowledge of their past, Champa, make a Cham person authentically Cham.

Balamon and Bani

There are two distinct groups of Cham in this region if we consider their religious affiliations. One group—called Balamon—adheres to an indigenized form of Hinduism. They worship the god Po Yang and their deified kings, and hold their ceremonies in the old Champa temples called *bimong*, which were built between the 14th and 16th centuries (Photo 3-2).

Photo 3-2. Po Klong Garai

Photo 3-3. A group of Balamon priests, *Halau Tamunay ahier,* outside of Hữ'u Dú'c

They are supposed to observe a taboo on eating beef. They are normally cremated when they die.[38] They are led by a body of priests, *Halau*

---

[38] However, those who die before the age of 15 are not cremated. The Balamon people from two small villages, Palei Rio and Palei Bingu, are not cremated when they die. The local scholars explain this by saying that the people of Palei Rio and Palei Bingu cannot be cremated because they are the descendants of landless slaves. At the time of my field research, the people of these two villages had their lands. However, because of a lack of good access to water resources, the villagers do not engage in wet-rice cultivation, as do the Cham in other villages. Instead, they cultivate sugar cane and corn, which do not have much market value compared to rice. For water for daily use, the villagers must go to a well which is about 1 km away. The well produces a small amount of water and the villagers have to wait for quite some time in order to collect a sufficient amount. The villagers did not give me any clear reasons why they do not go to the nearby Bani village of Văn Lâm to obtain their water, although I raised this question repeatedly. According to a legend among the Cham people in Palei Rio and Palei Bingu, their ancestors used to live around the northern part of Huế. For some reason, they sailed south and arrived in Panduranga where they are now. The north of Huế was about equivalent to one of the five regions of the Champa kingdom, called Indrapura. Indrapura was the first region that fell into the hands of the Kinh people.

Tamunay ahier (Photo 3-3). The other group—called Bani—adheres to an indigenized form of Islam. They worship Po Alwah *(*Allah) at their village masjid called *thang muki*. They are supposed to observe a food taboo on eating pork. When they die, they are buried without cremation. They are led by a body of priests, *Halau Tamunay awal* (Photo 3-4) (see Table 1).

Photo 3-4. A group of Bani priests, *Halau Tamunay awal,* in Phu'ớc Nho'n

Balamon	Bani
Po Yang	Po Alwah
Bimong	*Thang muki*
Cremation	Burial
Less Progressive (old)	Progressive (new)

Table 1. Balamon and Bani

In Ninh Thuận Province, all Balamon villages belong to one of three temples: Po Inu Nugar, Po Klong Garai, or Po Rame. However, Palei Rio and Palei Bingu do not belong to any of these three temples.

Ahier and *awal* as a male and female dichotomy

In Cham villages, the term Balamon is rarely heard. The Balamon Cham are simply known as Cham, by the same name as the ethnic group. The term Balamon is used only by scholars and researchers. A Cham scholar, Dohamide, mentioned that it is a Vietnamese word coming from the term "Brahman," although the term Balamon is never used by the Cham themselves in their daily conversation. However, in order to avoid confusion in terms—between Cham as Balamon and Cham as the entire ethnic group—I use the term Balamon in this book.

The French scholar Lafont reports that Balamon Cham called themselves *Cham jat* or *Cham harat* to indicate that they were the "pure race" of Cham to differentiate themselves from the Bani (1964: 158). All Cham are born as Balamon. But a particular group of Cham is scheduled to become Bani after their birth. The people of this group obtain their full membership through a ceremony of conversion to the Bani religion. Thus, being Balamon indicates an elementary form of existence in the world. Bani are not born as Bani but become Bani from Balamon. This, however, appears to me to be no more than a discursive distinction. In reality, the terms Balamon and Bani bear meanings that extend further than mere religious differences explainable by conversion. Membership in the respective group is determined from the time of an individual's birth. Since the matrilineal principle governs kinship, a person becomes Balamon because he/she was born to a Balamon mother, while a person becomes Bani because he/she was born to a Bani mother. It is possible to convert to religions other than Balamon and Bani—such as Buddhism, Christianity, Islam, etc.—but the convert will still maintain a certain identity as Balamon or Bani.[39] This identity not only indicates a difference of religion but also of the community into which the individual was born.

A difference that I found while observing rituals among both groups is that the Balamon's rituals are collective, while the Bani's rituals are individualistic. In each Bani village, there is one *thang muki*, while each Balamon village does not have its own temple but several villages belong to one Balamon temple. Deceased Bani people are buried individually, while deceased Balamon people are buried collectively. The Balamon people do not have individual tombs like the Bani (Photo 3-5). After the cremation of the body, nine pieces of bone are taken out of a deceased

---

[39] I have met a considerable number of Balamon men who have converted to Bani at the time of their marriage to their Bani wives. Recently, an increasing number of Bani are practicing Sunni Islam.

person's forehead. These nine pieces are kept for some time but then eventually buried with other pieces of bone of deceased people belonging to the same lineage in the same tomb called a *kut* (Photo 3-6).

Photo 3-5. Bani graves outside of Phu'óc Nho'n

Photo 3-6. Old *kut*

However, since Balamon and Bani do not share their daily lives in villages, they do not know much about each other's customs and traditions. The Balamon and the Bani do not live in the same villages[40] and previously, marriage between Bani and Balamon was strictly prohibited. Young Balamon and Bani students have opportunities to interact with each other at high schools or universities, but the old people, especially women, do not have many chances to communicate with each other. For example, my Cham language teacher was a Bani and his wife often invited me for lunch when I was working in her village. She was very curious about my impressions of the Balamon and often wanted to know what they fed me in their villages. She asked if I could eat their food. I told her that I had no problem eating their food, including ceremonial dishes. She expressed her surprise in the following terms:

> We [Bani] eat first and then conduct our ceremony, so our food is fresh and clean; meanwhile, the Balamon do the ceremony first, then eat afterward. That is why their food is not fresh and clean. Even though I am Cham, I don't dare eat Balamon food. You are not Cham, you're a foreigner, but you can eat their food. You are better than me. But you need to be careful about the food in Balamon villages. It's not as clean as ours.

This differing sense of hygiene seems to separate the two groups and provides a perspective on their relative degrees of "progress." Balamon ceremonies require complicated preparation and they are usually carried out over many hours. Many different kinds of offerings are displayed (Photo3-7). Sometimes, they are put out under the strong sunshine and are covered with sand, dust, and numerous flies. After the ceremony, these offerings are distributed among the people and consumed. To the Bani people, such Balamon ceremonies are not hygienic and they do not dare to participate.

The Balamon funerals,[41] which last for three nights and four days, are often the target of the Bani people's criticism. During that time, the body, which was dug out of the ground one or two years after death, is kept in a special ceremonial house (*kajan*). I often heard that Bani people commented: "They eat and drink in front of the dead body, it is dirty." I

---

[40] There are 22 Cham villages in Ninh Thuận Province. Among them, seven are occupied by the Bani people. One village, called Phú Nhuận, is an exception because in it both Balamon and Bani are living together. However, their residence is not intermingled. The village is divided into the Balamon residential area and the Bani residential area by a narrow street cutting through it.

[41] There are several kinds of funerals practiced among the Balamon people. See Appendix, Balamon funerals.

once met a Bani man at a Balamon funeral. He was married to a Balamon woman. The deceased was his wife's relative. He did not enter the funeral house to join in the ceremony, but sat instead in his relatives' house, drinking tea, smoking, and chatting. Occasionally, I saw other Bani people attending Balamon funerals. They never entered the funeral house. Perhaps they were afraid to approach the corpse, but their comments on the Balamon ceremony always related to the notion of hygiene: "dirty," "unclean," "unsanitary," and so on.

Photo 3-7. Balamon offerings at Po Klong Garai

For the few months that I was concentrating on observing Balamon funerals, I attended their funerals in different villages, about one every two weeks. I also held discussions with a Bani anthropologist on the sequence and variety of Balamon funerals. We had a few disagreements over the details of the ceremony, such as the number of pieces of bones to be removed from the cremation pile and the names of the invited deities. I thought that his knowledge was more or less based on beliefs popularly held by the Bani people about Balamon funerals. I suspected that he had not spent enough time observing actual ceremonies, probably because he did not feel comfortable attending them. In fact, I have never observed a Balamon funeral with him.

The Balamon, meanwhile, often agree with Bani criticisms of their religious practices. They admit that the Bani are more progressive, that their ceremonies are simpler. However, they also argue that they are unable to simplify their ceremonies as the Bani do because the Balamon must maintain the authentic cultural traditions inherited from Champa without alteration or simplification.

One of the aims of Vietnam's cultural policies is to preserve minority customs, traditions, and languages, while erasing obstructions to progress such as superstition, non-scientific practices, and outdated customs. The state thus urges the people to simplify and modify some of their more lavish religious ceremonies and customs. In the unitary "evolution scheme" of socialist thinking, in which the Kinh ethnic group is depicted as the most advanced and evolved among the 54 officially recognized ethnic groups, progress connotes assimilation to Vietnamese (Kinh) culture.

The Balamon reinterpret this unitary evolution scheme in terms of purity of culture and tradition. One of the poorest and most isolated Balamon villages in Ninh Thuận Province is called Bình Nghĩa. Here, certain ceremonies and traditions are different from those in other Balamon villages. The reason for this was explained to me in the following way. Bình Nghĩa village is located far from the Kinh communities and it is "backward" and very poor as a result. Of all the Cham villages, however, this minimal influence from Kinh culture has enabled them to maintain Cham customs and traditions in the purest form.

Harrell mentions a similar view on the Yi people of southwest China. The Yi people are considered to be one of the most under-developed ethnic groups in PRC. The Yi of Liangshan are considered to be particularly backward because of their isolation and slow development of the area in comparison to other areas. However, it is because of their slow development that their customs and culture are considered to be "the typical, the original, the untouched and unspoiled versions" (Harrell 2001: 180). Harrell attributes such a view to Chinese adoption of the simplified Marxist theory of historical stages.

Certain legends explain the origin of the Cham people's division into two groups and in these legends, Balamon and Bani are consistently identified as *ahier* and *awal*. Both words are of Arabic origin, with *ahier* meaning "back, behind, or after" and *awal* meaning "front or before." In the legends, *ahier* denotes Balamon and *awal* denotes Bani. In daily life, the Cham use these terms to differentiate between certain types of ceremony, or between people of the Balamon group and those of the Bani. They also use this dual principle in their cosmological explanations.

In the Cham lunar calendar, a month consists of 30 days. But the days are not counted from 1 to 30. Instead, the days 1 to 15 are counted twice. The first 15 days are called *bingun*. The second 15 days are called *klam*. The first *bingun* half of the month is denoted *ahier*, while the second *klam* half of the month is denoted *awal*. Both Balamon and Bani hold their wedding ceremonies on the Wednesday of the *klam* half of the month. Wednesday is seen as a day of balance. This notion of balance relies on the principles of *ahier* and *awal*. The Cham week consists of seven days, as in the solar calendar. The first three days—Sunday, Monday, and Tuesday—are considered to be *ahier*: fire and heat are attributed to these days. The last three days—Thursday, Friday, and Saturday—are *awal*: water and cold are attributed to them. Wednesday, on the other hand, falls between *ahier* and *awal*. Furthermore, the soil—representing growth and fertility—is attributed to this day, which adds to Wednesday's suitability for weddings.

These principles also govern other cosmological beliefs. For instance, the upper part of the human body, from head to navel, is called *akhar* and is considered *ahier*, while the lower part, from navel to feet, is called *tanuh riya* and is considered *awal*. The Cham imagine the sky as the body of a human being, hunched over with the hands and feet on the ground. They thus see the part of the day from dawn until noon (the sky's upper body, head to navel) as *ahier*. The period from noon until sunset (the sky's lower body, navel to feet) is *awal*.

Legends about *ahier* and *awal* suggest that this two-realm division is meant to bring peace upon Cham society. One version of a legend I collected reads as follows:

> A long time ago, the prophet Po Nubi Mohamat was an *ahier*. At that time, the *awal* became very strong and Po Nubi Mohamat was very impressed with them. So, he tried to change all the *ahier* people to become *awal*.

However, the *ahier* people opposed Po Nubi Mohamat, arguing that "In the world there should be men and women. If we have only women, how can we maintain the world?" Thus, a war between the *ahier* people and Po Nubi Mohamat broke out. They fought for seven days and seven nights. Then, Po Nubi Ichbrahim came between them as a mediator. He asked Po Nubi Mohamat, "Can you live with only one eye, only one hand, and only one leg?" Po Nubi Mohamat did not know how to answer this question and agreed that the rest of *ahier* should remain *ahier*, but he himself became *awal* on this occasion. After seven days and seven nights of battle, Po Nubi Mohamat felt thirsty. He brought out water by magic and shared it with all the *ahier* people, so peace between them was restored. (This legend was related to me by a Balamon shaman)

The dualistic tendency in Cham cosmology was pointed out by Blood. Of the two realms in the system she described, one belonged to the father and the other to the mother (Blood 1981: 43, 48). In the legend above, *ahier* is male and *awal* female. Many Cham people express a similar idea of *ahier* representing men and *awal* women and further explain that to function properly, society must have *ahier* and *awal*. An old man in a Bani village said that *ahier* means *yang* and *awal* means *yin*.[42] He unbuttoned his jacket and said that *ahier* and *awal* were like a button and a button hole; one had to have both a button and a button hole to wear a jacket. Others explained that *ahier* and *awal* are like plus and minus terminals of a battery, as we need to have both to make machinery run. Similarly, society must have *ahier* and *awal* to function. Thus, the *ahier* exists for the *awal*, while the *awal* exists for the *ahier*. The mutual dependence of the two realms holds the world of the Cham people together.

The male and female attributes of *ahier* and *awal* have many manifestations, which include the two groups' respective bodies of priests. For example, a local scholar of the Balamon told me the following story about the birth of his first child. After their marriage, he and his wife were childless for some time. His mother-in-law became concerned and sent him to a nearby Bani village to ask the Bani priests for help. He brought offerings of special candles and soup to the priests. They read the Qur'an for him. He made several trips to the Bani village, and he and his wife were then blessed by a son, followed by three other boys and four girls. He explained to me why

---

[42] A symbol mark of yin-yang is found in various places in Cham villages. I was told that the yin-yang symbol mark was introduced during the time of the Nguyễn dynasty (1802–1885) when the Vietnamese court established an administrative system modeled on the Chinese Confucian system (Woodside 1971). For the concept of yin-yang in Vietnamese society, see Jamieson (1993).

his mother-in-law asked him to see the Bani priests and not Balamon priests (the leaders of his own religion). It was because Balamon priests symbolize men and men cannot give birth. Only Bani priests, who symbolize women, could help the couple have children.

Photo 3-8. Bani women wearing *khan djram*

The gendered attributes of Balamon and Bani priests are also manifested in their behavior and clothing. When Balamon priests conduct ceremonies, they always sit with crossed legs in the way Cham men sit. Bani priests sit with their feet under them and to the side in the way Cham women sit.[43] Priests of both groups wear white turbans with red tassels at both ends, but on top of the turban, Bani priests add a cloth called *khan djram*. The *khan djram* is an item of clothing used by Bani women. The priests wear it in the

---

[43] Well-mannered Bani women will never sit with crossed legs. Belo makes a similar observation among the Balinese. She mentions little differences in physical appearance between men and women, such as clothing and hairstyles. She then discusses that gender differences were shown by certain rules of behavior, and she mentions that Balinese men sit cross-legged while women sit with both legs to one side (Belo 1949: 15).

same way as the women wear it (Photos 3-8 and 3-9). Bani priests shave their heads when they enter the priesthood, while Balamon priests wear long hair tied in a bun at the top of their head. When they are conducting ceremonies, the bun is covered by a white turban tied in a special way without red tassels. The turban is tied into the shape of a *linga* (Photo 3-10).

Photo 3-9. Bani priests wearing *khan djram*

Photo 3-10. A Balamon priest wearing a *linga*-like white turban at Po Klong Garai

Ahier–awal complementarity is also expressed in number cosmology. The Cham community identifies itself through a symbol called *hon kan*, composed of two numbers and two figures. The symbol's center is a circle representing the sun under which there is a crescent. The number 6 is set above the sun, and the number 3 below the crescent. The sun and the number 3 are considered *ahier*, while the crescent and the number 6 are *awal* (Figure 2). For the Cham, the number 9 is the largest number in the script. The *ahier* number 3 plus the *awal* number 6 join to form the number 9, which is the most complete number. Thus, the *hon kan* symbol—composed of *ahier* and *awal* elements—represents the most complete form of existence: unity, balance, stability, and peace. In other words, when *ahier* and *awal* co-exist, the world of the Cham finds unity (see Table 2).

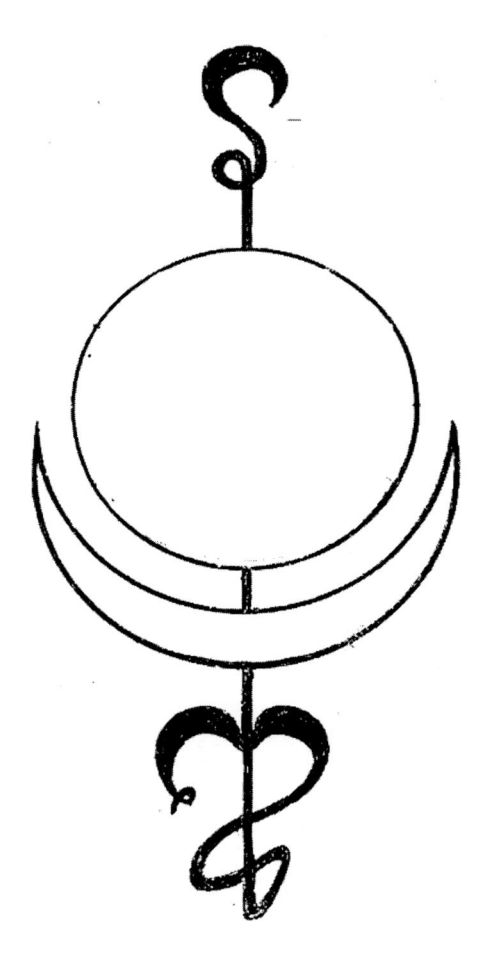

Figure 2. *Hon kan*

Ahier (before/front)	*Awal* (after/behind)
Balamon	Bani
Male	Female
Father	Mother
Upper body	Lower body
Sky	Earth
Sun	Moon
Fire	Water
Hot	Cold
Sunday, Monday, Tuesday	Thursday, Friday, Saturday
Death	Life, Birth
From dawn until noon	From noon until sunset
First 15 days of a month, *Bingun*	Latter 15 days of a month, *Klam*
Number 3	Number 6

Table 2. *Ahier* and *awal*

We may also pursue the idea of complementarity in the symbolism of the priesthood. As we have seen, Balamon priests symbolize men and Bani priests symbolize women. But they also bear attributes representing something from the opposite sex. The Balamon priest carries a yellow rectangle bag on his shoulder (Photo 3-11), while the Bani priest has three bags, which hang from his neck down onto his back. One of the three bags is slightly larger than the others, and the two smaller bags are tied by the same cord (Photos 3-12 and 3-13). The Balamon priest's bag symbolizes the uterus. The Bani priest's bags symbolize the penis and testicles. The bags associated with each religion symbolize the acceptance, within *ahier* and *awal*, of their counterparts.

The significance of the complementarity of the two sexes in other societies in Southeast Asia has been studied. Belo uses an example of Chinese yin and yang and explains that the theme of male and female is endlessly repeated in every context of the Balinese people's life, from the gods to the terms for a carpenter's joining (1949: 14). Hoskins, who studied indigenous notions of gender and agency among the Austronesian-speaking Kodi people of the western tip of Sumba in the Lesser Sunda Islands, also reports that gender is the most consistently evoked structuring principle within this "complementary dualism" (1987: 174). She argues that male and female, as abstract categories, provide a language for talking about ways of effective action. "Male and female are simply used to express contrasts which may be applied recursively. Male contains Female, Female contains Male. Inside contains the Outside, the Outside the Inside; Black, White, White, Black" (Hoskins 1987: 197).

Photo 3-11. A Balamon priest's bags

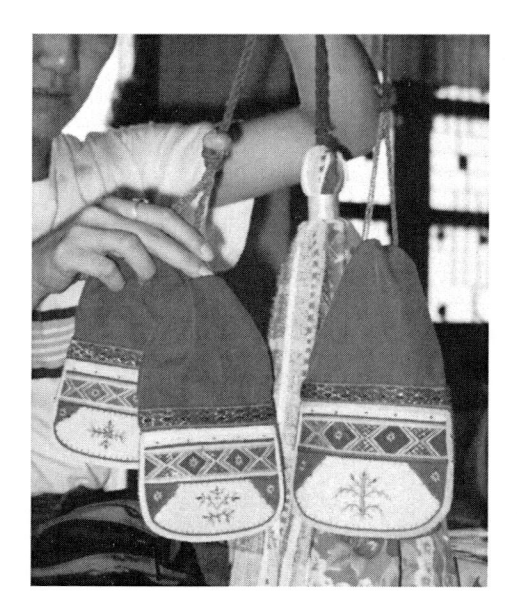

Photo 3-12. A Bani priest's bags

Photo 3-13. A Bani priest carrying the three bags

Such a notion of complementary dualism is observed in Cham ceremonies, but one peculiar thing is that we often find more *awal* elements in *ahier* ceremonies than *ahier* elements in *awal* ceremonies. For instance, during *ahier* funeral rituals, Balamon priests make a triangle by placing their hands above their forehead to pray to Po Nubi, Po Nubi Eta, Po Nubi Atam, and Po Nubi Mota, all of whom are *awal* deities. According to a Balamon priest, they must pray to invite *awal* deities to their funerals, weddings, and other ceremonies, as well as the celebrations held on the construction of new houses. On these occasions, the Balamon prepare two different sets of areca nut and betel leaf, which are essential offerings in every religious ceremony. One is called *hala kapu*, which is the *ahier* set. The *awal* set is called *hala tam tara* (Photo 3-14). While Balamon people often present both *ahier* and *awal* sets at their ceremonies, Bani people rarely present *ahier* sets. The only time I observed the Bani people using the *ahier* set was at a funeral.

Photo 3-14. Two *hala kapu* (*ahier* set) on the left and the two *hala tam tara* (*awal* set) on the right

According to Po Dharma, the strong *awal* (Islamic) influence in the *ahier* (Balamon) religion is a result of the political situation of Champa during the 17th to 19th centuries. Comparison of old documents kept among the Cham in Ninh Thuận Province with oral traditions led him to the discovery that *awal* deities were placed higher than *ahier* deities in the religious pantheon of Champa. He then came across documents on the origin of a ceremony called *Rija prong* explaining why the *awal* god Po Alwah took the place of the *ahier* goddess Po Inu Nugar. During that period, Champa tried to ally with military powers on the Malay Peninsula to fight against the Vietnamese, who increasingly threatened Champa. In order to maintain these alliances, in the context of ongoing Islamization of the Malay world, it was crucial for the court of Champa to show an interest in Islam. The replacement of *ahier* deities with *awal* deities in the state religious pantheon was made to meet political needs (Po Dharma 1990).

Po Dharma's argument is a convincing explanation of the existence of more *awal* elements in the *ahier* rituals. However, I would like to look more closely at the nature of the ceremonies, in order to understand how *awal* elements work in *ahier* ceremonies. I found that those *ahier* ceremonies which contained *awal* elements often bore meanings relating to life or birth.

During the Balamon's funeral ceremony, a shed called a *rap* is constructed to the northeast of the funeral house (Photo 3-15). The *rap* is usually occupied by musicians and craftsmen who make the ornaments for the cremation carriages. However, Balamon priests do not step into this *rap* because it is *awal* territory. The *rap* is built for the *awal* deity, Po Nubi Mohamat. Assisted by another *awal* deity, Ja Tin who holds a torch to light up the inside of the funeral house, Po Nubi Mohamat observes the sequence of the funeral ceremony from the *rap*. Ja Tin is symbolized by a torch-like object inside the funeral house (Photo 3-16). The *awal* deity, Po Nubi Mohamat, is present at the *ahier* funeral because the funeral contains the meaning of the rebirth.

Photo 3-15. A *rap* in Phu'ó'c Đồng

Photo 3-16. A torch-like object symbolizing Ja Tin

All participants in the funeral ceremony implicitly play the different roles involved in childbirth, including the newborn's parents, other relatives, godparents, midwife, and so on. On the first day of the funeral ceremony, a bowl of rice and a boiled egg are prepared for the deceased. This meal symbolizes the meal for a pregnant woman, and it means that the deceased impregnates a new life in his/her body.[44] When the deceased's skull is saved from the flames and the nine pieces of bones, *talang*, are removed from the forehead, the deceased gives birth to his/her new life in the other world. Immediately after this ceremony—whereby the nine pieces of bones are placed into the container *klong*—a ceremony symbolizing the newborn's first meal in the other world is performed. With both elements of *awal* and *ahier*, the life cycle—of which death is a part—is complete. Since an *ahier* funeral also connotes "rebirth," the female elements of *awal* must be included in their funeral ceremonies.

---

[44] In this symbolic context, the deceased's actual sex seems to be disregarded.

Awal, ahier, and akafir

Until now, I have discussed *ahier* and *awal* as religious distinctions between the respective groups of Cham people. However, within the Bani community itself, *ahier* and *awal* also mark differences in religious status. For the Bani, *awal* refers to the body of Bani priests, while *ahier* refers to the Bani lay people who do not enter the priesthood. Thus, the *awal–ahier* opposition, as it is used within the Bani community, distinguishes between the sacred and secular in the Bani religion.

At each Bani masjid, *thang muki*, there are usually 10 to 20 Bani priests. Eligibility for the priesthood is restricted to married Bani men who have accomplished the circumcision ceremony called *Katan* and know how to read Arabic script. In general, there is at least one priest from each of the village's lineages in attendance at the *thang muki*. On accession to the priesthood, the priest has to shave off his hair. From then on, he will always wear a special long white coat, which indicates his status as a Bani priest. He cannot drink alcohol nor eat pork. His food must be prepared according to the Bani religion, like *halal* food in Islam. Every Friday, the priests participate in prayers to Po Alwah at the *thang muki*, mostly attended by elderly women, one from each household. For the entire sacred month of *Ramuwan*[45] (Ramadan in Islam), Bani priests have to stay in the *thang muki*, away from their families. They fast and remain silent from dawn to sunset for the first three days of *Ramuwan* and pray five times a day throughout the month.

The terms *awal* and *ahier*, as used by the Bani people, also bear male and female attributes. But an attempt to unravel which realm bears which gender attribute can lead to considerable confusion. A Bani scholar explained that *awal* symbolizes male-right domain. According to him, since Bani priests belong to the *awal*, they mainly turn right (clockwise) in their ceremonies, while in the Balamon, who belong to *ahier*, priests turn left (i.e. the female realm, counterclockwise) in their ceremonies. However, in most of the ceremonies I observed, the Bani priests often turned counterclockwise, while the Balamon priests turned clockwise. Once, in discussion with the Bani, I repeated what I had learned in a Balamon village about the male and female realms indicated by the directions right and left. I had understood that a person's right hand belongs to the domain of *ahier*, indicating the

---

[45] The dates of *Ramuwan* are exactly the same as for Ramadan, but the Bani people organize various ceremonies four days prior to the beginning of *Ramuwan*. See Appendix, Ceremonies during *Ramuwan*, for a more detailed explanation.

male attribute, while a person's left hand belongs to the female domain of *awal*. This caused a big debate among the elderly men. Finally, the heated exchange ended with a bland sentence pronounced by a Bani priest, "*Awal* is male." The debate showed that my understanding of gender attributes of *ahier* and *awal* was incorrect. The confusion seems to come from the fact that the concepts of *ahier* and *awal* are highly contextualized. For the Bani religious community, *awal* (normally regarded as female), when used to refer to Bani priests, belongs to the male realm. *Ahier*, used in the context of Bani lay people, belongs to the female realm.

Being of the male realm, the Bani priests (*awal*) need assistance from the female realm (women and unmarried men cannot enter the priesthood). Within the priesthood, there are six different ranks,[46] and according to a principle of seniority, the Bani priest gradually climbs up the hierarchical ladder. The highest rank is *Ong Guru*, of which there is one at each *thang muki*. During the period of my field study, the *Ong Guru* of one Bani village had long since passed away, but the Bani priest in line to take the position had not been promoted. Without an *Ong Guru*, the village was unable to organize several important ceremonies, including funerals, led by the priests of their own village. The reason for this situation was that the wife of the candidate for the position of *Ong Guru* was very sick, lying in a hospital. Bani priests can be promoted only if they have good moral conduct and their wives are healthy.

A priest's promotion ceremony is performed on the last day of the month of *Ramuwan* (Photo 3-17). On this occasion, the wife of the promoted priest wears a cloth like the one she wore at the *Karah* ceremony, by which one enters the Bani religion. She wears as much gold jewelry as possible and sits in a guest house attached to the *thang muki* to observe the ceremony (Photos 3-18). If she is sick or in her menstrual period, she cannot attend the promotion ceremony and without her presence, her husband cannot be promoted to a higher rank in the priesthood. The Bani priest, as male, needs the assistance of the female. The ceremonies conducted by Bani priests require the presence of a woman called *Muk Poh*. In each Bani village, there are one or two *Muk Poh*. Most of the Bani rituals involve an offering of rice to the priests. When each household prepares the offering, an unmarried young girl is chosen from the household to do the preparations. Then, during the rituals, it is the *Muk Poh* who offers the rice to the priests. Bani priests cannot conduct rituals without the *Muk Poh*'s assistance. During Friday

---

[46] For more detailed information of the ranks of priests, see Appendix, Ranks of priests.

prayers, the first lay people to pray are *Muk Poh* and the wife of the *Ong Guru*. Their prayer acts as a signal to the other lay people to begin their prayers (Photo 3-19).

Photo 3-17. The priests' elevation ceremony at *kalaih Ramuwan* in Phu'óc Nho'n

Photo 3-18. Wives observing the priests' elevation ceremony in Phu'óc Nho'n

Photo 3-19. *Muk Poh* in An Nho'n

Within the Bani community, the gender attributes of *awal* and *ahier*—with *awal* as male and *ahier* as female—are consistent and possess their own internal logic. The reversal of the normal *ahier* and *awal* gender attributes within the Bani community can be explained by the continuity of *awal–ahier* principles. The Balamon are excluded from the *ahier* and *awal* categories used within the Bani community; they are classified instead as *akafir*. This term is equivalent to the Arabic term *Kafir*, denoting non-Muslims. The terms *awal*, *ahier*, and *akafir* are, however, used only for people belonging to the Cham ethnic group. Initially, as a Buddhist-Japanese, I thought I would be categorized as *akafir*. Yet, I was told that I was neither *ahier* nor *akafir* but Japanese. While Muslims generally use the term *kafir* without regard to a person's nationality or ethnic background, the Cham use these terms only within their own ethnic boundaries.

Let me attempt to summarize the discussion so far. Firstly, when these symbols are used in the context of the Cham religion as a whole, *ahier* (Balamon) is male and *awal* (Bani) is female (see Table 3). Secondly, within the specific religion of the Bani people, the gender attributes of *ahier* and *awal* are reversed. *Ahier* (lay people) is the female principle, while *awal* (priests) is male (see Table 4). Thirdly, when the terms *awal* and *ahier* are used in conjunction with the term *akafir* as a set of three, the first two terms lose their male and female symbolism. Instead, they indicate the degree to which one embraces the Bani religion. To the Bani, the relationship of *awal*, *ahier*, and *akafir* indicates the relative distance from Po Alwah. The Bani priests (*awal*) enjoy the greatest proximity to Po Alwah, the Bani lay people (*ahier*) are the next closest, and the Balamon (*akafir*) exist at the greatest distance. Thus, the distinction between *ahier* and *awal* reflects the different levels of multiple religious relationships. But in any case, when the two terms are used as a pair, they maintain the attributes of the male and female realms.

Cham Religion	
Balamon	Bani
Ahier	*Awal*
Male	Female
Right	Left

Table 3. The Cham religion and the division of *ahier* and *awal*

Balamon	Bani	
	Bani lay people	Bani priests
Akafir	*Ahier*	*Awal*
	Female	Male
	Left	Right

Table 4. The concepts of *ahier* and *awal* among the Bani people

Ahier and *awal* as the great tradition and the little tradition

Within the Bani religion, besides their symbolism of the male and female principles, and their representation of the degree of adherence to the Bani religion, the terms *ahier* and *awal* are sometimes used to refer to types of ceremony. Ceremonies conducted by Bani priests are called *awal*. However, some ceremonies cannot be performed by priests. The religious authority of Bani priests is limited to ceremonies relating to Po Alwah and Po Nubi. The *ahier* ceremonies, which are related to the ancestral spirits and other spirits, are conducted by ritual musicians and shamans called *Guru Urang*. Thus, *ahier* and *awal* sometimes indicate a distinction between the great tradition (religion) and the little tradition (spirit rituals).

Within the Balamon religion, by contrast, *awal* and *ahier* are not used to indicate any distinction between religion and spirit rituals. But despite the lack of terminology, a distinction between these two different types of religious practice is expressed by practitioners and through the materials used in ceremonies.[47] For instance, in Cham ceremonies, a grass mat called *chieu pang* is used by the priests and other religious practitioners. Usually, the *chieu pang* is kept rolled up. When the Balamon, as well as Bani, priests make their prayers, they sit on the inside face of the rolled *chieu pang*. This position of the *chieu pang* is called *padang* (Photo 3-20) When other religious practitioners, including the *Guru Urang*, conduct *ahier* ceremonies, they use the outside face of the rolled *chieu pang* (Photo 3-21). No religious cooperation ever takes place between the *Guru Urang* and the priests, either Balamon or Bani.

Photo 3-20. A *chieu pang* in the position of *padang*

---

[47] There is a group of musicians and dancers who play and hold significant roles in various rituals and whose associations with Balamon and Bani priests are strictly regulated. See Appendix, Relationships of priests and other religious practitioners, for a more detailed explanation of religious affiliations among them.

Photo 3-21. A *chieu pang* in the position of non-*padang*

Cham traditional religion

At a glance, Balamon and Bani seem like two completely different religions of Hindu and Islamic origins, but they are in fact two different outcomes of acculturation grown in the same ground. Balamon religious attributes make sense only when viewed in opposition to Bani religious attributes, and vice-versa. The terms *ahier* and *awal* are fluid. Their meanings depend on the context in which they are used. This fluidity differentiates them from very fixed terms like Balamon and Bani and illustrates the interdependency of the two religions. For the Cham people of south-central Vietnam, this binary principle is the dynamic that constructs their world.

Relations between the two groups also take literary forms. Within the tradition of Cham lyric poetry, there are three significant poems. One of them is called *Cham-Bani*, and it is a story of unfulfilled love between a young Balamon woman and a young Bani man. According to Inrasara, it was written around the end of the 19th century and became the most popular lyric poem among the Cham. It relates the story of how a Balamon and a

Bani fell in love, which was against the taboo of inter-religious relationships. Facing strong disapproval from her parents, the Balamon woman ran away and secretly went to live with the Bani man. Later, however, she was caught and brought back to her village and punished with death. During her funeral, her Bani lover jumped into the cremation fire.[48] They were reunited in the other world (Inrasara 1993: 175-181). The *Cham–Bani* lyric poetry symbolizes religious divisions of the Cham and at the same time, their inseparable nature.

Several folk songs among the Cham in Ninh Thuận Province broach the relationship between the Balamon and the Bani. One of my Cham teachers taught me the following song, which he often used when teaching Cham scripts to the Cham school teachers:

Balamon and Bani are not separated far
Actually, since long ago, we share the same blood
Which gods created us?
You are just a grain of rice and I am just a rice husk.

The song suggests that the two share the same origin, that they are different parts of the same thing. Another song describes the pumpkin and the gourd, their vines ever tangled on the same trellis. The pumpkin and the gourd, of course, symbolize the Balamon and Bani.

According to an old Cham text kept by a shaman, the Cham gods appear in different guises. They transform themselves from one form to another, crossing the boundaries between the two religions. For instance, one of the earliest and most supreme gods of the Balamon religion, called Po Ku, transformed himself into the goddess Po Inu Nugar, who is the mother goddess of Champa. She created human beings and the country of Champa. She also taught the Cham people agriculture, sericulture, and weaving. Po Inu Nugar transformed herself into Po Alwah, the supreme god of the Bani religion. In another example, a Balamon god called Po Alwah Hu transformed himself into Po Nubi Mohamat. But Po Alwah Hu is actually the name given to the god when he is in the sky, while Po Nubi Mohamat is the name given to him when he is on earth. In other words, the explanations of various deities found in the shaman's old text indicate that the Balamon and the Bani deities are the same (see Table 5).

---

[48] This can be considered as reversed *sati*, an act of sacrifice by a widow in the Hindu tradition.

Balamon	Bani
Po Ku ----> Po Inu Nugar ---------------->	Po Alwah
Po Alwah Hu -------------------------------->	Po Nubi Mohamat

Table 5. Transformation of Balamon deities

Despite their differences, the Balamon and Bani share the same system of beliefs—'the Cham religion'—and believe in the same gods. It might appear that they believe in separate gods. But in actual fact, their gods are the same but known by different names and worshipped in different ways by two different groups of Cham people. In Vietnam, they are more often represented—in the choices made by people involved in assembling museum collections, books on minorities, and other media—by the Balamon. Bani people see no problem in being identified as Balamon in the public sphere. The division of Balamon and Bani is like two faces of the same coin, and their differences are not understood as being ethnic by the Cham people. Sharing a belief system, a sense of belonging to Champa, and common ancestry, both Balamon and Bani assert a common ethnicity to outsiders.

Within the ethnic group, however, a clear boundary surfaces, which temporarily disappears when they relate to outsiders. Members of the Cham ethnic group know the differences between Balamon and Bani. Knowledge of this dual organization is a recognized token of membership in their society. This goes some way toward explaining why the Cham in south-central Vietnam often omit the Mekong Delta Cham when they talk about the Cham in Vietnam. The Mekong Delta Cham do not share this specific knowledge. This is why the Cham in the south-central region cannot identify them as the same Cham as they are.

Orthodox Muslim Cham

During the 1950s, there was a small movement among the Bani Muslim people in the Cham communities in Ninh Thuận Province to learn Orthodox Islam and redirect their religious practice. It was mainly motivated by their search for "true Islam" (Yoshimoto 2010: 240-247). Orthodox Islam was introduced and called *Jawa* by the Bani people. The Orthodox Muslim Cham in Ninh Thuận Province claim that they belong to *awal*. However, both Balamon and Bani do not agree with that, and the Orthodox Muslims are excluded from the *ahier* and *awal* dichotomy. They have become rather marginalized among the Cham communities in Ninh Thuận Province.

The person who played a significant role in proselytizing Islam among the Bani was named Mã Thành Lâm or Hosen (his Muslim name). He was born in the Bani commune of Phu'ớc Nho'n. He studied in Cần Tho' city in the Mekong Delta, and later, he found a job at the Office of Agriculture in Saigon. Whether during the time he was a student at Cần Tho' or while he was working in Saigon, he had opportunities to visit Muslim Cham communities in Châu Đốc. Seeing the Cham Muslims there keeping "genuine" practices of Islam, he wanted to correct "wrong" practices of Islam among the Cham back home (Nguyễn Văn Luận 1974: 272, 274). In Saigon, he got to know some Muslim people and learned Islamic teaching from an Indian Muslim named Mahamad Ally (Nguyễn Hồng Du'o'ng 2007: 148).

Wishing to carry out proselytization among the Bani communities, he contacted a Cham named Tù' Công Xuân. He was a teacher and, later on, was involved in politics and became a member of the Lower House of the Saigon government. He was originally from the Văn Lâm commune in Ninh Thuận Province. Tù' Công Xuân had become acquainted with an Indian businessman named Maideen and also Abdul Latif Moulawi, who was the *Imam* of an Indian masjid in Saigon called Jamia al Musulman or commonly known as Masjid Catinat.[49] Tù' Công Xuân was living in the district of Phú Nhuận in Saigon where many Cham from Châu Đốc had migrated. Then, he married a Muslim Cham from Châu Đốc and established a connection with *Mufti* Umar Aly in Châu Đốc (Nguyễn Văn Luận 1974: 272, 274). Tù' Công Xuân, Abdul Latif Moulawi, and *Mufti* Umar Aly went to the Cham communities in the south-central coast area. They first proselytized Sunni Islam among the Bani people in Phan Ri in Bình Thuận Province, but it was not very successful. They then moved further north to Ninh Thuận Province.[50]

Mã Thành Lâm himself also made tireless efforts to visit the Bani villages for proselytization (Nguyễn Văn Luận 1974: 274). By the 1960s, a separate masjid for the Orthodox Muslim people was constructed in the Bani communities of Văn Lâm, Nho Lâm, An Nho'n, and Phu'ớc Nho'n (Photo 3-22). Chapters of *Hiệp hội Chàm Hồi giáo Việt Nam* (Association of Cham

---

[49] Jamia al Musulman is located on Đông Du street near Đồng Khở'i street, which used to be called Rue Catinat after the French governor during the colonial time.
[50] Currently, there is no masjid in Bình Thuận Province. However, according to the *Hakim* of Văn Lâm, there were about 30 families who converted to Orthodox Islam before 1975 in Minh Mỹ village in Kánh Hoa district. There was a *Hakim* living in Phan Ri around 1974. Recently, approximately 40 Muslim families in Bình Thuận Province have filed a request to the authority to build a masjid.

Muslim in Vietnam) were also established at these masjids. *Hiệp hội Chàm Hồi giáo Việt Nam* was established in Saigon by the Cham Muslim migrants from the Mekong Delta. This organization facilitated social and cultural activities among the Muslim Cham in Vietnam. Nguyễn Văn Luận reported 2,000 members of *Hiệp hội Chàm* in Ninh Thuận Province in 1964 (1974: 275). Upon the request of Orthodox Muslim communities in Ninh Thuận Province, *Hiệp hội Chàm* assisted to make arrangements to send a group of Cham people from Văn Lâm, Phu'óc Nho'n, and An Nho'n to the Cham communities in Saigon or the Mekong Delta where they learned religious teachings of Sunni Islam. Upon completion of their studies, they would go back to their communes to proselytize Orthodox Islam among the Bani (Nguyễn Hồng Du'o'ng 2007: 166).

Photo 3-22. A masjid in Văn Lâm

As Orthodox Islam gained ground among the Bani, the antagonism between the converted Bani and the remaining Bani increased. Some sympathized with the Muslim converts. Most of these were relatives of Orthodox Islam converts, and they argued that religion should be chosen through an individual's will. These sympathizers were called *walai*. The villagers—including the priests—were divided between the *walai* and anti-*walai*. Antagonism within Phu'ó'c Nho'n village reached its peak between 1969 and 1971, when there were a few violent incidents. Orthodox Islam converts had to put up with various kinds of bullying from the Bani. One elderly person recounted that during that time of enmity, Orthodox Muslims could rely only on Allah and the local government.

The relationship between the Bani and the Orthodox Islam converts softened after Vietnam's reunification in 1975 when any kind of religious proselytizing was prohibited. Although Sunni Islam proselytization among the Bani people of Ninh Thuận has re-emerged since the onset of the *đổi mó'i* reforms (1986) and the number of converts is slowly increasing, the violent incidents of the past have not been repeated.[51]

The Bani tend to see Orthodox Islam converts as people who have abandoned their original religion and the Cham tradition. They are deemed to be committing a sin by neglecting *muk kay*, the ancestral spirits. According to the Bani, denying *muk kay* means denying oneself, as without the ancestors one would not exist. They also criticize the converts for abandoning the Bani religion to gain development and humanitarian aid from foreigners. The Orthodox Muslims in Ninh Thuận are connected to Muslim communities around the world and have received donations from foreign Muslim visitors and financial aid from foreign Muslim organizations. Because of such foreign connections, they teach English in

---

[51] In 2010, I carried out brief research on the lineage among the Bani communities. The lineage is a significant social unit for maintaining Cham people's tradition since it organizes various rituals and ceremonies and each lineage has its own taboos and customs. The knowledge of lineage is essential for the Cham to maintain their practice of exogamy: to avoid marrying a person of the same lineage. However, Orthodox Muslims have lost the knowledge of their lineage. None of the people who were born and raised as Orthodox Muslim who I interviewed could identify the names of their lineage. Only those who used to practice the Bani religion and later on became Orthodox Muslims could identify their lineage. The Bani people criticize that their loss of knowledge of lineage is an act to destroy Cham culture. I had one interviewee state that because of this, she hates the Orthodox Muslims. Relationships between the Bani and Orthodox Muslims are relatively moderate and friendly in Văn Lâm, while in Phu'óc Nho'n their relationship is tense and some Bani people completely cut off their relationship with close family members who are Orthodox Muslims. I suspect that Văn Lâm's more moderate relationship between Bani and Orthodox Muslims is due to the remaining of elements of Bani culture in their Orthodox Islam; for instance, having multiple numbers of *Imam*s at their masjid. In the masjid of Văn Lâm, there are four *Imam*s and this is a rare practice among the Orthodox Muslims (Nakamura 2014).

addition to regular Qur'anic study. I was often surprised to meet Cham students in their masjids who spoke to me in English. The converts' foreign connections and access to foreign aid provoke envy among the Bani people and it has become one of the reasons for their antagonism.

The Orthodox Muslims often become upset when they hear about such criticism from Bani people, and argue that they were practicing Orthodox Islam in order to "follow the right path," and not for monetary gain. One of the members of this group told me that following Orthodox Islam and the belief in it are a "revolution among the Cham." They believe that the Bani religion is a degraded form of Islam and that its practice is not right. It is steeped in superstition; it is unscientific and backward, and Orthodox Islam is scientific and more advanced. The Orthodox Muslims often consider themselves more educated, more scientific, and more developed than Bani people because they understand the theology of their faith and practice Islam "correctly."

Furthermore, although the Cham in An Giang Province have adhered to Orthodox Islam for much longer than the Cham in Ninh Thuận Province, the newly converted in Ninh Thuận claim that they are religiously superior. They admit that the Mekong Delta Cham can read the Qur'an more skillfully and are more familiar with the religious practice of Islam. But they also argue that the Mekong Delta Cham are narrow-minded and obsessed with religious practice, caring little about education, noting that few of their families send their children to school and their lack of scientific knowledge. The newly converted in Ninh Thuận further criticize that the Mekong Delta Cham cannot read *akhar thrah* and know nothing of the history of Champa.

Responding to the Bani people's criticism that they have renounced their Cham heritage, the Orthodox Muslim Cham in south-central Vietnam argue that they have no intention of abandoning Cham tradition and culture. By their efforts to preserve *akhar thrah* literacy and by participating in traditional ceremonies, such as visiting their ancestors' graves before the holy month of Ramadan, they preserve their cultural and historical traditions. Unlike the Cham in the Mekong Delta, whose ethnicity is constructed around the Islamic religion, the Muslim Cham in south-central Vietnam cannot use Islam alone to construct their ethnic identity. In the masjid at Phu'ó'c Nho'n village, all the posters on the wall were written in both Arabic and *akhar thrah*. The Muslim Cham in south-central Vietnam need to include elements of tradition connecting them to the ancient Champa, *akhar thrah*, and the Cham language holds a significant place in the construction of their ethnic identity.

Conclusion

The ethnicity of the Cham in south-central Vietnam has been constructed around a connection to the past Champa. Beyond their communities, they assert their ethnicity by claiming this heritage and by making links with the ancient Champa, which once established a civilization quite different from the Vietnamese. They assert their ethnicity by their respect for and preservation of cultural traditions through continued ritual practices, maintenance of cultural knowledge including the writing system *akhar thrah*, constant searching for the origins of the Cham culture, and a reluctance to marry non-Cham outsiders. Meanwhile, internally, their ethnicity is demonstrated by a highly contextualized fluid dualism, the concept of *ahier* and *awal*, the male and female realms. The fluidity of these terms illustrates the interdependency of the two religious groups, Balamon and Bani, and their construction of ethnic identity as Cham. The past-oriented ethnicity of the Cham in the south-central coast area is the most salient when it is compared with the ethnicity among the Cham people from the Mekong Delta, which I examine in the following chapter.

CHAPTER 4

THE CHAM OF THE MEKONG DELTA

In this chapter, the Muslim Cham of the Mekong Delta and their ethnic identity are discussed. In the eyes of the Cham in the south-central coast area, the Cham people in the Mekong Delta are the lost brothers who have forgotten their origin. As they have not kept their original writing system from Champa, they are often criticized as "cultureless." A local Cham scholar from Ninh Thuận Province who went to Châu Đốc to meet the Cham there during the 1960s informed me that he saw several books written in *akhar thrah* though nobody who could read the script. However, I did not come across a book written in *akhar thrah* during my field research in An Giang Province in the mid-1990s. Instead, the Cham in the Mekong Delta use the *jawi*, the Arabic alphabet.

The Cham people in the Mekong Delta are all Sunni Muslim. The religion of Islam is the focal point of the lives of the Cham here. Through Islam, to a certain degree, the Cham have managed to link two Cham communities: Ninh Thuận/ Bình Thuận and An Giang Provinces. The organization called *Hiệp hội Chàm Hồi giáo Việt Nam* (The Association of Muslim Cham in Vietnam) was responsible for such an endeavor. This chapter also discusses this short-lived organization to see the awakening of Cham ethnic identity among the Mekong Delta Cham.

Landscape of the Cham of the Mekong Delta

In contrast with the closed and isolated south-central coast Cham villages, the Cham villages in the Mekong Delta are quite open. Their villages are formed along the rivers or canals and next to the Kinh villages. The Southern Cham wooden houses are built on pillars, elevated about 1.5 meters above the ground. Their houses are not surrounded by any fences, and their entrances face the road running through the village (Photo 4-1). The Cham people often yell out to the street vendors, who are mostly Kinh people, from inside of their houses to get snacks, groceries, and other daily necessities. In contrast to the young Cham children in the south-central coast area who do not understand Vietnamese, the Cham children in the Mekong Delta seem to start to understand Vietnamese at an early age.

Photo 4-1. The Cham village of Châu Giang

The Mekong Delta Cham tend to be seen as having lost the Cham kinship principle of matrilineal and matrilocal systems (Phan Thị Yến Tuyết 1993: 250-251). Their living arrangements are rather ambilocal than strictly matrilocal. It often depends on the economic situation and access to the job market or education. However, their basic rule is matrilocal. The three-day-long Cham Muslim wedding reaches its culmination on the third day when the groom goes into his bride's house. There is a folk song which is supposed to be sung on the day when a groom departs from his natal home. The song teaches him how to behave toward his wife and his wife's parents at their house. People used to sing this song with tears since they had to say farewell to their son, brother, uncle, and nephew. At the bride's house, he takes off all his clothes given by his family and changes into the new clothes prepared by his bride's family. It symbolizes cutting off a tie with his natal family and becoming a new member of the bride's household.

In the south-central coast area, the Cham practice strict exogamy; they do not marry within the same lineage nor do they marry close relations on the father's side. Even cross-cousin marriage, which is technically permitted, is hardly found among them because they consider cousins to be too closely related. In contrast, the Cham in the Mekong Delta prefer endogamy; marriages among their own kin, especially with cousins. Traditionally in Muslim Cham communities, the parents arrange their children's marriages when they are still very young, and often the parents choose their children's cousins, both parallel and cross cousins, as their future spouses.

In the Mekong Delta, some Cham are engaging in wet-rice cultivation, but they do not have enough land to harvest rice to meet their needs. Some of them engage in fishing, mainly for their domestic consumption while others raise fish in the river which can bring a large profit. But it needs a certain amount of capital to start the business. A major source of cash income of the Cham in An Giang Province is small businesses selling old or new clothes and textiles. Many Cham women engage in such business and they play a significant role in the household economy.

During the mid-1990s, many Cham people in An Giang Province began selling *áo sida*, second-hand clothing, mostly shirts made in Japan, USA, Korea, Hong Kong, or Taiwan. Although they are second-hand, *áo sida* are still quite popular among the Vietnamese because of their good quality and reasonable price. The *áo sida* are sold throughout southern Vietnam. I suspected that *áo sida*[52] is clothing brought into Cambodia as aid by the UN. These aid materials are sold by the Khmer people and cross the border to be brought into Vietnam. The Cham people even bring them to the Central Highlands where the products are difficult to obtain because of the poor infrastructure. However, the *áo sida* business has begun to decline with the improvement of Vietnamese infrastructure. Currently, businesses catering to Malay Muslim tourists from Malaysia are popular in Ho Chi Minh City. Cham are making and selling *telecom* (women's prayer dress), *baju kurung* (traditional Malay dress), *tudung* (head cover), and other Islamic attires, and also selling *halal* foods (Islamically prepared foods) for their fellow Muslim tourists.

Champa or Angkor

In Ninh Thuận Province, I was told by the Cham people that the Cham in An Giang Province did not have "history," meaning that they do not remember Champa and do not keep any heritage of Champa. Some Mekong Delta Cham people I met in Ho Chi Minh City, however, were conscious

---

[52] In Vietnam, people use the French abbreviation *SIDA* for AIDS, which can be read as "aids" for humanitarian support.

about their heritage from Champa. These Cham people are educated and have more contact with the Cham from the south-central area and with foreigners. Two Cham women I met in Ho Chi Minh City—one referred to the Cham as the people of Champa—were both educated Qur'anic teachers who had many foreign friends. Some of the people had read or had knowledge of the book *Dân tộc Chàm Lu'ọ'c sử'* ("History of the Cham People") written by a Muslim Cham, which explained the history of Champa.

However, most of the Cham people from the Mekong Delta appeared not to know or care about their Champa heritage. At the beginning of my stay in the village of Châu Giang, I tried to collect information about the history of the village, or the history of anything about the Cham in the Mekong Delta. What I was able to collect was a series of Muslim people's names and their religious accomplishments.[53] For instance, I learned the story of an Arab man called Sayid Mustafa who first introduced Islam to the Cham people. Sayid Mustafa went to Phan Rang to teach Islam and Arabic script. He stayed in Phan Rang for two years, learned *akhar thrah*, and left for Cambodia. At that time, the Cham people living in Cambodia were followers of the Balamon religion.[54] Another more popular and recent story is about *Tuon Haji* Umar Ali who is responsible for establishing the basic Islamic orders in Vietnam which regulate all the ceremonies and religious activities among them. He later became a *Mufti*, the supreme leader of the Muslim community in Vietnam. His mother, *Haja* Amina, was pregnant with him in Mecca while she was making her pilgrimage. He started to study the Qur'an at the age of seven with one of the teachers in the Masjid Azhar of Châu Giang village. In 1921, he went to Mecca to study and stayed there

---

[53] Collins, who conducted field research among the Cham in Cambodia where a majority were Sunni Muslim, interestingly notes a similar understanding of history among the people. When he asked a question about Cham origins, he was answered with a story which described how Islam came to Cham (Collins 1996: 72).

[54] Mustafa's story continues as follows: In Cambodia, he introduced Islam among the Cham who were followers of the Balamon religion at that time. He was called *Chphoa*, which was one of the titles of the head of an administrative unit in French Indochina. The king of Cambodia heard about the reputation of Mustafa and recommended him for the real *Chphoa*. One of the ministers for the king was jealous of Mustafa and planned to expel him. Mustafa found out about the conspiracy and he killed the minister. He was arrested for the murder and executed by the king. He is said to be buried in Chrouy Changvar. During the next century, about six Cham people from Cambodia went to several places such as Kelantan (Malaysia), Patani (Thailand), or Mecca to study Islam and came back to Cambodia to teach Islam among the Cham.

for 12 years. He married an Arab lady whom he brought back with him on his return to *jama'ah* (Muslim community) Azhar of Châu Giang village in 1933.

I could only gather a few stories about Champa. One morning I met one of the shamans in *jama'ah* Azhar. I asked him that, seeing how Japanese people have their own country and so do the Chinese and many other people, how come the Cham do not have their own country? He answered that a long time ago, the Cham also had a country which was east of the country of Khmer and south of China. However, he had to spend some time remembering the name of the country: Champa. A village leader's family remembered the name of Champa where the Cham in An Giang came from, but they did not know where Champa was. When I mentioned about the old ruins of Champa along the south-central coast of Vietnam and said that Champa might be around the place of Phan Rang, one of them interrupted me and stated that Phan Rang was not Champa but *Chiêm Thành*, which is the Vietnamese word for Champa. Then his wife told us a different story of two boys from Malaysia who came to the Châu Đốc area by ship and started the Cham community.[55] Every time I hinted at a possibility that the Cham from the Mekong Delta might have originated in the Phan Rang area, the people became quiet and tried to find another explanation to convince me that my idea was not right. Finally, the head of the household decided to discuss this matter with other people in the village at their Friday prayer congregation. The answer he brought back surprised me. The people gathered at the masjid agreed that the Cham in An Giang came from Angkor, while the Cham around the Phan Rang area came from Champa.

After several failed attempts to find any signs of a connection between the Mekong Delta Cham to historical Champa, I was convinced that Champa did not provide any comprehensive link to their past. Champa provides one of the significant bases for the ethnic identity of the Cham in the south-central coast area and the official classification of the Cham people by the state. However, the Cham in the Mekong Delta, who do not bear the remains of Champa, would be marginalized in the Champa-

---

[55] On one other occasion, I was told that the Cham in the Mekong Delta came from Malaysia. I visited the Islamic Center of Ho Chi Minh City to see the preparations for the celebration of the Prophet Mohammed's birthday. I asked if they were going to invite the Muslim Cham from the Phan Rang area. An officer answered, "The Cham from Phan Rang area are different from the Cham from the Mekong Delta. The Cham Phan Rang had kings before and they had an original land, but we do not have kings. The Cham Phan Rang did not come from anywhere. They were there from the beginning, while the Cham Châu Đốc came from Malaysia."

centered classification. If they constructed their past around the historical Champa, they would become the people who had abandoned or neglected their "kings" and "original land." It is possible to see that their construction of the past around the religion of Islam is the Mekong Delta Cham's resistance against being marginalized in the construction of their ethnicity. They assert their ethnicity by constructing their past outside of Champa.

The Cham are Muslim

The religion of Islam is the focal point of the lives of the Cham in the Mekong Delta. In the Cham village, I lived in a traditional wooden Cham house. Every morning around five o'clock, I heard alarm clocks start to ring one after another from houses in my neighborhood. People were getting up for *Fajr*, the dawn prayer. Soon, I heard *Adhan*, the call for prayer, from a masjid in the village. A day in the Cham villages was punctuated by the prayers.

To the Cham in the Mekong Delta, being Cham and being Muslim are almost synonymous. The Cham children tell people that they are going to study Cham language at the masjid, by which they mean studying Arabic script and the Qur'an. They use the phrase "to study Cham" in contrast to "to study Vietnamese" which means the classes in the schools in the Vietnamese national education system. A boy living near my house heard a reading of the Qur'an from my short-wave radio and identified it as the Cham language. The Cham people use the term Cham and the terms Muslim or Islam interchangeably: "Is the person Cham?" means "Is the person Muslim?" We can find a reflection of such logic in the official ethnic category of the Cham people.

In Châu Giang village, there are two Cham *jama'ah* (communities). One is called Mubarak after the name of their masjid, and the other is called Azhar. The people in *jama'ah* Mubarak wear sarongs and head covers just like the other Cham people in *jama'ah* Azhar, but they do not speak the Cham language. They speak a language that the Cham call *Mien*, which is the Khmer language. These Khmer-speaking Cham people are classified as Java Kur, a sub-group of the Cham ethnic group, by the state. The Java Kur people are the descendants of the children of Muslim merchants from Malaya and local Khmer women. In Cambodia, the Java Kur are called Chvea[56] by the Cham to indicate that they do not speak the Cham language

---

[56] Zain bin Musa explains that Malays in Indochina are called Chvea in the Khmer language and Jva in Cham language in Cambodia (2011: 88).

(Collins 1996: 64). Some of the Chvea people might have been living close to the Cham communities in Cambodia, and they also came down to the Mekong Delta when the Cham migrated and settled beside them. The Cham in *jama'ah* Azhar are conscious about the differences between them and the Java Kur of *jama'ah* Mubarak. Yet they do not hesitate to call them Cham, and the Java Kur also identify themselves as Cham[57] since they are all Muslim.

The religion of Islam also enables individuals to join the Cham community. For instance, although a person was not born from Cham parents, the person becomes a Cham if he/she becomes a Muslim. I met a few people who "became Cham." One afternoon I was invited to have lunch at the house of the fiancé of my friend's niece. The food served was called *bánh xèo*, a southern Vietnamese dish. I wondered why this family cooked Vietnamese food instead of Cham food. It turned out that the fiancé's mother was from the Kinh ethnic group. She converted to Islam when she married her Cham husband and lived among the Cham people for over 20 years. At first glance, she appeared as a typical middle-aged Cham woman. She was wearing a sarong with a special kind of head cover that is unique to Cham women. Although she spoke little Cham, she did not seem to have any problem understanding the others' conversation in Cham. According to my friend, the fiancé's mother was a very good Muslim. She prayed five times a day and observed all other religious duties. She converted to Islam to marry her Cham husband, but she also had real faith in Islam and therefore she has become a Cham. Another example is the wife of a village official who was known for her business skills and for being hard-working. She had a small shop in front of her house where she sold noodles and sandwiches in the morning and various necessities throughout the day. She "used to be a Kinh" but became a Muslim when she married her husband. She learned to speak Cham and to practice Islam and was accepted as a member of the Cham community.

These women's ethnic change was initially engaged by their marriage to a Cham. However, the marriage itself cannot change their ethnicity from Kinh to Cham. It is their conversion to Islam and their diligent religious

---

[57] Collins notes that the Cham in Cambodia tend to think that the Chvea are ethnically different from the Cham because they do not speak Cham, and because of their Malay-Indonesian heritage. The Chvea in Cambodia tend to refer to themselves by the officially recognized term Khmer Islam, and also seem to think that they have different ethnic backgrounds from the Cham. They point out that because of their Malay heritage and their knowledge of Malay in which religious texts are written, they are religiously superior to the Cham (Collins 1996: 64).

practices which made them Cham. In other cases, a person's faith to Islam could transfer his/her ethnicity to Cham without having either marital nor kin relationships with the Cham people. For instance, Aisah introduced me to a spacious souvenir shop owned by a Cham family on the busy Nguyễn Thị Minh Khai street in Ho Chi Minh City. Though she indicated it was a Cham shop, when we entered we were greeted in Vietnamese. The shop was owned by the family of an *Imam* who was from the Chinese ethnic group (Hoa).[58] He had converted to Islam when he was very young. He had studied Islam in An Giang Province and was a devoted Muslim. He married a Kinh woman and she converted to Islam, and all their children were raised as Muslim. Aisah praised their religious practice and identified them as Cham.

Among the Muslim Cham people, the mixed marriage itself cannot be a reason to jeopardize one's membership to the Cham community. The important thing is not one's genealogical background but one's faith in Islam. It does not matter whether one's mother or father is Cham or Kinh. If a person has been raised in a Muslim household as a Muslim, he/she is a legitimate member of the Cham ethnic group.[59] Since practicing Islam constructs Cham ethnicity, not practicing Islam sometimes dilutes one's ethnicity as Cham. One afternoon, I saw a man visiting one of my neighbors. He was wearing a white shirt and gray pants, speaking in Vietnamese to the wife of my neighbor. It seemed that quite a serious conversation was going on and the man looked quite emotional. The man was the woman's lost nephew. Her brother married a Kinh woman and the couple lived outside of the Cham community. They had a son but unfortunately, the Cham husband died during the war. After the war, his wife tried to escape to a foreign country with her son, but they were separated and the son was raised as an orphan. When he was grown up, he started to search for his Cham relatives, and recently he found out that the wife of my neighbor was his aunt. Since he grew up in the Kinh community, he did not know Islam. My neighbor's family members classified their lost relative as a Kinh person since he was not a Muslim and did not speak Cham. His Cham blood-tie through his Cham father was not counted for his ethnic identity.

---

[58] His ethnic background as Hoa—Chinese descended Vietnamese, another ethnic minority person—may be more acceptable to the Cham community than being Kinh.
[59] Women seem to be playing a significant role in establishing "Muslim households." The degree of women's devotion to Islam influences their children's upbringing in the Islamic faith since they are the primary caretakers (Shaw 1988).

The ethnicity of the Cham in the Mekong Delta is constructed around the religion of Islam. It is the religious practice that holds the key to constructing a person's ethnic identity and an acceptance of the person's membership to the Cham communities. Instead of relying on priests or other people to practice their beliefs, individual Muslims have to practice their own beliefs. It is this practice which makes individuals as Cham. As long as a person is a good adherent of Islam, even if the person was originally from the Kinh or other ethnic groups and may not have a good command of the Cham language, people will not question his/her ethnicity as Cham. It is when a person's religious practices and their faith in Islam become questionable to other Cham that his/her ethnic identity will be re-examined.

It shows quite a contrast with the Cham in the south-central coast area, whose ethnicity is genealogically determined. For them, being Cham is like getting "stamped" on the day of their birth. If a person did not get stamped on the day of his/her birth, the person will never be able to receive the stamp. A person has to be from Cham parents and have a connection to his/her ancestors, and he/she also has to have a sense of the continuation from historical Champa. Further, inter-ethnic marriage in the south-central coast area causes a loss of membership in the Cham community. An inter-ethnic marriage which is often between a Cham man and a Kinh woman produces Kinh offspring, according to their matrilineal principle. Because of this, the Cham who marry Kinh are considered as though they have neglected their own people. While the religion of Islam, which the Cham in the Mekong Delta construct their identity around, not only legitimizes the Cham membership of children from the mixed marriage, it also transforms a person's ethnic identity from non-Cham to Cham in certain circumstances.

Non-Islamic religious practice among the Cham in the Mekong Delta

The Cham are not the only Muslims in Vietnam. There are non-Cham Muslim people who set clear boundaries between themselves and the Cham Muslim: Indian and Bawean. They are not officially recognized ethnic groups, but each group forms a small community in Ho Chi Minh City and its members live close to each other.

The oldest masjid in Ho Chi Minh City, which was established in 1885, is located in the first district.[60] It is called Masjidir Rahim and it is the

---

[60] Stokhof notes that it is actually not clear who built the first masjid in Saigon. He found the information in archives that said the Muslim people from current day

masjid of the community of the Bawean people who are descendants of migrants from Bawean Island in the Java Sea who were classified as *Malais* (Malay) by the French colonial government (Stokhof 2008: 35-36). According to the people of *jama'ah* Rahim, some Muslim people who were suffering under the Dutch colonial system escaped from Dutch Indonesia and came to Vietnam. There were also some Muslim merchants from British Malaya who came to Vietnam for business. These Muslim people intermarried within their groups and settled down in Vietnam by forming small pockets of Muslim communities.[61] The people at the masjid informed me that there are about 520 Vietnamese Muslims of Malaysian-Indonesian descent living in Vietnam, and there are about 100 people living around the Masjidir Rahim.[62]

The people at Masjidir Rahim have a distinctive identity as Malaysian-Indonesian Muslims, which differentiates them from the majority local Muslim population, the Cham.[63] For instance, the Qur'anic teacher at Masjidir Rahim showed a strong dislike of being identified as Cham. I asked his opinion about a claim among the Cham people in the Mekong Delta that they came from Malaysia. He immediately denied it. He argued that the Cham people came from Champa, while he and the people of *jama'ah* Rahim came from Malaysia. He further argued that the Cham community and the Malaysian-Indonesian Vietnamese Muslim community have different customs, traditions, and languages.[64] It was interesting to find that he knew the word Champa although the Cham people in the Mekong Delta had forgotten it. According to him, he learned the history of Vietnam, including the history of Champa, under the South Vietnamese regime. It implies that he had formal education and was more educated than the Cham people.

Pakistan and India first granted the land to build a masjid before construction of Masjidir Rahim by the Bawean (Stokhof 2008: 37).
[61] Stokhof explains that Bawean migrants to Vietnam were mostly men and they married local and non-local Muslim women. However, they did not interact with the small Javanese community in Saigon (Stokhof 2008: 37).
[62] Stokhof mentions that the Bawean people who lived close to Masjidir Rahim in 1976 were roughly around 2,000 in number and also estimates the same population in 2006, which is quite different from the population I gathered in the mid-1990s. I may have mistaken the number of households as the total population.
[63] In Stokhof's study, the people of *jama'ah* Masjidir Rahim identify themselves as Baweans; however, during my field studies, I did not hear them using this term to identify themselves. Instead, the country names, Malaysian and Indonesian, were used to indicate their foreign origin.
[64] The people of *jama'ah* Masjidir Rahim speak the Vietnamese language.

A Vietnamese Muslim of Indian descent showed a similar dislike of being identified as Cham. At Masjid Jamia Al Muslimin, commonly known as Đông Du mosque or Masjid Catinat in Ho Chi Minh City, there is a restaurant selling *halal* Indian food. The restaurant is owned by a Vietnamese Muslim of Indian descent, whose ancestors came from Tamil Nadu. When I asked one of the waiters if he was a Cham, he immediately denied it, and told me that he was Indian, not Cham.[65]

Ner notes that among the Muslim community, the most prestigious and richest people were Indian. Before 1975, the Indian merchants were actively involved in business in Vietnam. Along the coast of Vietnam, the *masjid* built by these Indian Muslim merchants' communities are found in the major port cities such as Nha Trang, Đà Nẵng, Hải Phòng, and also in Hanoi. Ner notes that the majority of Indian Muslims in Cochinchina were English subjects of southern India. They came from the coast of Coromandel, Madras, and Mayavaram. Some of them came from the region of Bombay. There were also Muslims of French India, Pondicherry, some of whom served as middle-level officials in the French colonial administration (Pairaudeau 2009: 87). The Indian Muslims were wealthy merchants who specialized in the business of textiles and money exchange. They supported other poorer Muslim people in Indochina. Ner comments that because of their charitable activities, these Indian Muslims were perceived as aristocrats among the Muslim community (1941: 152-153).

The Indian Muslims married in India, left their wives and children in India, and then frequently went back to India. Ner mentions that they considered it "dishonorable" to marry in Indochina. He quotes one Indian Muslim man who told him that only the Muslims of inferior class married local Muslims (Ner 1941: 152-153). This indicates that the Indian Muslims maintained their distinctive difference from the local Muslim population and did not assimilate into them.

Ner's account gives us a picture of status and class relationships among the Muslim population in Cochinchina, in which the foreign Muslim population formed the upper class while the indigenous Muslim population occupied the bottom of the social pyramid. Both Indian-descended Muslims and Malay-Indonesian-descended Muslims disliked being identified as Cham, perhaps due to the historical class differences within the Muslim population in Cochinchina and their feelings of superiority in understanding and practicing the religion of Islam.

---

[65] When I asked him the first time, though, he told me he was Malaysian, which indicates that the word Malay is used to indicate that he was Muslim.

The Muslim Cham, on the other hand, assert their ethnic identity by claiming that they have their particular cultural characteristics to differentiate them from the rest of the Muslim population in Vietnam. The cultural characteristics can be seen as non-Orthodox Islamic beliefs which can be classified as *mê tín* (superstition) by their communist government. Dohamide mentioned in our email correspondence that the non-Islamic elements in the beliefs of the Cham in the Mekong Delta are Sufism and some segments of the Cham communities are strongly influenced by it.

The Cham in the Mekong Delta believe in the existence of supernatural beings such as spirits other than Allah. Aisah built a new house in her village in An Giang Province. According to her and her mother, building a new house and leaving it empty was not a good thing to do. So, one of the family members should live there for a while to let the house get familiar with them. The Cham in the Mekong Delta believe that each house has a spirit called *patri*. All traditional Cham houses in the Mekong Delta have a center pillar in the house. It is the most significant pillar in the house and it is erected on the ground, piercing the center of the house and connected to the roof (Photo 4-2). A *patri* lives in this central pillar. In most cases, the *patri* is seen by the family members in the middle of the night, and often the *patri* appears as a beautiful young lady in white cloth and wearing lots of gold jewelry. There are male *patri* too, but I was told that the male *patri* do not bring much wealth into the family compared to the female *patri*.

Photo 4-2. A pillar of a house

Another supernatural being believed to be among them is *bun bat* who gives presents to the people who are innocent and honest. There was an honest but poor man among Aisah's relatives. One day, he went to the river to take a bath. In the river, he saw a small metal vase of the sort which people use to keep limestone powder in. He tried to push this vase away since it did not belong to him. However, no matter how hard he tried to chase it away, the vase always came back to him. He became scared and left. Later, the people who heard the story told him that it was *tualak*, a gift from the *bun bat*, and the vase was probably made out of gold.

Aisah had several stories of *bun bat* and *tualak*, but I had doubts about the stories and asked her to show me if she still kept her *tualak*. She was hesitant for a little while because the luck brought by *bun bat* will be weakened if a person shows or talks about the *tualak* to outsiders. But finally, she agreed to show me her *tualak*. It consisted of different kinds of things: two small stones, a centipede,[66] a small snake,[67] and a bunch of hair. The two small stones are called *matay ea* (jewelry of water). Aisah got them when she was 11 years old. It was during the flood season and the streets of Châu Giang village were under water. She was standing in the water enjoying the feeling of smooth mud underneath her feet. Suddenly, she felt something between her toes and managed to pick it up with her toes. It was two small stones. She showed them to her mother who took them to an elderly woman near her house. The elderly woman got breast milk from a lady who had recently given birth for the first time. She put the breast milk on her palm and placed the two small stones in it. The small stones absorbed the milk and she determined that they were *matay ea*,[68] which were gifts from the *bun bat*, and told Aisah's mother that among her children, Aisah would have the best future.

---

[66] The centipede was found in Aisah's house before 1975. Her sister saw it around the central pillar where they believed their *patri* was living. She was instructed to put a white cloth in front of it. If it was a *tualak*, then it would come onto the white cloth. The centipede subsequently came onto the white cloth and was proved to be a *tualak*.

[67] This snake was found in front of Aisah's house in Ho Chi Minh City. Since the snake was so shiny, Aisah first thought it was gold. She put a white cloth in front of it and it came onto the cloth to prove that it was a *tualak*. She wrapped the snake with the white cloth and has kept it since then.

[68] Aisah's *matay ea* that I saw were small marble-looking stones. Both of them were transparent and I could see a small air bubble in one of them. One stone was slightly larger than the other and the larger one was male and the smaller one was female, according to her.

Aisah's mother has many *tualak* stories. This indicates that she is honest and sincere and is liked by the *bun bat*. One of the *tualak* she was given is a lock of hair. This came when she had an overripe coconut. Inside of a coconut, there is a cake-like thing which the Cham call *ha kleh*. With a neighbor's advice, she ate all the *ha kleh* inside for good luck. A few days later her hair became matted as if it were alive and then became dreadlocks. She could not comb this part of her hair, so she cut it off and kept it for good luck together with Aisah's *tualak*.

The Cham also believe in ghosts, *bhut* or *jin*. Though Aisah often used the term *bhut*, I also often heard people use the term *jin* in Châu Giang village. There are two different kinds of *jin*: one is an Islamic *jin* and the other is non-Islamic. The Islamic *jin* are only observed around the masjid, while the non-Islamic *jin* live in the forest or in places covered by trees. An elderly woman in Châu Giang village told me that her husband often saw the Islamic *jin* around the village masjid. Her husband was very religious, and he went to the masjid to pray around three or four o'clock in the morning. Around that time, he encountered Islamic *jin* several times. One day, he saw a man praying in front of the masjid. When he passed by, the man disappeared. At a Friday prayer, he realized that the person praying next to him was a *jin*. When he looked at it, the *jin* suddenly disappeared. He claims that sometimes the masjid was packed with the Islamic *jin*. The Islamic *jin* only appear to the very faithful Muslim people. There are people who are also possessed by the Islamic *jin*. Once a person is possessed by an Islamic *jin*, the person becomes a very dedicated Muslim who spends days just reading the Qur'an.

In contrast to the Islamic *jin*, the non-Islamic *jin* or *bhut* are considered bad ghosts. They are born out of blood which was not properly taken care of, such as the blood that flows out of a dead body after an accident.[69] They often cause problems and sickness, or sometimes even kill people. In Châu Giang village, I became friends with a young girl whose father had passed away and whose mother remarried. She did not get along with her stepfather, so she was staying with her grandfather and aunt's family. I was told that her father was quite an educated Muslim Cham from Cambodia. But nobody mentioned how he died. Later on, I found out that he had committed suicide by jumping off the top of a masjid in Ho Chi Minh City. Suicide is one of the bad deeds in the Islamic faith. The people who told me the story of his death attributed his suicide to a non-Islamic *jin*. He had escaped from

---

[69] The belief that inappropriately disposed of blood is the cause of ghosts is also found among the Cham in the south-central coast area.

turmoil under the Pol Pot regime. He saw many dead people and a lot of blood in Cambodia that made him possessed by non-Islamic *jin* which eventually killed him.

In order to purify the contamination and to remove the non-Islamic *jin*, a shaman called a *Guru* practices a ritual, *tana*, in which the *Guru* lights a candle and reads verses from the Qur'an. The Cham people also rely on a *Guru* when they know that Western medicine cannot do much to cure an illness. Aisah's mother was suffering from epilepsy attacks and had been to several doctors, but her condition was not improving. Aisah became very skeptical about Western medicine after fruitless visits to doctors and spending lots of money buying prescribed medicines. Finally, she decided to invite a *Guru*. The *Guru* came to diagnose her mother, and Aisah brought betel leaves to him. He asked her to choose one out of the ten betel leaves. She tried to choose the best-looking leaf. When she chose one, the *Guru* looked at it and told her that her mother's sickness was due to her mental problem, which was exactly the same diagnosis that the doctors at the hospital told her after numerous exams.

While Aisah's mother's health was declining, Aisah's sister became very sick and she was diagnosed with cancer. She was hospitalized and had been lying in a hospital bed without having any effective treatment for about two months. Aisah gave her a bottle of water and asked her to drink it all. Before preparing the water, Aisah cleaned her body, and then she chanted a certain verse from the Qur'an and blew air into the water. She repeated this 100 times. Aisah believed the water had a magical power to cure her sister's illness, and her sister said she felt better than before every time she drank the water.[70] Aisah had been taught some shamanistic practices by her father. He was a well-respected *Hakim*, a religious leader, and at the same time he was a famous *Guru*, trained in Cambodia where their magic is generally believed to be more powerful than that of the Cham in Vietnam.

The *Guru* of the Mekong Delta seems to be an equivalent to the *Guru Urang* of the Cham in the south-central coast area. In Ninh Thuận Province, the sphere of gods and the sphere of spirits/ghosts are clearly demarcated. The priests of both the Balamon and Bani religions cannot be a *Guru Urang* at the same time. While a *Hakim* can be a *Guru* at the same time, among the Cham in the Mekong Delta there is not such a division between gods and spirits. Yet, the practices of *Gurus* are considered as non-mainstream religious practice, which may be the target of state criticism as superstition. Although the shamanistic practices among the *Guru* of the Cham in the

---

[70] However, the water could not cure her illness and she died four months later.

Mekong Delta appear to be similar to those of the *Guru Urang* of the Cham in the south-central coast area, the Cham people in the Mekong Delta argue that there is a significant difference between the two. While the *Guru Urang* in the south-central coast area can practice sorcery and witchcraft, the Cham *Guru* in the Mekong Delta can only practice exorcism.

An old man who was one of the religious leaders in Châu Giang village was a *Guru*. His daughter told me that the Kinh people at her workplace liked him because he always helped them. He fixed one man's broken leg and cured another who was suffering from a bad toothache. He even fixed a broken marriage. Her father overheard our discussion and showed us several *azmat*. An *azmat* is a talisman against evil. There are many different kinds of talismans, but all of them consist of Arabic scripts. The Cham people asked him to write *azmat* to hang in their houses to prevent theft or sickness, or to carry around while they were traveling to avoid accidents. The *azmat* can only be made on a Friday. Before starting to create the *azmat*, he would light incense and read the Qur'an for about two hours to ask Allah his permission to prepare the *azmat*. When I mentioned to him that I also saw similar *azmat* in Phan Rang, his daughter argued that "The magic in the central area is to lay a curse, while the magic in the Mekong Delta is to undo the curse." She asserted that the magic in the south-central coast area often caused bad things among the people, but the magic among the Cham in the Mekong Delta caused good things. The magic in the Mekong Delta can only be practiced after a *Guru* prays to Allah, and only practiced in order to help people. Her explanation reminded me of an incident I had heard about a man who went to Ninh Thuận Province to proselytize Islam. This Muslim Cham from the Mekong Delta was not liked by Bani people. He suddenly became very ill and returned to his home, where a *Guru* found out that he was cursed. The *Guru* practiced exorcism to "undo" the sorcery and he was saved.

Although the *Guru* among the Cham in the Mekong Delta was said to practice exorcism to only help people, there are many stories which indicate the practice of sorcery among the Cham there. Aisah often attributed the failure of her marriage to sorcery. Her ex-husband had a Cham lover in Châu Đốc before he married Aisah. When he decided to marry Aisah, the family of his former lover was jealous of her and sent someone to Cambodia. He brought back two mud dolls; one was male and the other was female. They put the male doll in a Buddhist temple and the female doll underneath Aisah's house. Once they were married, Aisah's husband was never at home. He always spent his time at the temple where the male doll was placed, while she always stayed at home. When they were apart, they missed each other, but when they got together, they spent most of the time quarreling or he often became sick. First, he suffered from severe headaches and then stomach aches. He asked Aisah to perform an exorcism. She brought a bowl of water, read some verses from the Qur'an, and blew air into the water, then dumped the water on the top of his head. After her exorcism, he felt better and also became a kind husband who stayed at home and helped her with her business. However, his good attitude toward her did not last. She attributed this to the other black magic cast by the sisters of his former lover in Châu Đốc.

Though the religion of Islam provides a significant foundation for the establishment of the Mekong Delta Cham's ethnicity, the non-Islamic beliefs peculiar to these people also provide a ground for them to differentiate themselves from other Muslim groups. I was often told that religion and culture are two different things: the religion of the Cham people is Islam, while they have culture and traditions which are only understood by the Cham people in the Mekong Delta. The phrase "Cham believe" was often used when they introduced non-Islamic practices in order to particularly stress the practices of the Cham community. However, the Cham in the Mekong Delta tend to hide their non-Orthodox Islamic elements from outsiders as they formally pronounce to others that they are Muslim. The knowledge of their non-Islamic practice is enclosed within the community as if it were a secret among them. It is this quietly shared knowledge among them that sets the boundary around the Cham in the Mekong Delta to differentiate them from the rest of the Muslim community.

Hiệp hội Chàm Hồi giáo Việt Nam (The Association of Muslim Cham in Vietnam) and the awakening of Cham ethnicity

The Cham who engaged in small business traveled around various regions. They started to have a small area in Saigon that they could use as a relay station before traveling to other regions and could stay in while supplying merchandise from wholesale markets in the Chinese-Vietnamese district of Chợ Lớn. Because of the intensity of the Second Indochina War and also by seeking employment in Saigon, the number of Muslim Cham migrants from the Mekong Delta to Saigon increased, and the temporary stations became more permanent settlements for the Cham in the city. Most of these Cham migrants did not have sufficient formal education to process necessary paperwork such as filling out job applications or resident registrations. They desperately needed some assistance by an organization that could take care of the bureaucratic paperwork. They also needed to have an organization to identify them as the Cham ethnic minority to prevent them from being conscribed into the army.

The organization called *Hiệp hội Chàm Hồi giáo Việt Nam* (The Association of Muslim Cham in Vietnam), or *Hiệp hội Chàm*, was formed in 1961. Upon establishment of *Hiệp hội Chàm*, it carried out various activities to assert the ethnic identity as Cham based on the religion of Islam, and its membership reached 15,000 by the mid-1960s (Nguyễn Văn Luận 1974: 275). During the 1960s, the political environment worked preferably for the ethnic minority to form their own organizations such as *Hiệp hội Chàm* and to manage them by themselves. After the assassination of President Ngô Đình Diệm in 1963, a new constitution was proclaimed. Under the new constitution, the Council of Ethnic Minority (*Hồi đồng cách sác tộc*) was established under the Ministry of Development of Ethnic Minorities (MDEM). One third of the members of the council were appointed by the government and the rest were selected by the ethnic minority themselves through elections. The council's work included drafting statutes of ethnic minorities. Four Cham individuals from different regions participated in the council.

Since *Hiệp hội Chàm* was recognized by the former Saigon government, current Vietnamese scholars see it as an anti-communist or anti-revolutionary organization, or a conspiracy of ethnic divide of the US puppet regime (Mạc Du'ò'ng 1978: 37-40; Trần Thị Minh Thu). Such criticism is rather conventional Communist Party discourse without careful examination of the social movement. *Hiệp hội Chàm* did not receive any financial aid from the USA or the Saigon government. It was managed by membership fees and donations. Each member of *Hiệp hội Chàm* paid 30 piasters when they joined and then paid 10 piasters each month (Nguyễn Văn Luận 1974: 273).[71] There are only a limited number of studies examining the establishment of *Hiệp hội Chàm* and these studies are quite sketchy and some facts are mixed up.[72]

The development of *Hiệp hội Chàm* and its activities reveal the process of the awakening of Cham ethnic identity among the migrant Cham in Saigon. While becoming a visible ethnic group in the urban center, the

---

[71] *Hiệp hội Chàm* had about 15,000 members in the mid-1960s. By a simple calculation, it was supposed to have about 150,000 piasters revenue from each. It also received some aid from the Malaysian government in goods and services.

[72] I have been trying to gain access to the national archives to look for information on *Hiệp hội Chàm Hồi giáo Việt Nam* since 2011 but my request has not been approved by the authorities.

Cham from the Mekong Delta had gone through the process of defining who they were. *Hiệp hội Chàm* played a significant role in such articulation of their ethnic identity as Cham in Saigon. It was also an attempt to integrate themselves into the Vietnamese society and, moreover, it was the earliest effort of two different Cham groups living in different regions to reach out to each other.

Establishment of Hiệp hội Chàm

Many early Cham migrants to Saigon depended on the support of a person named Danh Mal or *Haji* Mamod (popularly known as Ông Bài Mốt) in the district of Nancy where the earliest Cham migrant community was formed (Nguyễn Hồng Du'o'ng 2007: 162). He was a Java Kur and a well-known fortune teller, and he attracted a number of followers. He financed the construction of a small masjid in Nancy and also helped to establish the Association of Malays of Cochinchina (Dohamide & Dorohiem 2004: 67-68).

Though Danh Mal was not Malay, he used Malay for the association's name. It was probably for practical reasons. The Cham as an ethnic minority from the Mekong Delta were unknown in Saigon. When they looked for employment in Saigon Bay or in French factories, the Cham called themselves Malay, a much more familiar term in Saigon (Dohamide & Dorohiem 2004: 68). It was easier for the Cham to get employment when they indicated that their ethnic background was the more familiar term of Malay. It is probably also due to the relatively negative image of the Cham compared with the Malay. Malay holds religious superiority among the Muslim Cham (Ner 1941: 158), and the word Malay connotes economic and religious superiority among the Cham.

The small masjid in Nancy that Danh Mal built was burned down together with people's dwellings in the mid-1950s (Dohamide & Dorohiem 2004: 69; Nguyễn Hồng Du'o'ng 2007: 162). In order to rebuild a new masjid, the Nancy community needed to obtain permission from the government to establish a religious center, and for that they needed to have an organization representing them. Naturally, Danh Mal's organization, the Association of Malays of Cochinchina, could be the negotiation agent. However, Danh Mal did not agree to change the association's name from Malay to Cham. Under the Ngô Đình Diệm regime, Malay people had been classified as foreigners. But for the Cham to enjoy the benefits given to ethnic minority people, the organization had to bear the name of Cham, the ethnic minority of Vietnam, not Malay. Thus, a separate organization was to be formed.

Photo 4-3. Mr. Dohamide

Around 1951, prior to the establishment of *Hiệp hội Chàm*, small French and Vietnamese language classes for the Cham youth had been organized in Nancy. In order to gain employment, mastering these two languages was crucial (Dohamide & Dorohiem 2004: 70). The language classes were organized by the Cham bureaucrat named Dohamide whom Nguyễn Văn Luận introduced as the mastermind of *Hiệp hội Chàm* (Nguyễn Văn Luận 1974: 272, 274, 280) (Photo 4-3). The classes had around 15 students who showed their interest in learning about the history of Champa (Dohamide & Dorohiem 2004: 70) and they also discussed the problems of the Cham communities. Dohamide had intentions to teach the youth the significance of self-empowerment and of organizing social activities through the classes. During our email correspondence, he stated that through the language classes he could "successfully instill in their minds the new way of community operations to be based on the decision of the majority instead of the fake general consensus they had experienced so far at home." [73] Dohamide's language classs fostered the spirit of communal activities

---

[73] Email correspondence with Dohamide, December 28, 2010.

among the Cham youth of upward mobility and laid the foundation for the establishment of *Hiệp hội Chàm*. It was the materialization of Dohamide's visions of self-empowerment of the Cham community and of the improvement of its status in Vietnamese society.

Dohamide was born in Katambong and his father was a teacher under the French system. Katambong is one of seven Cham communities in the Mekong Delta. Though it is an economically less privileged community, the Cham from Katambong put a high value on education, and many Cham who have achieved higher education came from there. In 1949 he moved to Saigon to enter secondary school. Because he did well in school, he enrolled in Petrus Ký high school (current day Lê Hồng Phong High School for gifted students). After he completed his high school education, he lived with his elder sister's family in the district of Nancy and took a job at a military welfare office to support her family. During this time, he participated in writing competitions organized by a newspaper, and his articles won prizes. He was invited to write articles on the Cham community in Châu Đốc in the daily newspaper *Buổi sáng* (*The Morning*). He also published his opinions on social issues in the Sunday newspaper *Thế Giới* (*The World*).

Dohamide passed an exam to work in South Vietnam's premier's office (*Thủ hiến Nam Việt*). Working in this office was quite prestigious and he gained people's respect. The office was located in front of the national library where he became acquainted with the head of the library, Trân Quang Tấu, who provided assistance for his research on the Cham and Champa. Dohamide wrote a history of Champa based on the French material and published the book titled *Dân tộc Chàm Lu'ọ'c sử'* in 1965. It is the first history book on Champa written by a Cham. His wish to educate the public on the history of Champa and to allow Muslim Cham from Châu Đốc to know their historical heritage of Champa motivated Dohamide to publish this book. His concerns about Cham people's history and his attempt to connect the Cham of the Mekong Delta to Champa must be due to his exceptional achievement of higher education outside of Islamic education.

In 1956, Dohamide entered the Institute of Administration and studied at the Committee of Highlands (*Ban Cao Nguyên*). Upon graduation, he worked in the Ministry of Interior, then moved to the Ministry of Finance. Although many bureaucrats of ethnic minority backgrounds were transferred to outposts away from Saigon such as Quảng Trị or Huế due to the outbreak of the anti-government ethno-nationalist movement (FULRO), Dohamide remained in Saigon and worked at the High Commission of Peace and Pacification (*Phủ phó thu trung Đặc trách bình Đnh*). In this office, he worked as a service chief at the bureau of research and studies at the service of ethnic minorities. After the coup set up by Nguyễn Cao Kỳ, he was transferred to the attaché of the cabinet of the Prime Minister's Office. Then, he was selected to study in the USA. He studied at the University of Kansas and completed his master's degree. Though he planned to continue his studies for a Ph.D., he was called back to Vietnam in 1967 and became the Director of Logistics. He assisted the advisory group from Michigan State University and also helped researchers from the University of Chicago who worked in a village in Long An. His attainment of a higher degree in education and his successful career as a high-ranking government bureaucrat was quite exceptional among the Muslim Cham.

Hiệp hội Chàm was established to be a self-supporting organization for the Cham migrants to live in the new urban environment. Though most of the significant decisions were made by consulting with Dohamide, his name was not listed as a founding member[74] of *Hiệp hội Chàm*. It was because Dohamide wanted to establish a new type of organization with a democratic system. The traditional Cham organization was hierarchical. With their virtues and religious knowledge, the religious leaders often headed the organizations. Dohamide wished to establish a flatter organization with no hierarchy, so that every member in *Hiệp hội Chàm* could express their opinion freely. *Hiệp hội Chàm* also organized an election to select their officers later on. Dohamide, as a very high-ranking government bureaucrat, was afraid to disturb this flat organization and thus he remained low profile.

Hiệp hội Chàm's main activities

Hiệp hội Chàm's main activities were to issue Cham identification cards, assist Cham migrants and their religious activities, increase the popularization of Islam, and reach out to the international Muslim communities. One of the biggest problems that the Cham faced under the Saigon government was military service. The South Vietnam government had conscription and all young men over 18 years old[75] had to join the military. The Cham people feared this because it is quite difficult to keep Islamic commandments once a person joins the military. They especially feared the possibility of eating pork and the inability to bury their deceased immediately upon death in the battlefields. The Saigon government followed the French colonial administration's special treatment of the

---

[74] Most of the founding members of *Hiệp hội Chàm* were the Cham from Katambong.
[75] University students could delay their military service.

Central Highlands as the *Pays Montagnard du Sud-Indochinois* (PMSI) (Salemink 2003: 146), which meant ethnic minority people in the Central Highlands were all exempt from conscription.[76] *Hiệp hội Chàm* managed to gain the same status for Muslim Cham people. Upon this agreement, *Hiệp hội Chàm* issued identification cards for the Cham Muslim people.

The members of *Tổng Hội Hồi Giáo Việt Nam* (Muslim Association of Vietnam) established by Tù' Công Xuân, a Cham from Văn Lâm and member of the Lower House of the Saigon government, also joined *Hiệp hội Chàm* as they needed to have the Cham identification card to be exempt from military conscription. Dohamide at first approached Tù' Công Xuân in order to obtain government approval for the establishment of *Hiệp hội Chàm*. Though he supported Dohamide's idea, Tù' Công Xuân himself did not participate in *Hiệp hội Chàm*. Instead, he established his own organization, *Tổng Hội Hồi Giáo Việt Nam*, with the people of Ba Cum. Ba Cum is a place outside of Ho Chi Minh City where a group of Kinh Muslims who had converted to Islam of their own free will lived.[77] The Ba Cum people migrated to Saigon and lived in a small community in the district of Hoà Hu'ng in Saigon.[78] By losing its members to *Hiệp hội Chàm*, however, *Tổng Hội Hồi Giáo Việt Nam* had become a nominal organization. Later on, the task of issuing a Muslim Cham identification card was transferred to the MDEM where Dohamide's younger brother, Dorohiem, was working.

During the war, organizing gatherings met various restrictions. Various religious activities in which many Muslims congregated in one place required approval from the authorities. *Hiệp hội Chàm* took care of this paperwork so that the Muslims could enjoy their gatherings without any trouble. *Hiệp hội Chàm* also took responsibility to make reports to the authorities after the events, as well. The police also carried out inspections of resident registrations among the households. There were incidents where Cham individuals were arrested because they could not produce proof of residence. In this case, *Hiệp hội Chàm* became a guarantor of the arrested individuals and also provided paperwork for these individuals to have a resident registration.

Dohamide published a series of articles on Islam in a prestigious magazine called *Bách Khoa* from 1964 to 1965. He had the intention to teach the Vietnamese population about Islam because they did not have

---

[76] Khmer and Chinese-Vietnamese (Hoa) were not exempt from military service at that time.
[77] Ner reports that Ba Cum is located 21 km outside of Chợ Lớn (1941: 161).
[78] The headquarters of *Tổng Hội Hồi Giáo Việt Nam* was located there.

accurate information about it. Islam was understood as a somewhat esoteric religion since most Vietnamese were familiar with it through fortune-telling or sorcery carried out by the religious practitioners (*Gurus*). Dohamide also wished to facilitate a better understanding of Islamic teaching among the Cham people. Considerable numbers of Cham men took a second wife[79] whom they became acquainted with during their prolonged business trips away from home. Most of the second wives were non-Muslim Kinh and some were Catholic. Bringing their second wives back into Cham villages often created commotion. *Hiệp hội Chàm* tried to correct such a practice and organized talks on Islam and provided books to further educate Cham Muslims for a better understanding of Islam. *Hiệp hội Chàm* also supported Qur'anic teachers by providing them with salaries.

Reaching out to the international Muslim communities to improve Cham communities was also one of Dohamide's hidden agendas for the establishment of *Hiệp hội Chàm*. As a government-recognized organization, *Hiệp hội Chàm* became an international representative of the Muslim communities in South Vietnam. *Hiệp hội Chàm* was responsible for processing paperwork for the people who made pilgrimages to Mecca and also to participate in various international Islamic events, such as Qur'an reading competitions in Malaysia and Islamic conferences.[80]

Muda and *Tua* conflicts and *Hiệp hội Chàm*

Hiệp hội Chàm had Umar Aly as the supreme advisor for mostly religious matters. Umar Aly was from *jama'ah* Azhar and had spent many years studying in Mecca. He became the *Hakim* of *jama'ah* Azhar and established a religious school (*madrasah*). He taught many students who, later on, became religious leaders, and *jama'ah* Azhar became the center of religious education. His reputation was rising and shadowing the influence of *Saykhol* Islam which was a local position under the French colonial rule and somehow survived after the French left.[81] During the French colonial period, the French adopted a position, *Saykhol* Islam from the British

---

[79] Polygamy was prohibited during the time of President Ngô Đình Diệm.
[80] Dohamide participated in the International Islamic Conference of Southeast Asia and the Far East held at Kuala Lumpur, Malaysia, in 1964 and the International Islamic Conference held in Saudi Arabia in 1974.
[81] Nguyễn Văn Luận quotes an open protest of *Saykhol* Islam by Tăng Khạo Mat in a newspaper article in which *Hakim* Umar Aly was mentioned as the representative of the Muslim community (1974: 291 footnote 1). This incident seemed to be the initial reason for organizing the meetings.

colonial government, which established this in the state of Trengganu of British Malaya. *Saykhol* Islam, or *Chef des Malais* in French, was a leadership position to control the Muslim communities in the Mekong Delta region. Traditionally, *Saykhol* Islam was held by a person from Java Kur's *jama'ah* Mubarak (Dohamide & Dorohiem 2004: 63). Even after the French left, the title of *Saykhol* Islam remained and continued to be held by an individual from *jama'ah* Mubarak (Nguyễn Văn Luận 1974).

Compared to the Cham people in other *jama'ah*, the Java Kur people were economically better off. In the *jama'ah* Mubarak, there was a ferry terminal on the Bassac river (Hậu Giang) and many people went there to catch the ferry to the city of Châu Đốc, where they bought daily supplies at the market and Cham students went to school. A few Java Kur people owned tug boats and some of them loaned money to other Cham with high interest rates (Dohamide & Dorohiem 2004: 64).

The rivalry between Umar Aly and *Saykhol* Islam became serious and, finally, a meeting to resolve the conflict was organized in 1960. The conflict between the two sides was revealed to be complicated because of the involvement of another conflict between *muda* and *tua* (Nguyễn Văn Luận 1974: 292-294; Nguyễn Hồng Du'o'ng 2007: 179). As a result, the Council of *Hakim* (*Hội Đồng Giáo Cả*) was established and replaced the old French colonial appointments. *Hakim* Umar Aly was elected as *Mufti*, the paramount leader of the Muslim community (Dohamide & Dorohiem 2004: 79).

Though the *muda* and *tua* conflicts among the Cham have not yet been systematically investigated, the competition between *muda* and *tua* created various social conflicts among the Muslim Cham community in the 1960s around the time that *Hiệp hội Chàm* started its activities. *Muda* and *tua* are Malay words meaning young (new) and old, respectively. The *kaum muda* (new group) was the Malay religious reformist group that emerged around the beginning of the 1900s which challenged the conservative religious doctrine and the religious authority of the traditional group, *kaum tua* (old group), including Malay aristocracy and nobility (Bedlington 1978: 55; Nagata 1986: 37). *Kaum muda* opposed the feudalistic structure of Malay society and called for the total reform of it. The group also demanded to reduce the sultans' power over religion by arguing that they should be subordinate to *syariah* (Islamic law) and on decisions of religious matters, they should rely on the council of *ulama* (religious authority) (Kamarulnizam 2003: 41-42). The *kaum muda*'s teaching clashed with the state religious authorities on every aspect of religious and social life, including the use of savings banks and women's education. The conflicts between *muda* and *tua* divided Malay Muslim communities and it was reported that there were no villages without arguments and disputes between *muda* and *tua* in Malaya (Roff 1994: 78, 87).

According to Cham religious leaders, the different practices of religion between *muda* and *tua* can be summarized as 12 points, including the number of Prophets and the frequency of *rakat* (prescribed movements of prayer) in the *Tarawat* prayer during the fasting month[82] (Nguễn Văn Luận 1974: 294; Nguyễn Hồng Du'o'ng 2007: 178). The *muda* group also denied some local religious practices such as vigils for the dead, saint worship, belief in magic, and spirit and holy relics (P. Taylor 2007: 126-127).

The *muda*'s reformist teachings were introduced to the Muslim Cham community in Vietnam in the late 1950s. The Java Kur people who studied in Malaysia came back and introduced the *muda* teachings.[83] *Muda* gradually spread. Before 1975 there were 37 *muda* followers,[84] which steadily increased and, according to a book by Nguyễn Hồng Du'o'ng, *muda* now occupies about 20% to 25% of the Cham Muslim population (2007 179).

The antagonism between *muda* and *tua* was quite strong and very emotional. Once a person was recognized as *muda*, he/she would be excommunicated. There was no communication or interaction between *muda* and *tua*, even among relatives, and there were no marriages between *muda* and *tua* individuals prior to 1975. Since *tua* did not agree that *muda* people could come and pray in the same masjid, the *muda* group established two masjids of their own in the hamlets of Châu Phong and Đa Phu'ó'c (P. Taylor 2007: 123-127).

---

[82] For *muda*, there are 23 Prophets and 8 times of *rakat*, while for *tua* there are 25 Prophets and 20 times of *rakat*.

[83] According to Cham intellectuals, the first person who followed the teachings of *muda* was *Hakim* Idress from *jama'ah* Mubarak who studied in Malaysia. *Hakim* Idress had several students, one of whom was *Haji* Hosen from Châu Phong hamlet. *Hakim* Idress, *Haji* Hosen, and a person named *Haji* Ayob of Châu Phong are the three main figures who were responsible for spreading *muda* teaching among the Cham Muslims around the 1950s. *Imam* Yusof, the late *Imam* of masjid Musulman Jamia Al Muslimin in Ho Chi Minh City, remembered that it was around 1955 when the *muda* was first introduced to the Cham community in Vietnam. Zain bin Musa attributed the wave of *kaum muda* movement in Indochina to a Cambodian-born Cham, *Imam* Musa (Ly Mousa), who spent some time in Bangkok and was educated in Patani, Thailand, and in Kelantan, Malaysia (2008).

[84] Interview with a religious leader in Ho Chi Minh City in 1994. However, Nguễn Văn Luận indicated that according to Jacob, the secretary of *Hiệp hội Chàm*, there were 37 families instead of 37 people of the *muda* teaching (1974: 290 footnote 1).

Meetings to resolve the conflicts between *muda* and *tua* continued to be organized between 1964 and 1966 and a stone monument was erected to remember the solidarity of the Muslim people at the end of the process. Yet the members of the Council of *Hakim* were all *tua* and they opposed the *muda* teachings (Nguyễn Văn Luận 1974: 293-294). Having the Council of *Hakim* as religious advisors, *Hiệp hội Chàm* took the side of *tua*. One of the founding members of *Hiệp hội Chàm*, Mousa Misky, was an intellectual and a teacher who had learned about *muda* teaching and begun to practice it. Due to that, he was expelled from *Hiệp hội Chàm* (Nguyễn Văn Luận 1974: 281).

Muda movements, which predominantly gained followers among the Java Kur community, can be seen as the resistance to the new socio-political order among the Cham. The Java Kur community, which held prestigious official positions linking the Muslim community with the authorities during the French colonial period, had lost such positions during the rise of the Cham people's religious and social movements. *Jama'ah* Azhar, which was located next to the Java Kur's *jama'ah* Mubarak, became the center of religious education, and the *Hakim* of *jama'ah* Azhar became the *Mufti*. *Hiệp hội Chàm* took on the role of socio-political representative of the Muslim Cham community and it negotiated with the Saigon government for the Cham community's well-being. The Java-Kur-centered old political structure in the rural Mekong Delta had been replaced by a Cham-centered urban-based secular organization, *Hiệp hội Chàm*. The *muda* movement, which challenged the traditional teaching of Islam, can be interpreted as the resistance of the old political structure among the Muslim community in the Mekong Delta. By adapting new teachings of *muda* from Malaysia, well-learned religious leaders from the influential families among the Java Kur people asserted and tried to retain their traditional leading position and influences among the Muslim communities in the Mekong Delta.

The meaning of *Hiệp hội Chàm*

Establishing *Hiệp hội Chàm* embodied Dohamide's wish for the Cham not to feel shame about their ethnic background but rather to gain pride for who they are. It lasted for 14 years under the Saigon regime and was responsible for several important achievements in the Cham communities. The establishment of *Hiệp hội Chàm* and its activities created an awakening of Cham ethnic identity among the Muslim Cham of the Mekong Delta. Having moved to Saigon, their ethnic identity was redefined and asserted in the new socio-political context. With the religion of Islam, it connected the

Cham from the south-central coast area and the Cham from the Mekong Delta. It also connected relatively isolated Muslim Cham communities to the international Muslim communities. One of the most important achievements of *Hiệp hội Chàm* is that the Cham took the initiative and established a secular organization which was different from their traditional organization based on religious hierarchy. *Hiệp hội Chàm* also stressed the significance of secular education, which was necessary to survive and to integrate better into Vietnamese society. To think of the current minority people's position in Vietnam, an establishment that is initiated, organized, and managed by an ethnic minority is something that cannot be materialized. Yet prior to 1975, the Cham had managed to do the impossible.

Conclusion

The Cham people in the Mekong Delta assert their ethnicity by being Muslim rather than by being descendants of Champa. The Java Kur people, who do not trace their genealogy back to Champa, identify themselves as Cham largely because they are Muslim. It is not their connection to Champa but to Allah which gives the people their Cham ethnic identity. It is not the knowledge of historical Champa but the knowledge of Islam which constructs their ethnic identity. Having Islam for the foundation of their ethnicity, they are no longer a peripheral sub-group of the Cham community. With Islam, the Cham of the Mekong Delta can re-center themselves as equally "genuine" Cham as the Cham from the south-central coast area.

Practicing the religion of Islam also transforms a person's ethnic identity to the Cham. In this regard, one can contrast the past-oriented, genealogically based ethnic identity of the south-central coast Cham to the present-oriented, religiously based ethnic identity of the Mekong Delta Cham.

However, within the Muslim community, their non-Islamic beliefs and customs peculiar to the Cham people differentiate them from other Muslims. With their knowledge of non-Islamic beliefs which are only shared among the Cham in the Mekong Delta, they draw an ethnic boundary around themselves which excludes non-Cham Muslim people as well as others.

Hiệp Hội Chàm was the earliest organization that articulated Islam-based Cham ethnicity in Vietnam. Having the ethnic name of the Cham as part of the organization's name, *Hiệp hội Chàm* made these people visible in Vietnam. It also demonstrates the potential of an ethnic minority's strong initiative for self-empowerment that challenges the current passive status of these people as mere recipients of state-made ethnic minority policies.

Dohamide's efforts to connect the Cham of the south-central coast and the Mekong Delta are persistent. Long after his migration to the USA, in 2004 he published a book titled *Bangsa Champa* in the USA. The cover of this book depicts Cham ladies in traditional clothes dancing around one of the most famous existing Hindu temples, Po Klong Garai. He has chosen Champa vestiges and traditional Cham dancers for his book cover because he wants the Muslim Cham from the Mekong Delta to remember their past. On the cover, a group of female dancers carrying jars on their heads are coming out of Po Klong Garai temple, headed by a young woman who is wearing clothes with a stand-up collar and gold chains different from the other dancers (Photo 4-4). This leading dancer is named Jyasmine Tham, a Bani Muslim who later on joined Orthodox Islam. Having Champa's heritage as a background, Jyasmine is performing traditional Cham dances and she is looking ahead to the future of the Cham people, which Dohamide believes is the religion of Islam. He wishes the Cham to know their past and to move forward and organize their society based on Islam.

I cannot agree that the religion of Islam can be the sole common foundation for the Cham people in Vietnam to construct their ethnic identity. However, Islam has re-established or re-articulated an ethnic boundary among the Cham people who left Vietnam. Many Bani or Balamon Cham became followers of Orthodox Islam when they migrated into Cambodia and other countries. Almost all Cham people in the diaspora are Orthodox Muslim.[85] The dynamics of the ethnicity of Cham Muslim people reveal their resilience. Siu-Woo Cheung, who studied the impact of Christianity on the society of Miao minority people in PRC, describes how a new religion could unite the Miao people who used to be scattered and loosely related to each other. It strengthened their common ethnic identity and they became a

---

[85] Collins names a process of redefining Cham communities in Cambodia to include other Muslim people who are not ethnic Cham, that is to include the Malay or Chvea, as "Malaysianization" of the Cham. It suggests that the Cham in Cambodia may redefine themselves as Khmer Muslim instead of Cham in the future. One of Collins' informants told him that "Many Muslims were now feeling that even the Cham language or any remaining Cham culture could also be abandoned, and it would not matter because they were Muslim" (Collins 1996: 96). The article published in 2011 by Zain bin Musa indicated that the Cham and the Malay in Cambodia form a homogenous community which is known as "Khmer Islam." The decision to name the community not based on their ethnic denomination but on their religious affiliation was decided in 1954 by the Sihanouk government (Zain bin Musa 2011: 1).

unified, well-organized people, able to handle their own affairs through formal administrations under strong church leadership (Cheung 1995: 243). Similar to the Miao case, the religion of Islam probably has created a firmer base for the Cham refugees to re-establish their community on foreign soil and maintain their ethnic identity in new foreign environments.

Photo 4-4. A cover of *Bangsa Champa*

CHAPTER 5

CHAM ETHNIC IDENTITY AND *DÂN TỘC* CHAM

In this chapter, Cham ethnicity in the context of the Vietnamese nation-state is examined. The Vietnamese words *dân tộc* are used to indicate ethnic groups. The words *dân tộc* are from the Japanese word *minzoku* (民族) created during the Meiji period (明治時代) when Japan was in a hurry to modernize itself to become a nation-state recognized by the Western powers. The Japanese use the word *minzoku* to indicate both ethnic groups and the citizens of a nation. Since the Japanese state has created a myth that the nation of Japan originated from one ethnic group (or one "race"), the ambiguity of the word *minzoku* has never been so problematic. However, the word *minzoku* has kept its ambiguity and a difference from terms such as race and citizens (Morris-Suzuki 1996: 88). This word was introduced to Vietnam through China (Harrell 1996b: 276) as *dân tộc*, which is used to indicate both people of a nation and also an ethnic group.

The Vietnamese state has been engaging in the project of classifying people living in its territory by their ethnic identities. The state has adapted Stalin's definition of nationality to the ethnic classification. According to his definition, a nationality is a group of people who have a common territory, common language, common economy, and common psychological nature. Adapting Stalin's definition and especially the language classification, the population of Vietnam was classified into 64 *dân tộc* in the 1950s but the number was reduced to 58 in the late 1970s (Yoshizawa 1982: 14) and finally defined as 54 by the 1990s.

The means of classification of *dân tộc* have been examined and have received some criticism by Vietnamese social scientists. Later, Vietnamese ethnographers recognized the significance of people's self-conscious identity in determining a person's ethnic identity (Phan Ngoc Chien 1993: 48-50). However, *dân tộc* is still considered as being rigid and static in Vietnam. A child who has parents belonging to two different *dân tộc* must choose one of his/her parents' *dân tộc* as their own. In other words, a person cannot be half Cham and half Kinh, but must be either Cham or Kinh. The state does not allow a person to have more than one ethnic identity, and changing ethnic identities requires approval from the authorities (Phan Ngoc Chien 1997: 5).

The description of each *dân tộc* found in books and museums tends to depict culturally homogeneous groups without paying much attention to their regional and religious differences. The Cham are also described as monolithic: the people of the "ancient Kingdom of Champa" and the culture of the Cham in the south-central coast area have been depicted in the Cham *dân tộc* in Vietnam. The Cham people from the Mekong Delta are treated as a sub-group. As the previous chapters demonstrated, the Cham are not a culturally homogenous group. Actually, various scholars have already pointed out the problems of seeing an ethnic group as a cultural group (Leach 1964; Moerman 1965). Diversity of an ethnic group and dynamism of ethnicity cannot be explained in the state classification of *dân tộc*. Yet as long as one is a Vietnamese national, one must slot oneself into one of the 54 *dân tộc*. In this chapter, I focus on how the different Cham ethnic identities are negotiated in the public sphere. By examining the representation of the Cham people in the public domain, I try to understand the interplay between the Cham communities and the state of Vietnam over their identity.

Văn nghệ as a culture-manufacturing arena

During my field research, Vietnamese officials encouraged me to attend *văn nghệ*[86] (cultural shows) to learn about Cham culture. *Văn nghệ* were usually organized by various administrative offices: the People's Committee, Department of Office and Information, Department of Labor, The Front of Father Land, Institute of Social Science, and so on. The shows usually consisted of singing, dancing, short plays, and sometimes a fashion show, and an introduction of some minorities' customs. The ethnic minorities' performances were always popular because they provided different flavors to the show which mostly consisted of the majority Kinh performances.

In the beginning, I was reluctant to attend *văn nghệ*, but later I realized that it was an arena of creation and demonstration of the ethnic minority people's "correct" (*chính xác*) culture. Similar to the gender differences that are produced through systems of representations and discursive practices (P. Adams 1979: 52), the ethnic identity of a particular group of people is also constructed through the representation of cultural differences in the public domain such as *văn nghệ*. The ethnic minority cultures performed on the

---

[86] *Văn nghệ* is a short form of *văn học nghệ thuật,* meaning literature and art. In this chapter, I use *văn nghệ* to indicate cultural performances at the theaters.

stage are the result of filtering out their "unwanted" characteristics such as "backwardness" (*lạc hậu*), poverty, social disadvantages, a problematic political position, and their ambiguous relationship to the majority group. This is a sterilized culture which is not "contaminated" by social problems.

For the Vietnamese organizers, what they are looking for in the minority performances is authenticity. Every five years, the Vietnamese government organizes a large-scale cultural festival of ethnic minority people in Vietnam. The one held in Phú Yên Province in 1995 had a theme of "genuine ethnic culture," that is, culture not influenced by the majority Kinh people. At the festivals, many minorities' dances, songs, and clothes have been criticized by the Vietnamese officials for having lost their originality under the Kinh cultural influence.

However, what is "authentic" is very problematic since the represented "supposed to be" genuine culture of a minority is not a representation of reality but of an already preconditioned image of who they are. The Vietnamese organizers are the judges of the cultural authenticity and, in the end, it is the state which has the authority to recognize the "authenticity" of the minority culture. The authenticity is determined as the distance from the majority Kinh culture: something unusual, unfamiliar, archaic, and exotic.

The *văn nghệ* are organized and supervised by Vietnamese officials, but each cultural presentation allows the Cham people a certain degree of freedom to decide the content, theme, and style of performance. Moreover, in contrast to museum displays, in cultural shows the Cham people are the ones who perform their culture which also involves a certain degree of freedom of choice in their repertoire, costumes, and stage settings. K. Adams argues that preparing cultural activities for outsiders to see makes an ethnic group become self-conscious about their culture. Her study of the impact of tourism among the Toraja people in upland Sulawesi demonstrates that in the process of unifying their culture and history which are to be presented to the tourists, the Toraja ethnic consciousness was evoked. Their cultural prestige in the nation was enhanced, any criticism of the Toraja for being "backward" was denied, and their "backward" customs were justified (K. Adams 1997: 318). In *văn nghệ*, the Cham were not just a passive object to be presented but they could engage in the construction of their culture, markers, and identity. The *văn nghệ* which are supposed to promote "the original form of minorities' cultures" become arenas for manufacturing them. It provides a particular time and space where the ethnic identity and their markers are negotiated and re-articulated.

Cham fan dance

Historically, Champa was known to have rich music and dance traditions. Their dance called *Linyu gaku* (林邑楽) was introduced to Japan through China during the Nara period (奈良時代) (710–794) and it is still performed in Japan. The Vietnamese court was also interested in their dance and music, and there are historical documents recording that in 982 during the Lê dynasty (黎朝 980–1009), a number of singers from Champa were brought to Đại Việt. In 1044, Emperor Lý Thái Tông (李太宗 1028–1054) captured and brought back to Hanoi around 5,000 prisoners including a number of court dancers. They knew Indian-style dance and the emperor built a special palace for them. These captured musicians and dancers from Champa performed at the Đại Việt court, and Emperor Lý Nhân Tông (李仁宗 1072–1127) grew up listening to the music and seeing the dances from Champa at the court (Trần Quốc Vu'ọ'ng 2011: 268, 272-273).

At *văn nghệ*, Cham dancing performed by the south-central coast Cham is quite popular. They have various repertories such as the fan dance, the fetching water dance, the scarf dance, the fishing dance, and the royal court dance which has been popularized as the Apsara dance. Traditionally, Cham from the Mekong Delta, especially women, do not dance because of their religious background. Islam has been seen by Vietnamese scholars as well as some Cham as a plague which killed the original Cham culture among those in the Mekong Delta. Phan Thị Yến Tuyết, who studied the Cham in the Mekong Delta, argues that by following the religious rules and rites, the Cham people there practice a simplified version of the original Cham tradition. Further, she criticizes that Islam overshadows the ethnic characteristics of the Cham, makes them lose their original culture, and molds the Cham culture into something different (Phan Thị Yến Tuyết 1993: 266-274).

However, the Cham from the Mekong Delta do still have music traditions and music groups which sing religious songs. Aisah has had a long singing career. By 1975 she and her cousins had formed a band and as the lead vocalist, she was one of the first female Cham singers to appear on TV (Photo 5-1). After 1975 she organized her own *kampulan qasidah* (music group) and it became quite popular in Ho Chi Minh City. Aisah was interviewed by several newspapers about her music and her group was invited to perform in different programs organized by various ministries, districts, and a TV station. As they have become increasingly popular, their singing style has become more refined and they have adapted more entertainment elements, such as dancing.

Photo 5-1: A music band prior to 1975 (courtesy of Ustazah *Haja* Basiroh *Haji* Aly)

Initially, her group did not dance with the music, but then they started to dance while they were singing, and at last, they created dance pieces. The first dance piece has the theme of fetching water. Slow music is played and Aisah starts to sing with the music. Three females wearing Malay-style clothes called *baju kubaya* made from batik come onto the stage holding vases in their hands. They place the vases down and sit on the stage making a gesture of wiping sweat from their faces. Then the music changes to an up-tempo beat, the ladies look at each other, and start to enjoy the music. Finally, they stand up and start to dance with the music while Aisah sings next to them. In this performance, her group adapted a theme of popular south-central coast Cham dance: the fetching water dance. Their Malay-like clothes made out of batik and wearing head scarfs connote their religious identity as Muslim. By retaining their religious identity and adapting the dance theme from the south-central coast Cham, they have created a new Cham cultural performance (Photo 5-2).

Photo 5-2: The water fetching dance

Soon after they created the fetching water dance, the group created a piece entirely attributed to dancing. For this performance, they have adapted fans. A Vietnamese choreographer, Đặng Hùng, points out the significance of fans in Cham rituals and folk dances, and mentions that the fan is like a language in their dance. It expresses their feelings and emotions. He further argues that the Cham people's fan dance is quite unique among the people of Southeast Asia (Đặng Hùng 1998: 130-131). The fan, which determined the dance styles in the Cham rituals in the south-central coast region, has been adapted by the theatrical performances and fans have become an indicator of Cham ethnic elements on stage.

In the new dance performance by Aisah's group, five females dressed in Malay dress called *baju kurung* with full head covers dance with a big fan in each hand to instrumental music somewhat reminiscent of Central Asian tunes. There is no singing. Some fan movements and a pattern of steps are similar to those of the Cham fan dance from the south-central coast area.

The popular theatrical Cham dance from the south-central coast area provides the ground for this new Cham Muslim dance to be identified as a Cham dance. The audience can recognize the elements of the south-central coast Cham culture, which they are more familiar with, in this Muslim Cham dance (Photo 5-3).

Photo 5-3. The fan dance by Cham Muslims

As discussed in previous chapters, the Cham from the south-central coast area and the Cham from the Mekong Delta have different foundations for their ethnic identities: one is Champa and the other is Islam. Aisah's *kampulan qasidah* has been creating performances by emphasizing their Islamic background. They included somewhat Arabian-style movements in their dance which reflect their connection to the Middle East through their religion. Many songs they sing or use are from Malaysia or other Muslim countries which she has translated into the Cham and Vietnamese languages. These songs are all introduced as Cham music. Yet in order to articulate their ethnic identity to the non-Cham audience, they co-opted the ethnic markers of the Cham from the south-central coast area despite the fact that they usually do not want to be identified with them. By adapting the cultural markers of the Cham from the south-central coast area, the Cham of the Mekong Delta can articulate their ethnic identity as one of 54 *dân tộc* in Vietnam.

The royal court dance: the Apsara dance

At one of the *văn nghệ*, I saw a Cham dance piece performed by three females dressed in decorated bikinis with Khmer-style head-dresses with very slow music. The dance was called Siva dance. Historically, Siva-worshipping was widespread in Champa, and the Siva statue at the entrance of the Po Klong Garai temple is one of the well-known markers of the Cham people as well as the temple itself. The Cham might have the dance of the god Siva, but I wondered about the relationship between these three female dancers in skimpy costumes and the god Siva.

The Siva dance, or later on renamed as the dance of Apsara (a celestial nymph) (Photo 5-4), turned out to be the Champa's royal court dance created by Đặng Hùng, a Vietnamese "people's artist" (*Nghệ sĩ nhân dân*) who was a native of Bình Định Province. He had studied dance and theater in Hanoi, North Korea, PRC, USSR, Bulgaria, and Cuba. A newspaper article introduced Đặng Hùng and his creation of the Cham royal court dance as "the only choreographer who has successfully restored the Cham royalty's most exotic dance" (*Viet Nam News* 1997). Because of his birthplace, Bình Định Province, a former territory of Champa, Đặng Hùng emphasized his connection to Champa: "Since childhood I was completely captivated by their statues of dancers and the stocky Cham towers in the province and that raised me, Cham culture is still alive in me now" (*Viet Nam News* 1997).

Photo 5-4. The Apsara dance (courtesy of Trần Kỳ Phu'o'ng)

Đặng Hùng calls his works a restoration of the royal court dance (*phục hồi múa cung đình*). According to him, there used to be three types of dances that were known to the people of Champa: religious dance, folk dance, and royal court dance. Among these three, the royal court dance has been forgotten and is no longer performed, while other Hinduized Southeast Asian countries like Cambodia, Laos, and Thailand have kept their royal court dances. He legitimized his restoration of the Cham royal court dance by arguing that the restoration met the decision of the 8th National Assembly where the culture and arts policies of the new era were discussed. They agreed to encourage "exploring and displaying people's traditional culture and art, and also making their culture and art more progressive, and rich" (Đặng Hùng 1998: 15).

Đặng Hùng restored the royal court dance by observing religious dance performed by the Cham and also referencing sculptures from the vestiges. He also added various decorative elements to meet the requirements of court rituals and to reflect the aesthetics of the aristocrats of a particular era (Đặng Hùng 1998: 141-143).

The Apsara dance demonstrates that Cham culture is exotic and ancient. The dancers' costumes and suggestive movements are erotic and exotic, and the dance brings the audience back to the time of Champa when kings, royal families, and foreign envoys were entertained at the royal court. It even evokes the image of Champa's captured dancers dancing in front of emperors at the Đại Việt court. The dance also highlights Hindu heritage, which was the oldest and also the state religion of Champa. Such characteristics of the restoration of the Cham royal court dance are a result of Vietnam's civilizing project.

Harrell, who has worked among the ethnic minorities in PRC, describes that the state policies on ethnic minorities as civilizing projects were "a kind of interaction between two actors, the civilizing center and the peripheral peoples, in terms of a particular kind of inequality" (Harrell 1995: 4). PRC's civilizing projects have developed along with its history. Harrell called its current version "the Communist civilizing project" (1995: 9).

The Communist civilizing project is, in theory, quite different from other civilizing projects. The Communist civilizing project does not have a prior assumption that its center consists of a particular group of people which is superior to the rest of the population. In the Communist project, the goal is not to assimilate the minority group into the majority group, but "to bring them to a universal standard of progress or modernity" (Harrell 1995: 23). Yet, despite the ideology of the Communist civilizing project, the majority

Han inherited an innate sense of superiority over the minority people due to their prior (Confucian) civilizing project.

According to Confucian thought, civilization is characterized by being "cultured." The degree of being cultured is judged by the level of one's literacy. Therefore, the scholar officials who served the imperial state were the most civilized beings. At the same time, there was the possibility that non-Chinese-speaking people could learn the language, a requisite knowledge to being "cultured," and could enter the civilized world. This possibility of teaching them to be "cultured" gave the center a belief of the moral rightness of this approach (Harrell 1995: 18-20).

Harrell mentions that as long as such an innate sense of Han superiority remains, the actual program of the Communist project will be based on the unconscious assumption that Han ways are better and more modern (Harrell 1995: 26). The Han, as the most progressed group, are leading other ethnic groups who are encouraged to catch up with the Han. The civilizing project is carried out first to define and objectify the subjects of it as inferior to the Han and thus in need of civilization. In the process of defining subjects of the civilizing project, the "inferior" ethnic minority groups are eroticized, historicized, and juvenilized (Harrell 1995: 3-17). They have cultures distant from Confucian morality.

Eroticization and historicization of Cham culture can be understood as the process of the Vietnamese state's similar civilizing project. The Vietnamese civilizing project classified people living in the territory of Vietnam into the different *dân tộc*, and each of these is categorized and ranked by its level of progress. In the process of classifying *dân tộc*, Cham culture is perceived as ancient, exotic, and erotic. It is distant from the majority Kinh's Confucian-based tradition. By eroticizing and historicizing Cham culture, the Cham are included as the subjects of the Vietnamese state civilizing project and become one of the *dân tộc* of Vietnam.

During my field research in the mid-1990s, the Cham royal court dance was not very well received by Cham intellectuals who claimed that it was a total misrepresentation of their culture. According to them, the traditional Cham dances are very modest. The Cham women would not show much skin to others, and they are not supposed to raise their hands higher than their shoulders. The Cham intellectuals also found that it is not accurate to call this performance a traditional or classical dance (*múa cổ truyền* or *múa cổ điển*) of Cham as the way it is usually introduced at *văn nghệ*.

However, this dance has become so popular that it has gained a position in Cham traditions. When newspapers or magazines introduce Cham culture, they always include a picture of dancers performing the Cham royal court dance, now popularly known as the Apsara dance. When a Cham painter, Đàng Năng Thọ', held his first art exhibition in Hanoi, the Apsara dance was performed at the opening reception as an introduction of the Cham culture to the people of Hanoi. Cham university students in Ho Chi Minh City performed the Apsara dance when they organized a cultural show (Photo 5-5). I also saw this dance performed by the Cham Muslims in Ho Chi Minh City at their cultural show to celebrate the completion of the fasting month. Since an adult female Muslim Cham could not dance in such a costume, a very young girl, six or seven years old, performed this piece.

Photo 5-.5: The Apsara dance performed by the Cham students at HCM City

The newly created ethnic markers become pervasive and they become a part of ethnic identities recognized and adapted by the Cham people themselves. By acting out their culture as being erotic and ancient at *văn nghệ*, the Cham demonstrate their acceptance of the officially constructed ethnic identity and being one of the Vietnamese national minorities. It further connotes their submission to the Vietnamese state civilizing project.

The stereotype: ridicule as "the weapon of the weak"

In *văn nghệ*, I saw Cham people's production of a culture of *dân tộc* and their acceptance of Vietnam's civilizing project. However, I also encountered various occasions when their act of accepting being a *dân tộc* of Vietnam could be interpreted as a sort of passive resistance. It was a joke on stereotypes of ethnic minority people.

Perkins' article "Rethinking Stereotypes" gives insightful critiques on the studies of stereotypes and her definition of stereotypes provides a useful tool to examine the relationships among the stratified group of people in a society. Perkins first raises ten aspects of misleading assumptions about the nature of stereotypes (1979: 18). As opposed to seeing stereotypes as simple and rigid, she argues that the stereotypes are social; they reflect complicated social relationships involving social roles and statuses. It implies knowledge of a complex social structure. For instance, the words "dumb blonde" imply more than just hair color and intelligence: "it refers immediately to her sex, which refers to her status in society, to her relationship to men, to her inability to behave or think rationally" (Perkins 1979: 139-141).

The stereotypes are social; they are group concepts, describing groups and held by groups. They are evaluations held by a group about a group. In this sense, stereotypes are ethno-, class-, and status-centric (Takezawa 1988: 386). The stereotypes of minority people in Vietnam tell us about their roles and statuses in the society and their relationships to other groups, especially the dominant group.

During my field research, I did not find any particular stereotypes of the Cham people but I did of minority people in general. The most common stereotype of the minority people is their "dark skin" (*da đen*). The ethnic minorities, including the Cham, were depicted as the people of dark skin. The significance of the stereotype of dark skin is that it immediately brings up other stereotypes of minority people: a lack of hygiene, backwardness, less intelligent, simple, honest, child-like innocence, heavy drinkers, and so on.

The Cham people have adapted the majority Kinh's such stereotypes of the minority people. The shade of skin color corresponds to the level of progress. The most "progressive" ethnic group has the least dark skin; the darker skin they have, the more backward they are. While the Cham people consider themselves to have darker skin than the Kinh, they see themselves as having lighter skin than the other ethnic minorities, especially the people living in the Central Highlands. Similar to the Kinh, the Cham pay little attention to the differences among the minority groups living in the Central

Highlands and indiscriminately apply the adapted stereotypes to them. The Cham comment that the highland minorities are simple and more honest than the Cham themselves.

By adapting the discourse of stereotypes of the minority people in Vietnam, the Cham make statements of their more progressive social status to the other minority groups. When they use stereotypes to describe other minority people or different Cham groups, they are putting themselves in the position of the Kinh people in a social evolution scheme to stress their "progress" and superiority. Their adoption of stereotypes of the minority people indicates their acceptance and submission to a position inferior to that of the dominant Kinh group.

However, when the Cham people apply the stereotypes of minorities to describe themselves in comparison with the Kinh people, it does not really demonstrate their submission to their inferior status to the Kinh. It can be considered as an act of resistance against such an inferior status by ridiculing the Kinh perceptions of minority people. Scott argues that the people in the subordinate class cannot afford to engage in open, organized, political acts of resistance; instead, they use ridicule, irony, petty acts of non-compliance, and so on (Scott 1985: xv, 350).

One of my Cham friends, Hai, told a story at a dinner gathering of preventing a big accident. He was on a long-distance bus. He wanted to go to the bathroom, so he asked the driver to stop the bus. All the people listening to his story laughed. They mimicked Hai by raising their hands like school children calling to their teacher in a classroom and said out loud, "*mạt tiêu lắm*" (I got to pee). They burst into laughter. Hai—as a Cham, an "unsophisticated" ethnic minority—did not have any shame to tell of his physiological needs, so the driver stopped the bus for Hai. While the driver was waiting for Hai, he realized that something was wrong with his bus. Apparently, the bus had a serious mechanical problem. If he had continued to drive the bus, it could have exploded, and many people would have been killed. Thanks to Hai's call to stop the bus, an accident was prevented. The bus driver hugged Hai when he came back from the bathroom and thanked him vigorously. The ending of Hai's story created more laughter.

We can find a sense of resistance in the people's laughter about Hai's story. His unsophisticated manner, in which he did not have any shame to tell of his physiological needs in public, was contrasted with the Kinh people who are "polite" and "well mannered." They would not ask to stop the bus but probably would wait until the next stop to go to the bathroom. They laughed about what Hai did because they know that, from the Kinh point of view, it was an object of social ridicule and, at the same time, they laughed at the Kinh's politeness and belief of superiority over the minorities. Hai's unsophisticated "typical" minority manner saved people's lives, while Kinh people's politeness would have killed many of them. Such ridicule of the Kinh in the Cham people's self-condescending jokes can be seen as their resistance to the Kinh social norms and cultural values which are the basis of their evaluation of other ethnic groups.

Hai had another bus story. A man sitting in front of him was a Cham person who advised him to put his head against the back of his seat to sleep. Hai did so and fell asleep. When he woke up, he realized that the inside of the bus was a mess. The bus had tipped over and the passengers were lying everywhere. He saw a woman with long hair lying unconscious and covered with blood. Hai crawled out of a window of the bus. Luckily, he was not injured, but his white shirt was dyed red by other people's blood. He started to walk to the next town. When he got to an inn, the people there asked what happened to him. However, he temporarily lost his memory because of the aftershock of the accident. The only answer he could give them was, "I am a Cham person from Phan Rang." The bus which Hai took was found at the bottom of a cliff five days after the accident and the people inside the bus were all dead.

This story made the Cham at the dinner gathering laugh for two reasons. The first reason was that Hai lost his watch in this accident. Under such a circumstance, some people might take advantage of the unfortunate individuals in the bus to gain something but Hai lost his watch, instead. He was quite "dumb," which was the reason for the laughter. The second reason was because of Hai's response to people's inquiry at the inn. Despite the traumatic accident, he could only answer, "I am a Cham person from Phan Rang." It was due to the temporary memory loss, but the contrast between the catastrophe of the accident and the fact that he did not understand it was what made the people laugh. Hai's bus accident story, which tragically ended with the death of the entire busload of passengers except Hai, was nothing to laugh about. Yet the Cham people at the gathering laughed about Hai's behavior because in this story Hai was shown as a stereotype of an ethnic minority person. He was simple and naive. He was not capable of understanding the danger and seriousness of the accident and did not deviously take advantage of it. By talking about or seeing Hai's behaviors through the Kinh people's perspective, the people laughed about Hai and his story, but at the same time, they were ridiculing the stereotype as well. In the end, Hai was the only survivor from the horrible accident.

Hai's two survival stories reflect a belief held by the Cham people. Among the Cham, there is a sense of being special, or specially protected, people. Various survival stories of the Cham people during the Vietnam War are known as proof of the Cham's special status as being protected by supernatural beings. For instance, a group of Cham was working in a forest where a bomb was dropped. They all lay face down with fear, yet nothing happened. When they timidly opened their eyes, they saw an unexploded bomb half-buried in the ground. None of them was killed or injured.

I was told that if there was a unit of 100 soldiers and among them only five or six people could survive, most likely those few survivors would be the Cham. Hai used to be a soldier in the South Vietnamese army. His unit lost their way in the Central Highlands and ended up wandering around the jungle for 15 days. Their supplies were exhausted, and they had to live on leaves and grasses. He and other Cham people in the unit, three from Châu Đốc and four from Bình Thuận, made a pledge to one another to bring the body to their families if any of them died. In the end, many Vietnamese soldiers in his unit did not survive, but all eight Cham returned safely.

The director of the Cham Language Editing Committee (BBSSCC) was educated during the French period and presents himself as a man of science. He admitted that, to start with, he did not believe any of the above-mentioned survival tales known to the Cham people. But one experience of his own made him believe that the Cham are somewhat special people. He was in a *thang muki* as an interpreter for a French visitor who was observing a ceremony. He was a little absent-minded but was told to pray. He prayed while asking the god, Po Alwah, about the causes of several difficult family problems he was facing at the time. During this time while he was praying in the *thang muki*, an elderly man in white clothes visited his wife at home and told her to inform her husband that there was nothing he did wrong, and he should stop worrying about it. Shortly after this incident, his problems were solved. This experience convinced him that the Cham were specially chosen people who were protected by supernatural beings.

He attributed this to their religious practice in which they paid such respect to their gods and ancestors, although this was seen as wasteful by the state officials. On the other hand, his explanation elucidates a stereotype of the Kinh people held by the Cham. While the Cham are religious and spiritual, the Kinh people are materialistic and running after material comforts. They only care about money to gain a better material life at the price of their spiritual life. This is why they are cunning, opportunistic, and greedy. Similarly in Châu Giang village in the Mekong Delta, I was told by my Cham neighbor that every Muslim Cham would go to Heaven (*Soruka*) after their death, while every non-Muslim (*Kafir*) Kinh (*Yuon*) would go to Hell (*Noruka*). This is because the Cham bear the hardships of life and accumulate good deeds in order to go to *Soruka*, while *Kafir*/Kinh go after worldly pleasures and do not care about their afterlife. My neighbor's talk also reflects a similar stereotyping dichotomy: the Cham people live spiritually, while the Kinh people live materialistically.

Scott states that the dominant ideology held by a dominant class is considered to be pervasive, but the subordinate group has a different set of cultural values (1985: 329). While the Cham accept the stereotypes of the minority people, they also have stereotypes of the dominant Kinh people which were created by their own social norms and cultural values. The Cham people are conscious of the power relationships in which they have been embedded and of what kinds of roles they are playing and statuses they are holding. However, they are not just submissive to such power relationships. Joking and ridiculing, which may appear to be trivial acts in everyday affairs, are the denial of the dominant values and ideology imposed upon them and the assertion of their own socio-cultural values.[87]

Conclusion

In this chapter, the negotiation of the Cham ethnic identity within a framework of the nation of Vietnam is examined. In order to demonstrate and represent who they are, the Cham need to appropriate their ethnic identity which is relevant to the state-given definition of *dân tộc* Cham and also not contradict with their other identity as Vietnamese nationals.

Champa has been co-opted into Vietnamese history and is considered to enrich the cultural history of the country. The state has designated several vestiges from Champa as historical heritage (*di tích lịch sử*) and cultural heritage (*di tích văn hóa*), and has integrated them as properties of Vietnamese historical heritage. The Cham people are presented by highlighting their cultural antiquity in the public domain: "The people of ancient Champa." The Kinh-appropriated ethnic markers of the Cham people, such as the royal court dance, which is a product of a Kinh fantasy about ancient Champa, became a part of the culture of *dân tộc* of Vietnam. The Cham negotiated to apply the given ethnic markers to demonstrate their ethnic identity as a national minority (*dân tộc*) in the public domain.

The Cham from the Mekong Delta have a problematic discrepancy between their ethnic identity and their identity as *dân tộc* of Vietnam. In order to be seen as one of the recognized Vietnamese *dân tộc*, they have to

---

[87] Nishimoto reports a similar narrative by Christian Lafu people in northern Thailand (2000: 438-440).

establish their connection to Champa. Yet the Cham from the Mekong Delta have detached themselves from the history of Champa. Their attempt to create their new history around Islam is to situate their past outside of Champa, and as a result, outside of the nation of Vietnam. They sometimes appear to have an identity as foreigners, instead of being an ethnic minority of Vietnam. For instance, after the reunification of the north and the south, all the citizens had to register their ethnic identity. A considerable number of Cham from the Mekong Delta registered themselves as Malay. Aisah's *kampulan qasidah* was invited to sing for the celebration of Vietnam joining the ASEAN disguised as an Indonesian singing group.

In order to demonstrate their identity as *dân tộc* Cham, they have adapted some ethnic markers particular to the Cham from the south-central coast area. Through demonstrating their similarity to the Cham from this area, they connected their past to Champa and "fit" themselves into the category of *dân tộc* Cham. The given classification and definition of the Cham people by the Vietnamese state works to make two groups of Cham people from two different localities into one unified ethnic group. Being *dân tộc* Cham of Vietnam, the Cham people whose ethnic identities have been constructed differently identify themselves as a single ethnic group.

By becoming one of the national minorities of Vietnam, the Cham hold a particular position in relation to the majority Kinh people in Vietnam's civilizing project. The Cham reconcile their inferior and less civilized position based on socio-economic progress. They have adapted Kinh people's stereotypes on ethnic minorities to describe other ethnic groups whose inferior position to the Cham is emphasized. Yet the Cham do resist their inferior status rather passively by joking about minorities' stereotypes and ridiculing the Kinh social norms and value system which they covertly look down upon. Their quiet resistance by making self-tormenting jokes implies their predicaments of submission to Vietnam's civilizing project. In the following chapter, the possibility of widening the space for the Cham's resistance to their minority position in the post-*đổi mớ'i* (renovation) Vietnam will be discussed.

Chapter 6

The Cham Under *Đổi Mớ'i*

In the late 1980s, the government of Vietnam adopted new economic policies coined as *đổi mớ'i* (renovation). The adoption of a market economy through the *đổi mớ'i* policies brought significant changes to Vietnam and it has pushed the country into an irresistible wave of globalization. The Vietnamese people are now enjoying a higher standard of living, driving new motorbikes or cars, eating out in fast food restaurants, shopping at malls and department stores, talking to friends by cell phones, and connecting to the world through the Internet. Villages at the outskirts of Hanoi and Ho Chi Minh City have transformed into new residential areas filled with multi-storey condominiums. Vietnam, which once was known for its prolonged wars, has now become one of Asia's favorite destinations for its beautiful sceneries, luxurious resorts, and exotic minority cultures.

Two years prior to the implementation of the *đổi mớ'i* policies, then-Secretary General of the Communist Party Nguyễn Văn Linh organized a meeting with artists and cultural cadres. At the meeting, they complained about the state's tight control over artistic activities. The Politburo Resolution Five that was released a month later admitted that their policies on art and cultural management were "simplistic, coarse and superficial, and undemocratic" (Jamieson 1996: 25). Since then, the state has relaxed its control over arts and cultural activities. As a result, many traditional rituals, rites, religious pilgrimages, and other ceremonies have been resurgent (Hy Van Luong 1992; Kleinen 1999; Malarney 2002). Such changes were brought to the ethnic minority groups as well.

In 1991 the Vietnam government released Notice No. 3 of the Central Politburo on policies toward the Cham ethnic group (*Thông tri của Ban Bí thu' về công tác đối vớ'i đồng bào Chăm*). It stated that the government of Vietnam would conserve and protect the Cham people's historical and cultural heritage, establish cultural centers, popularize Cham script education, and encourage mass-based artistic activities. This notice implied that the state respected Cham tradition and supported regulation to deal with communal issues (Shin-e 2001b).[88] Some Cham rituals which were banned after the reunification of Vietnam under the communist regime were now allowed and Muslim Cham could participate in religious pilgrimages to Mecca.

In this chapter, I discuss the process of mainstreaming the Cham culture as part of Vietnam's national culture. Until the beginning of the 1990s, Cham culture and Champa were something foreign and rather too problematic to be a part of Vietnamese history. Now, the Cham and Champa are used to represent the nation of Vietnam. For instance, the Cham are well known for their textile production. Their hand-woven textiles are used to make various kinds of souvenirs with "Made in Vietnam" labels for tourists. The Cham festival *Kate* is now well publicized as one of the important "Vietnamese people's festivals" and the image of it and the Champa vestiges are used to promote tourism in Vietnam.

Đổi mớ'i has led the market-driven national integration of ethnic minority cultures. As Mukerji argues, the "tastes" of consumers determined the demand of the products which eventually control the pattern of economic development (1983:28). By responding to the globalized market demand, various "ethnic items" have become popular. However, mainstreaming of ethnic minorities and their culture is ironically causing their marginalization as cultural agents. Minority cultures are detached from their owners and circulated in the market at the same time as commodities and images of

---

[88] Ito argues that Notice No. 3 indicates the failure of the integration of the Cham ethnic minority people (2009b: 51). She further argues that after reunification, the Vietnamese government did not pay as much attention to the ethnic minorities as before when they were important for mobilizing the war effort. After reunification, they were considered to be obstacles for socio-economic development, especially ethnic minority people that had been left behind living in the mountainous areas. The government changed its indifferent attitude toward the ethnic minority people by releasing the decision of the Central Politburo on socio-cultural development in the mountainous regions in 1989. The uprisings of the ethnic minority people in the Central Highlands in 2001 and 2004 proved that such changes in government policies came too late. The uprisings were the result of the negligence of the government and its misunderstanding of ethnic minority people's socio-economic problems. These problems were caused by the loss of their land and livelihoods triggered by the massive migration of the Kinh majority and other ethnic minority people from the north and other parts of Vietnam to the Central Highlands. Instead of admitting their failed policies toward the ethnic minority people in the Central Highlands, the state simply believed that it could tame the people by providing economic subsidies and therefore not have to change their top-down approach (Ito 2009a).

ethnic minority people themselves are commodified and circulated. In this context, I explore the possibility for the Cham to take back their culture into their own hands by examining the works of a Cham artist. I suggest that the changes brought by *đổi mới* in the art scene provide a space for the ethnic minority people to express themselves by their own symbolic vocabularies.

Mainstreaming Cham culture and alienation of the Cham people

According to the standard of culture set by the state, minorities are encouraged to maintain certain cultural items of their traditions. One of these approved cultural items is minority handicrafts. Encouraging ethnic minorities' handicrafts also has some economic purpose. In the early 1990s, something described as "ethnic" did not have a positive meaning. For example, my language teacher at university was carrying around a backpack made out of Cham-woven textile. A classmate and I commented on how beautiful it was, yet she told us that only foreign students at the language center appreciated her backpack. All her Vietnamese friends criticized it as ugly. In the same year, I visited Đà Lạt, a famous resort city in the Central Highlands. I saw some ethnic minority people selling their hand-woven textiles to the tourists. They wandered from hotel to hotel at night looking for customers. I became friends with a man of the Koho ethnic group who married a Cham woman from Ninh Thuận Province. One night I saw him trying to sell his weavings to some Westerners at a restaurant. One of them almost bought two weavings; I saw him pulling his wallet out of his pocket. Suddenly, a group of Vietnamese women came into the restaurant and greeted the Westerner. They seemed to be acquaintances of his. Among them, one woman spoke English and asked him if he was going to buy the weavings. The Westerner asked her opinion and told her that he would not buy them if she did not think the weavings were good. She immediately answered that they were of poor quality. He put his wallet back in his pocket. The Koho man looked at me and said, shaking his head, "The Kinh do not understand [the value of the hand weavings]."

At that time, the Vietnamese much preferred factory-manufactured textiles in the same way they preferred plastic dishes over potteries. They saw these products as modern and fashionable since they were industrially mass-produced with modern technologies. Ethnic minority handicrafts, including hand-woven textiles, were neglected by the majority population and officials alike.

The year 1994 seems to have been a turning point for ethnic minorities' weavings. This year witnessed an increase in the numbers of foreign tourists in Vietnam (Kennedy & Williams 2001: 139), who appreciated ethnic handicrafts and became the major buyers of them. In the same year, I saw many young female students carrying cloth bags made from traditional Cham weavings. Previously, these bags were only sold in a limited number of museum shops or souvenir shops carrying a few minority products. But in 1994, people could buy them on every corner in downtown Ho Chi Minh City. The price was lower in 1994, about 15,000 đồng to 20,000 đồng ($1.50 to $2.00), compared to about 25,000 đồng to 45,000 đồng ($2.50 to $4.50) in 1993.

The young Vietnamese generation has adapted to the tastes of foreign tourists in a very short period of time. They wear blue jeans, t-shirts, and sneakers, and carry backpacks on their shoulders. With the popularity of minority weavings among the foreign tourists, the Kinh tailor shops, which predominantly have expatriates as customers, started to use textiles woven by minority people. I had a dress made out of a Cham textile. The owner of the tailor shop quickly noticed that the material I brought in was woven by the minority people, and to my surprise, she praised how beautiful it was. The Koho man's business in Đà Lạt had experienced a drastic change as well. When I revisited the city in 1995, he displayed weavings on the street with other ethnic minority people near the city's central market. He cheerfully told me that his business has been going so well that he did not need to go around hotels to look for customers. "Instead they come to me," he commented.

There is a small kiosk run by a Cham from Mỹ Nghiệp village in the state department store in downtown Ho Chi Minh City. The owner of the kiosk is a Cham lady who was once a fighter for FULRO. She knew of the disadvantages for the Cham weavers who used to sell their weavings so cheaply to the Kinh middlemen. She gathered the Cham weavers in Mỹ Nghiệp together, and sold the weavings made into different products and shared the profit among them. This kiosk expanded after 1994. Prior to then, the basic merchandise consisted of simply designed bags and sarongs. Now, it has various kinds of merchandise made out of Cham weavings, backpacks, wallets, various shapes of bags, caps, slippers, book covers, pillowcases, pen cases, and so on. Every time I dropped by the shop, it had a new item. The weavers also created new patterns by reviving forgotten old ones. A young female Cham shopkeeper told me that their business had been flourishing and sometimes they had shortages of merchandise. They began to receive large orders from foreign trading companies in Germany, France, and Japan. The owner managed to get some funding from the state in 1995 and expanded her business to get more weavers in the village into her cooperative. She had about 70 Cham weavers after a year.

Some NGOs in northern Vietnam have been interested in ethnic minorities' handicrafts as an income-generating project. Their target markets for handicrafts, especially weavings, were foreign tourists or expatriates in Vietnam. In 1994, three NGOs set up a booth to introduce a few ethnic minorities' handicrafts, predominantly hand weavings, at the Christmas party of the International Women's Club in Hanoi, which was organized by the spouses of expatriates. The handicrafts were a hit at the party. Many women rushed into the booth and fought over pieces of cloth. Every year since 1995, several NGOs have cooperated to set up a one-day bazaar of ethnic minorities' weavings in Hanoi. It has become very popular among the expatriates in Vietnam, and it is also mentioned in popular travel guidebooks.

In December 1995, the Vietnamese fashion company, Legafashion, held a show in Ho Chi Minh City in which they introduced clothing such as cocktail dresses, business suits, and mini-skirts all made out of Cham hand weavings. Two Cham weavers from Mỹ Nghiệp were hired to demonstrate their weavings in the background of the show.[89] This fashion show aimed

---

[89] Both Cham in the south-central coast area and the Mekong Delta produce hand-woven textiles. While the textiles woven by the Cham people from the south-central coast area became very popular, those from the Mekong Delta remained rather unknown to outsiders despite the rapid commercialization of the minority textiles. The reason, I think, for this is because they are lacking a certain quality to be identified as a "minority" product. The Cham in the south-central coast area use two different kinds of looms. One is a rather simple back-strap type loom which is popular among the highland minorities. It is easy to disassemble and move from place to place. The other type of loom has a long (2 to 3 meter) crosspiece, and it is used to weave narrow strips of cloth. In the Mekong Delta, the Cham use a sophisticated upright loom. The quality of the Cham textiles from the Mekong Delta is closer to the industrially manufactured textiles than those from the south-central coast areas. Also, many Mekong Delta Cham weave well-known check-patterned thin scarves which are used by the people living in the Mekong Delta regions, including some parts of Cambodia, and may not be seen as "minority" products. The minority textiles have been promoted as an "ethnic marker" by the state because of their economic potential and also their "exotic" patterns, colors, and textures which are distant from the industrially manufactured textiles that the Kinh people are familiar with. The ethnic markers indicate the distance of the cultural tradition of a group from one of the dominant groups. The Cham textiles from the Mekong Delta may not have a sufficient distance from the textiles of the Kinh people to be an ethnic marker.

to demonstrate that minority weavings could be used to make fashionable modern clothing. The new clothes introduced in this show were reported on in a magazine called *Thờ'i Trang* (*Fashion*) and it asked readers to vote for the best style among them. The Cham weavings have thus been elevated from a simple, non-industrialized, and non-fashionable product to a unique and fashionable product of Vietnam. This gave a kind of pride to the Cham people. One of the Cham weavers at the Legafashion show was interviewed and stated that the Cham textile designs "are more attractive than those of other ethnic minorities" (Bang Thanh 1995: 7).

The new global market has pushed the items of the Cham and other ethnic minority people, who have been a marginalized and highly localized population of Vietnam, into the mainstream national culture. However, it does not mean that the ethnic minority people themselves have been mainstreamed. In early 2000, I began to notice at the various tourist attractions that there were souvenirs made from the Cham textiles bearing the name of places such as Điên Biên Phú', Mỹ So'n, or Huế (Photo 6-1). The Cham type of textile is perhaps used for souvenirs because of its distance from the dominant Kinh culture. Tourists make trips to other unfamiliar places where weather and customs are different from their home. They remove themselves from their mundane life and do, see, hear, and eat something different. The Cham textile is generalized as Vietnam's ethnic minority textile and it is used to invoke the distance that people experienced during their trips away from their daily life. Cham textile souvenirs remind them of an unusual time and place that they were in. However, these Cham textiles for the souvenirs are factory-made. Vietnamese textile factories copy the Cham patterns and produce Cham-patterned textiles on a mass scale. Once the Cham textile has become integrated into the national culture, the Cham seem to lose ownership.

The creation of the Cham court dance, popularly known as the Apsara dance, is another example of the alienation of the Cham from their own culture. As I discussed in the previous chapter, the Apsara dance created by the Vietnamese choreographers has been accepted by the Cham as a part of their cultural tradition and it has become quite a popular cultural marker of the Cham in Vietnam. It has been performed at various events including international conferences, in restaurants, and other tourist attractions with theatrical performances. However, the Apsara dances I saw after 1995 were all performed by Kinh dancers.

Photo 6-1. Souvenirs made out of the Cham textile

There is a restaurant called "Apsara" in the city of Đà Nẵng where the famous museum of Cham sculptures is located. The restaurant is in a colonial-style building and stone garden lanterns light the short pathway to the entrance. In their garden, there is a replica of the Champa temple which is also lit by gentle light. They create a mysterious and somewhat nostalgic atmosphere. When I visited the restaurant, it was packed by groups of Japanese tourists who enjoyed the Cham dances, including the Apsara dance, over dinner (Photo 6-2). I also saw a similar but less sophisticated Cham dance performance in a restaurant in the booming tourist city of Hội An. All these Cham dances were performed by Kinh people who were probably trained in various forms of ethnic dance in Vietnam. As the Vietnamese government claims that it supports ethnic minority people to practice and preserve their culture and tradition, the Cham royal court dance has been revived and preserved but without Cham people as the cultural agents. Here, the Cham royal court dance has become a mere genre, style, or taste within the Vietnamese theatrical performance.

Photo 6-2. The Cham dance at the restaurant "Apsara" in Đà Nẵng

By responding to the globalized market demands, various "ethnic items" have become popular. However, the commodification of Cham and other ethnic minority people's cultures in marketing Vietnamese culture for the global audience removed these people as the cultural agents. The more that an ethnic minority culture has become popular and more visible in the public space, the more that the ethnic minority people have become detached from it. The marketed ethnic minority culture does not bear their voice; it is like an empty shell without its master.

Several lacquer paintings I found in Ho Chi Minh City symbolically reflect the loss of substance of ethnic culture. They are pop-art-like paintings, which show a series of ethnic minority women's portraits that are almost identical in facial depiction yet wearing different headgear, dresses, and jewelry. This series of lacquer paintings implies that ethnic minority culture has nothing to do with people, their life, or their identity, but purely the style of headgear, clothing, or jewelry. They have become simply a style of expression (Photo 6-3).

Photo 6-3. Lacquer paintings of ethnic minority people

The lacquer paintings further indicate the commodification of minority culture and the fact that ethnic minority people themselves are a national commodity. Images of ethnic minority people are now representing the entire nation of Vietnam. The portraits of ethnic minority people, often women, in colorful traditional dresses in a natural background with mountains, streams, traditional housing, or rice paddies, for example, are circulated and consumed in the art markets.

Portraits of ethnic minority people

In the pre-*đổi mới* era, paintings were considered as a tool to propagate communist ideology and to facilitate national unity. The principles of Vietnamese art under the Communist Party were established during anti-colonial struggles and were to combat against bourgeois decadence in art. For this, the art should be: scientific (meaning "abandoning religious themes, mysticism, and idealism and popularizing the Marxist perspective"); national (meaning "dedicated to the needs and aspirations of the Vietnamese nation, putting one's art in the service of the revolutionary cause"); and popular (meaning "producing works that would simultaneously appeal to and educate the vast majority of people, laborers, farmers, and soldiers, inciting them to be loyal and to be ready to sacrifice for the revolution") (Jamieson 1996: 19). The dominant style of art was called Socialist Realism and abstract paintings, including Cubism, Fauvism, and Surrealism, were banned.

Art was closely affiliated with the Vietnamese nation-building project such as national defense, national unity, and national integration. All the artists belonged to the centrally controlled *Hội Mỹ Thật* (the artists' association) and were to serve the nation through their artistic talent. The artists painted and sculpted glorifying images of Vietnamese people who were united to defeat the foreign invaders, to build their nation, to improve their lifestyle, and so on (Jamieson 1996; N. Taylor 2009: 15-17). The ethnic minority people appeared in these paintings in this context.

After the adoption of *đổi mới* policies, the style of artistic works has become rapidly diversified; abstract paintings are no longer prohibited, installation arts have become popular, and some artists carry out performance arts in public spaces (N. Taylor 2007). The free market economy made Vietnamese art become a commodity. The artists could sell their works through private galleries in Vietnam or even overseas. Although the number is limited, there are artists who can make their living just by selling their artworks in private galleries without joining the artists' association of Vietnam. While Vietnamese art is being diversified, the rapid modernization and wave of globalization has pushed the Vietnamese to redefine their art; "What is Vietnamese art?" The dominant buyers of Vietnamese art have been foreigners, and some art critiques censured that these artworks have been formed by the international market (N. Taylor 1999: 247, 2009: 9; Kraevskaia 2005: 9, 22-23). The foreigners want to buy "Vietnamese art" that often depicts things to remind them of Vietnam which is not the post-*đổi mớ'i* urbanized Vietnam but the pre-modern Vietnam that is an agrarian-based rural society.

In the emerging and rapidly growing foreign-clients-oriented Vietnamese art market, the paintings of ethnic minority people have become popular. They have little to do with national defense, unity, or solidarity. In Ho Chi Minh City, there are several art galleries on Đồng Khở'i street where many foreign tourists visit to purchase high-end souvenirs (Photo 6-4). Almost all of these art galleries display paintings of ethnic minority people. The paintings done by Dinh Ngoc Thang are such as this and can be found in an art gallery on Đồng Khở'i street. Dinh Ngoc Thang was born in the north and educated at the University of Fine Arts in Ho Chi Minh City. His paintings of ethnic minority ladies from northern Vietnam are some of the best-selling works at the gallery.

Photo 6-4. An art gallery on the Đồng Khở'i street

Dinh Ngoc Thang's short biography given by the gallery mentions that he made a tour of Vietnam in 2003 and was enchanted by the beauty of the highland's scenery and people. His gaze cast upon the ethnic minority people is similar to the foreign tourists' gaze. According to the gallery attendance, almost all the buyers of his works are foreign visitors and they buy them because "they want to buy paintings that remind them of Vietnam." Dinh Ngoc Thang's romanticizing of the life of the ethnic minority people in the highlands and the nostalgia for the pre-modern life of Vietnam reflected in his paintings appeal to foreign buyers who are looking for an image of a "traditional, authentic" Vietnam. Ethnic minority people are used to create images of pre-modern Vietnam because of their "less developed status" and their unique cultural tradition in Vietnam (Photo 6-5). As the famous paintings of Hanoi streets by Bùi Xuân Phái—which have been recognized as masterpieces of Vietnamese modern art—provided images of Hanoi that foreign visitors desire (N. Taylor 1999), the images of ethnic minority people provide images of Vietnam that foreign visitors fantasize about.

Photo 6-5. A painting of Ding Ngoc Thang (courtesy of Ngueyn gallery)

The Cham painted by Cao Thị Đu'ọ'c

The Cham ethnic minority people are also painted to provide images of Vietnam. They are often depicted in connection to the historical Champa. Cao Thị Đu'ọ'c, a female Kinh artist, is known for her series of paintings of Cham women and has painted Cham people for decades. She was born in Bến Tre, a city in the Mekong Delta, and graduated from the Ho Chi Minh City Fine Arts University in 1990 (Nguyễn Kim Loan 2007: 128-134). She began to paint the Cham people due to her teacher's work. Her teacher, Sỹ Hoang, who used to carry out fieldwork in the Cham village of Mỹ Nghiệp in Ninh Thuận Province, exhibited his work at the university. Đu'ọ'c was quite inspired by his work and went to Mỹ Nghiệp and also the nearby village of Bàu Trúc which is well known for traditional pottery production. She stayed in Bàu Trúc for three months and produced her graduation work, "Cham market" (*Chọ Chăm*). Almost every year since, she visits Bàu Trúc for sketches with her students. Later on, she also produced a series of paintings on the Cham.

Đu'ọ'c often depicts Cham females; Cham males are rarely seen in her works. This is because she feels sympathetic toward Cham women who, according to her, have been tied down to the various social restrictions and constraints and enjoy little freedom compared to the majority Kinh women. She also finds beauty among the Cham women who engage in hard labor. Most of the works produced by Đu'ọ'c are oil paintings. Usually, she does not use any models when painting but she practices figures and portraits by pastel color. Her pastel drawings probably provide models for her oil paintings.

There are distinctive differences in the depiction of the Cham in her oil paintings and her pastel drawings. Her pastel drawings of Cham women were exhibited at the gallery of Ho Chi Minh City Fine Arts University in May 2010. The titles of the portraits were the names of the models. On the models' portraits, there was nothing to indicate their ethnic minority origin. Looking at the portraits and their titles, one would not know that the models belonged to the Cham ethnic group unless one was told so (Photo 6-6). While her oil paintings carry the theme of the Cham, Đu'ọ'c depicts them as people of darker complexion, with connected eyebrows like Champa sculptures, and with thick lips. They decorate themselves with earrings, bracelets, and necklaces, but are often bare-breasted which can be seen as an emblem of ethnic minorities connoting their close proximity to nature, or primitiveness, and their distance from civilization. None of her oil paintings have the names of the models as titles. Most of the titles are simply

Photo 6-6. A pastel painting by Cao Thị Đu'ọ'c (Picture taken at the gallery of Ho Chi Minh City Fine Arts University)

"A Young Cham Woman," "An Old Cham Woman," or such like (Photo 6-7). Kennedy and Williams examined tourism in Vietnam and discussed how the images of Vietnamese women, who were depicted as "Heroic mother and female guerilla fighters" before, have been depoliticized and marginalized as "ornamental and sexual" (Kennedy & Williams 2001: 158-159). Similar comments can be made on Đu'ọ'c's oil paintings of Cham women. They are anonymous, decorative, retrospective, mythical, and sensual. In her oil paintings, the Cham become a style projecting the images of ethnic minorities whom others wish to see.

If the Kinh artists paint the Cham based on their perception of images of ethnic minority people, what about the images created by the Cham themselves? I examine two Cham painters' works.

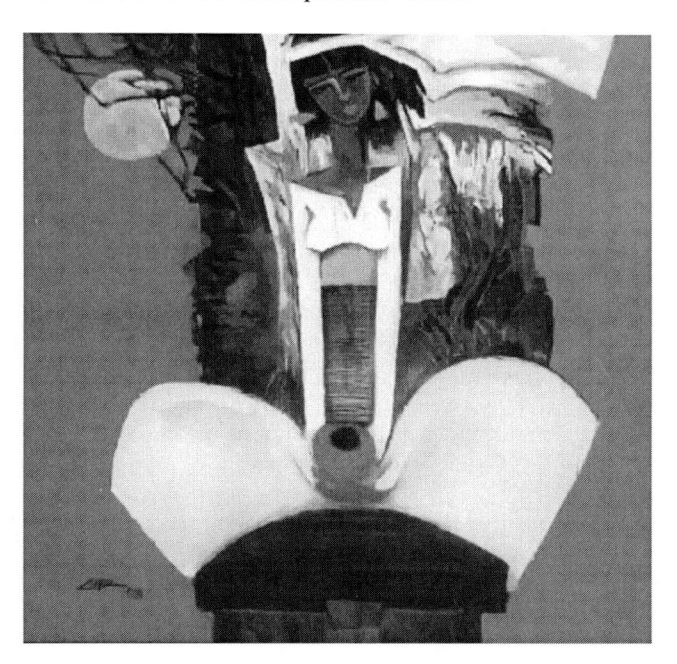

Photo 6-7. An oil painting by Cao Thị Đu'ọ'c (From Cao Thị Đu'ọ'c's postcards)

The works of Chế Thị Kim Trung

Chế Thị Kim Trung is a female Cham artist whose works have received various prizes from the Vietnamese government. Her prized works have been purchased by the national museums,[90] and a national TV channel has

---

[90] One of her paintings, titled "*Làng Chăm o'n Bác*" (Cham village thanks to Ho Chi Minh), has received a national prize and was purchased by the National Museum in Hanoi. It is a painting of Ho Chi Minh standing in front of Po Klong Garai temple

broadcast a program about her life and works. Kim Trung has become one of the most popular Cham artists in Vietnam.

She was born in the Bani village of An Nhơn in Ninh Thuận Province. She studied at a teachers' college and became an art teacher. Because she could not give up her desire to study art, even after her marriage, she enrolled at Ho Chi Minh City Fine Arts University in 2002 as a mother of two children.

Some of Kim Trung's paintings reflect national policies on minorities, unity, and solidarity, such as paintings on the celebration of the liberation of Phan Rang city and ethnic minority women preparing food for soldiers. This might be due to her proximity to the Communist Party. She is a public-school teacher and her husband is a Communist Party cadre. But most of her paintings are about Cham people and their traditions and religious activities. She has expressed that she paints Cham rituals and traditions to pass on the Cham people's rich historical heritage to the next generations. However, Kim Trung's works reveal that she has adapted Vietnamese signifiers of the Cham people. She paints along the lines of the Kinh majority people's image of the Cham: they are the people of Champa, people of the past, people of colorful dresses and strange traditions. She has adapted their gaze cast onto the ethnic minority groups.

One of her most well-known works is titled "*Kate* festival" (*Lễ Hội Katê*) from 2007. *Kate* is one of the most important ceremonies of the Cham people and probably the nationally best-known Cham religious ceremony in Vietnam. This painting was a prize at the national exhibition of the Vietnamese art association, and purchased by the Ho Chi Minh City Museum of Fine Arts (*Công ty quảng cáo truyền và du lịch thanh niên*). However, when I saw the painting, I wondered about her knowledge of the Cham culture. Most of the people depicted in her painting do not play any roles in an actual *Kate* ceremony. Kim Trung painted a male dancer in the center who is wearing a red jacket and holding a stick in his hand. He is *Ong Kaing*, who dances for other religious village ceremonies, together with a drummer who plays a tambourine-like drum. None of the musicians

---

surrounded by Cham people. This painting created some discussion among the Cham people due to the issue of copyright. The title of the painting is the title of a song composed by a Cham musician, Âm Nhân, in 1985. Parts of the lyrics in the song, "*Hồ chí Minh trong trái tim ngu'ò'i Chăm*" (Ho Chi Minh is in the hearts of the Cham people) and "*Hồ Chí Minh trong trái tim Việt Nam*" (Ho Chi Minh is in the hearts of Vietnam), are also painted on the plates placed above the god Siva on the temple which made some people upset because it was considered as disrespectful (*Inrasara*).

depicted in this painting would be found at an actual *Kate* ceremony, yet the most significant musician, *Ong Kathar* who plays the two-stringed instrument, is not found (Photo 6-8). During an interview, Kim Trung explained that she paints for the continuation of Cham culture and tradition and for passing these down to the next generations. But what are the culture and tradition that she is going to pass down if she does not depict them as practiced?

Photo 6-8. *Kate* festival by Chế Thị Kim Trung (Picture taken in the Ho Chi Minh City Museum of Fine Arts)

Kim Trung's painting on the *Kate* festival reveals a striking similarity to the paintings done by a Kinh painter named Nguyễn Công Văn from Ninh Thuận Province. He also produced a painting titled "*Kate* festival" (*Lễ Hội Katê*) in 2003. Nguyễn Công Văn depicted a male dancer, *Ong Kaing*, at the center and groups of female dancers and musicians surrounding him in front of Po Klong Garai temple. The same as Kim Trung, Nguyễn Công Văn also did not include the musician *Ong Kathar*, although his performance is an essential part of the *Kate* ceremony (Photo 6-9).

Photo 6-9. *Kate* festival by Nguyễn Công Văn (From Hội Văn Học Nghệ Thuật Ninh Thuận 2005.)

It is said that there are several kinds of ritual systems in the Cham tradition. There are various musicians, dancers, and other religious practitioners involved in conducting the Cham rituals, and who can work with whom is strictly determined. However, to the majority Kinh people, such an intricate cultural system does not mean much unless they are ethnologists or anthropologists. The important thing for the painting of the *Kate* festival is to convey two things: the Cham and the festival. Both Kim Trung and Nguyễn Công Văn successfully convey such a message by painting Cham temples, Cham dancers wearing traditional clothes, and musicians playing the traditional instruments. They did not need to paint the *Kate* festival with detailed information.

Kim Trung's adaptation of the Kinh gaze upon the Cham seems to be due to her position in the Cham community and also her ambition. She has been away from her native Cham village and living in the capital city of Phan Rang for the last 15 years. Her house is a newly constructed three-storey building on one of the main streets in the city. The first floor of her house is an art gallery where she exhibits and sells her various paintings. Along with her paintings, Kim Trung also sells souvenirs such as Cham textiles and potteries from Bàu Trúc which she paints designs on.[91] Though she has not yet found a gallery in bigger cities where she wants to send her paintings, her small art gallery is an attempt at putting her works on the art market. In order to make her paintings marketable, she has to adapt the majority tastes and their way of seeing things. She paints the Cham in a way that outsiders can recognize as the ethnic minority culture. Her paintings appeal to the Kinh majority people because her depictions of the Cham ethnic minority people satisfy the Kinh's image of the Cham.

The works of Đàng Năng Thọ'

The other Cham painter is Đàng Năng Thọ' who is the most well-known contemporary Cham artist. According to the art historian Trần Kỳ Phu'o'ng, who has been working on Champa art, the works by Thọ' are the crystallization of the essence of Cham ethnicity. Phu'o'ng calls Thọ's works, especially his terracotta sculptures, "ritual objects." He describes that the works of Thọ' have excellent composition and are refined, but at the same time bear some primitiveness. The works reflect the strong nature of the Balamon religion and express sacredness and awe. The history and religion

---

[91] Traditionally, potteries from Bàu Trúc are fired only once and are without coloring.

of Champa and the Cham people are condensed in his works and he expresses them in a highly mature manner (Photo 6-10). The Cham people painted by Cao Thị Đu'ọ'c and Chế Thị Kim Trung are both the images of the Cham perceived by the majority Kinh people. They are etic and pastiche.

Photo 6-10. A terracotta sculpture by Đàng Năng Thọ' (courtesy of Trần Kỳ Phu'o'ng)

However, Đàng Năng Thọ' expresses images of the Cham differently, and his works demonstrate the possibility of art as a contested space for the ethnic minority people to express their identity and culture through their own symbolism and artistic vocabularies.

Đàng Năng Thọ' was born in 1952 in a Cham village called Bàu Trúc, which is well known for its earthenware production in Ninh Thuận Province. His family made a living through agriculture. His father was also good at carpentry and his mother made the village's earthenware. She was also one of the ritual dancers of her lineage. Thọ' had two other siblings but they both died when they were small and so he grew up as an only child. According to Đàng Năng Thọ', he was not a very sociable child and used to play alone at home, and considered his mother as his only childhood friend. He liked to observe funeral ceremonies when he was a child, and was fascinated by the stories of kings, princes, and princesses of Champa as told by village elders. He studied at Po Klong High School for Cham ethnic minority people and became known for his paintings of Po Klong Garai temple. He painted many of his classmates by their request and these paintings opened up a new life in art for him.

Immediately after the liberation of South Vietnam in 1975, the Ministry of Culture in Hanoi dispatched a group of scholars to the south in order to eliminate any publication that displayed the thoughts of the Saigon government. An ethnologist, Phan Đăng Nhật, was one of the scholars on this mission. He took advantage of his assignment in the south and visited some Cham communities. He has written a thesis on the epic of the Ede ethnic minority called Dam San. There was an argument that the Dam San originated from an epic Cham story. Phan Đăng Nhật did not support this argument but since it was during the wartime, he could not travel to the south to gather information. After the war, he wanted to find out if his opinion was right.

What he discovered in the Cham communities was a young man with artistic talent. He saw paintings of Po Klong Garai temple in various Cham homes which led him to meet Đàng Năng Thọ'. Phan Đăng Nhật believes that the DNA of a group of people will pass down to future generations and that is the way the cultural characteristics of an ethnic group will be continued. He argues that Champa achieved highly sophisticated arts and the Champa people's artistic DNA should be inherited among the contemporary Cham people. He tried to support the little-educated young Cham man who had a talent for art. Upon his return to Hanoi, Phan Đăng Nhật met a friend working at the Ministry of Culture who was also a member of the Central Committee of the Communist Party, and made preparations for Thọ' to be admitted to the University of Fine Arts in Hanoi. However, Thọ' had financial difficulties and his wife did not like him to go away as far as Hanoi. As a result, Phan Đăng Nhật then rearranged for Thọ' to study in Ho Chi Minh City.

The post-1975 government had policies to promote ethnic minority people and to integrate them into the newly unified nation of Vietnam, and there was a movement to include elements of ethnic minorities into art (*Tính dân tộc trong nhgệ thuật*).[92] Such a political environment worked favorably for Đàng Năng Thọ' to pursue art. He entered Art College (*Cao Đẳng Mỹ Thuật*) in Ho Chi Minh City in December 1975. Almost all of his fellow students were former soldiers from the front. He was the first and only student from an ethnic minority background at the school. He recalled how well he was treated at the college. Upon his graduation from Art College, he went back to his home town and worked for the Office of Culture at Thuận Hải Province (former Ninh Thuận and Bình Thuận Provinces). During his work there, he had opportunities to visit various Cham villages in the region. After serving for several years, he enrolled at the University of Fine Arts in Ho Chi Minh City in 1987.

The story that Đàng Năng Thọ' told about himself, how a poor boy growing up in an ethnic minority village had become a well-known artist, has some analogies to Cham legends. He considered meeting with Phan Đăng Nhật as his fate. He could achieve his lifelong dreams because of Phan Đăng Nhật's help. He could study art at university. He could hold his first exhibition in Hanoi in 1995. He could go to India to participate in an art conference which adapted one of his terracotta sculptures for the cover page of the conference pamphlet. He could have his sculpture purchased by the Museum of Hanoi. In some Cham legends, people who are born with unusual talent or supernatural ability will become rulers or important people in society with the help of a person who has the ability to understand extraordinary characters hidden in the protagonists. What Thọ' emphasized during the interview was how ill-educated and naive he was when he met Phan Đăng Nhật. He was working in a field covered with dust when he met Phan Đăng Nhật for the first time. He did not even understand the word art (*Mỹ thuật*) nor paintings (*Hội Họa*). He was asked to write a letter in which he expressed his desired to study art, but he ended up writing words dictated by Phan Đăng Nhật like a faithful pupil. The contrast between his lack of social skills and unsophisticated and naive manner and his extraordinary hidden artistic talent gives legend-like charm to his story.

---

[92] Interview with Trần Kỳ Phu'o'ng in May 2011.

Thọ' described his artistic talent and aesthetic value as a gift. It was not learned but was given at his birth. He can "feel" good arts from the bad arts, according to him. Since he believes his aesthetic talent to be a gift, producing paintings or sculptures seems to be a kind of religious experience for him. He explains that he is usually in a trance-like state while creating his works. He cannot hear or communicate with others and can only hear his inner voice. He believes that his artistic expression is to allow his soul to express itself, and his ethnic background is quite significant for this.

His graduation work is called "Pray for Rain." In it, a lady visits a ritual musician, *Ong Kathar*, who is sitting in front of a brick temple. The female statue in the background tells that she is Queen Bia Thanh Chi and the temple is enshrining her husband King Po Rame.[93] Thọ' painted the background with an orange and red color which indicates fire, especially cremation fire for the Balamon people. The color also implicates the sun (Photo 6-11).

Photo 6-11. The original painting of "pray for rain" by Đàng Năng Thọ' (courtesy of Đàng Năng Thọ')

---

[93] Po Rame temple was established between the 16th and 17th centuries.

Ninh Thuận Province is one of the driest places in Vietnam. Murderous rays of sun dry out the land where cactuses are growing. The Cham villages where irrigation canals have not yet reached only harvest rice once a year, while other irrigated areas can harvest two to three rice crops a year. The rain is an important source of the Cham people's livelihood. In the work by Thọ', the Cham woman, who is considered to be the source of life among the matrilineal Cham, has visited the temple to pray for rain. The painting has two hidden notions of fire (sun) and water (rain), which leads to the most significant symbolism of the Cham people: *ahier* and *awal* dualism. However, due to the disapproval of his committee members, Thọ' altered the background by painting several women carrying their offerings to the temple (Photo 6-12). The altered painting has more perspectives and also has a classic look, but it has lost significant symbols of the Cham characteristics.

Photo 6-12. The revised painting of "pray for rain" by Đàng Năng Thọ' for his Graduation (courtesy of Đàng Năng Thọ')

One can see this dualism as the base of Đàng Năng Thọ's works. He uses ethnic symbolism or ethnic vocabularies. His artworks are created through the emic point of view and are filled with a coded message which can be read by the people who have knowledge of Champa history and Cham tradition.

Let us compare the paintings of Chế Thị Kim Trung and Đàng Năng Thọ' of a ceremony called *Rija prong*. The *Rija prong* is organized by the kin belonging to the same lineage and in this ceremony, a female dancer called *Muk Rija* dances to a song performed by a ritual drummer called *Ong Muthon*. There are different types of *Rija prong* ceremony: one is a *Rija prong* of a mountain group, the other is of a sea group.[94] In Kim Trung's painting of a *Rija prong*, a *Muk Rija* is sitting on a swing and this indicates that she painted the *Rija prong* of the sea group.[95] The *Muk Rija* is surrounded by the musicians[96] and a woman is also praying beside her. The painting is descriptive and explains what *Rija prong* is like to the viewers (Photo 6-13).

Thọ's painting of a *Rija prong* shows no dancer or musician. He painted only red wooden structures, a sun, and a letter-like figure with a blue background (Photo 6-14). If one knows the *Rija prong* rituals, one can decode the painting and can tell it is of the sea group. Three red wooden structures indicate the supporting frame of a swing and the blue background indicates the sea. There are three red frames for the swing because a *Rija prong* ritual sequence, which lasts two days, is performed three times among the sea group. For each, the sun and the letter-like figure indicate a part of the *hon kan* symbol which is a mark of the Cham people. We can also read the symbolic dualism of Cham culture in this painting. The blue background color indicates the sea (water) and the frames for the swing where the *Muk Rija* sits symbolize the female realm (*awal*), while the red color, the sun, and the letter-like figure symbolize the male realm (*ahier*).

Thọ's paintings intellectually include people who can read his hidden codes and exclude people who cannot. Finding the cultural codes hidden in his paintings creates intimacy between the viewers and the painter: "I could read your message, I understand your symbolic language, and what you are

---

[94] For the historical significance of the *Rija prong* ceremony and other *Rija* ceremonies, see Truong Van Mon (2008).
[95] The *Rija prong* of the mountain group does not use a swing and their ceremony lasts fewer days than the *Rija prong* of the sea group.
[96] In Kim Trung's painting, five musicians are playing the four different instruments. In the actual *Rija prong* ritual, only the tambourine-like drum is used.

178 Chapter 6

expressing in your paintings." Sharing the symbolic codes with the painter produces a sense of "in-group" identity. Both the painter and the viewers belong to the same community.

Photo 6-13. *Rija prong* by Chế Thị Kim Trung (From Chế Thị Kim Trung's gallery pamphlet)

Photo 6-14. *Rija prong* by Đàng Năng Thọ' (courtesy of Đàng Năng Thọ')

During interviews, Đàng Năng Thọ' explained that the Cham who appear in his works are the people from pre-1975, and this is because the Cham who lived before this time were more beautiful than the contemporary Cham. He believed that the pre-1975 Cham kept their genuine traditions from the ancient times and were closer to the gods. They were more religious, more fearful of gods, and more respectful. Before 1975, under the Saigon government, the Cham had control over their communities and culture to a certain degree. They could study their own culture together with the French priest, Father Moussay, at the Cham cultural center. Cham students went to their own Po Klong High School. They could form Cham units in the military which worked side by side with the US soldiers; the Ministry for the Development of Ethnic Minorities had Cham people holding high-ranking positions; the Muslim Cham formed their association, and so on. The Cham lost all of that after 1975.

They have been placed in the socialist framework, and have been taught, guided, and controlled to become citizens of the Socialist Republic of

Vietnam. After the reunification of the two Vietnams, some Cham religious traditions were abandoned under the instruction of the government which carried out policies to protect ethnic minorities' cultures yet also to abolish so-called backward customs and unscientific superstitions. The agrarian lands were collectivized which caused many of the Cham rituals relating to the rice fields and the agrarian cycle to be forgotten. With the impact of *đổi mớ'i* policies, Cham traditions and historical heritage have been commodified under the name of tourism. The more that the Cham culture has become mainstreamed by being recognized as a part of Vietnamese national cultural heritage, the less that the Cham can assert ownership of their culture. The traditional Cham hand-woven textiles are now woven in factories. Traditional Cham dances are performed by Kinh people. One of the biggest Cham religious celebrations of the *Kate* festival is organized by the prefectural Office of Culture which "invites" Cham priests to carry out the ceremony in their own temple. Champa vestiges have been renovated and transformed to something else[97] (Shin-e 2001a: 234-236, 2001b: 244 footnote 12; Tran Ky Phu'o'ng 2006: 22-23), and Po Klong Garai temple has been getting Vietnamized[98] to list just a few examples of the Cham people's marginalization from their own culture.

Đàng Năng Thọ's portrait of a Balamon priest seems to be making a comment on the current Cham situation. In this painting, a priest wearing a white gown and standing with a fire-red background indicates the Balamon's symbol of cremation fire. Behind him, there is a Cham village

---

[97] Hoa Lai temple is located approximately 14 km north of Phan Rang city along the National Highway No. 1. Hoa Lai temple originally consisted of three towers but the central tower was destroyed by bombardment during the war period. Hoa Lai temple has gone through several renovations. The renovations were done by the Ministry of Culture, Sports and Tourism of Ninh Thuận Province in mid-2000 and caused an outcry among Cham intellectuals. An American writer, Mike High, wrote a short article expressing his concern about poor conservation works on Hoa Lai temple in 2009. However, the English newspaper, *Vietnam Times*, refused to publish his article and it was never subsequently published either.

[98] The Balamon temples, like Po Klong Garai, of the Cham people were only open four times a year. The rest of the time, few Cham visited the temples because they respected and feared the power of the gods. The Champa vestiges are now under the care of the provincial museum which belongs to the Ministry of Culture, Sports and Tourism of the province. The Po Klong Garai is now open year-round for tourists. Inside, the temple is decorated with illumination and the *linga* is covered by the king's attire. There are flowers, incense, a donation box, and other offerings, and none of these practices is part of Cham tradition. Tourism seems to push the Vietnamization of Cham people's historical and cultural heritage.

The Cham Under *Dổi Mổ'i* 181

in the distance painted with green which hints at life and people living in it. The priest is painted from above the thigh and slightly diagonally on the canvas, which gives the impression that he is looking to the side of viewers. The priest is wearing a white turban with a red scarf on top of it, hinting that he is taking leave from his ritual duty. His wrinkled face gives the impression that he is frowning to express his discontent or disagreement in taking leave from his pre-1975 Cham community to look into the contemporary world, in which he gives disapproval of the current Cham and their loss of religious traditions and culture (Photo 6-15). In this painting, Thọ' expresses his mourning and lament about the loss of Cham culture and tradition.

Figure 6-15: An old Balamon priest by Đàng Năng Thọ'

While many artists are trying to make a living with their works, Đặng Năng Thọ' is not interested in selling his pieces. In fact, many of his works have been lost or he does not know their whereabouts.[99] He values the process of creating art more than the finished work. As mentioned earlier, creating art is an almost religious experience for him in which he can travel in time, so to speak, and be with the sacred beings of Champa. At the same time, the process of creating art is to pray for the sacred beings and the great ancestors of Champa. It is to play a requiem to the lost Cham culture and traditions and to the Cham people who have lost ownership of their culture.

Conclusion

Gladney, who studied Muslim minority populations in PRC, argues that the majority group's ethnic identity has been constructed in opposition to the image of ethnic minority people. The majority is an unmarked entity which does not possess any unique, exotic, or "bizarre" culture or customs in comparison with the ethnic minority people who are decorated with colorful dresses and "unusual" culture (Gladney 2003: 51-98). In Vietnam, the image of less developed, pre-modern, nature-friendly traditional ethnic minority people provides a contrast to the modernized majority Kinh population, and such images of ethnic minority people are favored by the foreign-oriented art market and tourist industries. In order to provoke an image of traditional, pre-modern Vietnam, national ethnic minorities have become an essential national item.

While ethnic minority culture and their images have been mainstreamed, ethnic minorities themselves have become detached from their own culture. They have remained subjects of the government's top-down policies. What is good or what is bad for them is all decided by the government and they remain as passive recipients of government aid and guidance. Their lack of control over their socio-cultural life reveals that the ethnic minority people remain as a passive body on which the state practices its policies (Ito 2009a, 2009b).

---

[99] Most of his works are now his former wife's property. His works exhibited in Hanoi were put up for sale and have been kept by one of his acquaintances in Hanoi. However, this acquaintance has passed away and Thọ' does not know what happened to his paintings. The works exhibited in India were not returned to Vietnam and he does not know their whereabouts.

Ethnic minorities themselves have adapted the images of ethnic minorities created by the government and used state vocabularies to express their own identity. It is as though the colonized people do not have the vocabulary to explain themselves other than the vocabularies given to them by their colonial masters. This is related to the question raised by Gayatri Spivak, "Can Sabaltan speak?" to which she herself answered negatively (Loomba 2001: 75). However, the works of Đàng Năng Thọ' may be able to demonstrate that they can break the spell on ethnic minority people and they can talk about themselves with their own artistic vocabularies. The art whose horizon has been opened up by *đổi mới* has become a contesting arena for cultural agencies. It has become a platform for the Cham and other ethnic minority people to express their own identity and thoughts with their own artistic vocabularies.

CONCLUSION

IN THE NAME OF CHAM

As I found out, the variety of ethnic identities among the Cham people from different regions—what it is that constitutes Cham—will always be shifting along the course of history. The only common and most prominent characteristic of their identity is their proper name, Cham. All the Cham I met in Vietnam referred to themselves as Cham regardless of where they were from. Shils notes that the name of a society is important to its members especially when they are in contact with people from other societies. By means of the name, they create a boundary between 'them and us' and at the same time, they declare that they share something of "undefined but significant quality" among them, but not with others (Shils 1980: 164).

The name of the Cham became their "official" name after 1975 when the Vietnamese government made conscious efforts to make ethnic autonyms into official names.[100] Once a name is chosen over others used by various neighboring groups as the proper name by the state, the group officially exists in the territories of the nation. Harrell states that once an ethnic category was created in the state discourse of ethnic classification and in history, it became a vocabulary item used in the practical language of ethnic identity, and this would gradually shape the people's own ethnic consciousness (1996a: 111, 1996b: 279).

Cham as an interactional identity

Ethnicity is "a process of dialogical interaction" between one's identity and state-defined or state-recognized identity (Gladney 1998: 120). The Vietnamese state's ethnic classifications sometimes do not correspond to the ethnic classifications which people experience in daily life, and therefore they have to negotiate between their ethnic identity and the one given to them by the state.

---

[100] In South Vietnam, Cham used to be called Chàm with a longer vowel sound with a falling tone.

Ethnicity is an interactional concept; it is a process and communication between different groups and individuals. Social contacts and relationships are essential to ethnicity. The people have to draw and redraw ethnic boundaries around themselves when they encounter various "others." Li Tana studied the historical development of the Vietnamese southern expansion (*nam tiến*) and argues that the Vietnamese migrants into the south lived much closer to other ethnic groups like the Cham (1998: 101-131). K. Taylor explains that the Vietnamese could retain their separate identity from the Chinese despite the 1,000 years of Chinese occupation because of their contacts with other ethnic groups such as the Cham and Khmer (1983: 299).

Cham ethnicity becomes most salient in opposition to the Kinh majority. Although ethnicity is not a structure that should be defined by oppositions (Tonkin et al. 1989: 9), in reality, ethnicity is experienced in a dyadic relationship: majority and minority (Macdonald 1993; McDonald 1989; Tonkin et al. 1989; Wallman 1979). This is because the context of interaction with others is destined to stratify and hierarchize the groups interacting: one is more powerful than the other, one is more prestigious than the other, and so on. Ethnicity cannot escape from inequality and be neutral in reality (Glazer & Moyniham 1975: 11-12; Tonkin et al. 1989: 16). The Cham people describe the characteristics of themselves in opposition to the Kinh majority: minority vs. majority, poor vs. rich, backward vs. developed, illiterate vs. educated, matrilineal/matrilocal vs. patrilineal/patrilocal, spiritual vs. materialist, and so on. The Cham people are not only an ethnic group (*dân tộc*) but at the same time also a minority (*thiểu số*) whose lower socio-economic condition is a national project for the state to tackle.

Cham as an invention

The state plays a significant role in the formation of the ethnic groups. Gladney reports that the Hui people in PRC are an officially recognized ethnic group, while the same group does not exist in Taiwan where its government is reluctant to recognize them as a separate ethnic group but rather as the Chinese group that follows Islam (1998: 128). According to the late 1950s classification of ethnic groups in Vietnam, there were 64 ethnic groups living there, but the number was reduced to 58 in the late 1970s and finally to 54 (Yoshizawa 1982: 14). What happened to the groups that disappeared in the later classifications? Did they all die out? The development of the ethnic classification of Vietnam indicates that ethnic groups and their ethnicity are inventions of the state. The state can dismantle an ethnic group and at the same time, it can create one (Sollors 1989).

The state's authority in various media such as the national census, school textbooks, maps, museums, and national academies legitimizes the ethnic groups as "scientific" facts. It is not a statement itself but, as Foucault argues, what governs the statement is that which makes it scientifically acceptable. Anthropologists "who are charged with saying what counts as true" (Foucault 1984: 54, 72) have played a significant role in defining various ethnic groups. It is the academic authority which scholars and researchers hold that makes their analysis and interpretation reliable and in extreme cases, the "truth." A Vietnamese anthropologist, Du'o'ng Bích Hạnh, told a story at a conference that a Black Thai woman living in the northern part of Vietnam changed her identity to White Thai simply because an ethnographer from Hanoi came into her village and told her that she was actually a White Thai.

Eriksen argues that ethnicity is the creation of anthropologists. He demonstrated the different level of interest in ethnicity studies in Western countries. In French anthropology, the concept of *ethnicite* is understood differently from the way that it is understood in British and American anthropology. Eriksen points out that in the *Dictionaire de l'ethnologie et de l'anthropologie* by Bonte and Izard (1991), there is no entry for ethnicity, but only for ethnic groups and ethnic minorities. The connotation of "ethnic groups" in France is something similar to the notion of races or cultures. Such differences in understanding ethnicity reflect that "ethnicity is a social and cultural product which anthropologists contribute to creating" (Eriksen 1993: 161).

The Hui people on Hainan Island in China call themselves Utsat in their local language. Benedict points out the similarity between the Utsat people's language and the Cham's language and alludes that the Utsat of Hainan originated in Champa (1941). By examining Chinese documents, Tasaka argues that the Muslims on Hainan Island are the descendants of Champa who escaped turmoil caused by wars in their mother country (1952: 57-58). Thurgood, another linguist, has also come up with the similar argument that the Utsat are descendants of merchant-class Muslim Cham who sought refuge in the north after the fall of Champa's northern capital (2007).

Anthropologist Keng-Fong Pang, who conducted her field research among the Utsat people, notes in her dissertation that these people now accept Champa as their land of origin, and one Utsat person indicated to her that he wanted to go to Vietnam to learn the Cham language and to understand what he viewed as the pure version of their culture (1996: 199-200). She ascribed the Utsat people's awareness of their Champa background to their encounters with the Cham people during their pilgrimages to Mecca. However, I suspect that Pang and her research may also have influenced their awareness of the Champa connections.

At the first gathering of the Chamic studies group of the Association of Asian Studies held in Chicago in 1997, the people working on Cham populations were encouraged to exchange their field data to create a comparative study of the Cham diaspora. However, among those classified as Champa-descended populations in different parts of the world, I believe some may not be conscious of their origin or they may not be so interested in it. My study of the ethnic identity of the Cham people in Vietnam and my presence in their communities evoked certain aspects of Cham ethnic identity and, in a way, pressured them to articulate their ethnic identity. In this way, anthropologists will evoke ethnic consciousness and change people's ethnicity or even create an ethnic group.

Sacrifice for the state

As the national minority group, the Cham people's homeland faces a serious threat to its existence because of the Vietnamese national nuclear energy program. The myth of nuclear energy as an ideal, safe, and clean energy of the future has been proved to be false by Japan's Fukushima nuclear disaster in 2011. There is no such thing as safe and clean nuclear energy. Three years after the disaster, there are approximately 130,000[101] people who still cannot return to their homes in Fukushima. The fishing industry of Fukushima is still suffering from the leakage of radiation-contaminated underground water from the nuclear reactors to the sea.

Nuclear plants require internal and external sacrifices. In the daily operation of nuclear reactors, the workers at the front line cannot avoid minor exposure to radiation on a regular basis. They place their health in danger for economic reward. Once there is an accident, the people who live around the reactors and the surrounding environment will be exposed to radiation. In the case of Fukushima's nuclear reactors, around 70% to 80% of the workers were local people who were, at the same time, the victims of earthquake, tsunami, and nuclear disaster (Takahashi 2012: 37-38, 63, 66). Some scholars have pointed out a kind of colonialism in this system. During the rapid Japanese economic development of the 1970s to 1980s, the

---

[101] This is an estimate based on the data found at the following sites (retrieved April 30, 2014): www.pref.fukushima.lg.jp/sec/16025b/shinsai_higaijokyo.html; www.pref.fukushima.lg.jp/uploaded/attachment/61491.pdf

Fukushima prefecture contributed to this development by providing laborers, food, and energy to the urban center. Yet Tokyo, the urban center, and Fukushima, the agrarian periphery, have never had an equal partnership. The agrarian periphery was subordinated to the urban center for its development (Shimizu 2012: 186). It is an exploitation of the periphery by the center. Tokyo burdens the risk of nuclear reactors on to Fukushima and at the same time, receives the benefit of the power generated. The electric company and the nuclear industry have enjoyed large profits from this operation (Takahashi 2012: 195).

To build a nuclear reactor, there must be an economically disadvantaged region which dares to agree to have the nuclear reactors in its backyard despite the possible risks. Historically, the northeastern region including Fukushima was considered to be an uncivilized area inhabited by rebellious people called Emishi (蝦夷) who refused to submit themselves to the court of Yamato (Japan). Often, the Emishi are depicted as physically and culturally distinctive from the Yamato people, just like Japan's indigenous people, the Ainu. In the modern era, Japan's northeastern region has remained an under-developed periphery. It is the people's backwardness and poverty that made this region accept or desire to take over what the center did not want, such as nuclear reactors and nuclear waste.[102]

According to Kainuma, who calls Fukushima a "nuclear village" in the context of Japan's post-war economic development, once the nuclear plant was established, the local economy was drastically changed. Not only did people find employment at the nuclear reactors, but also local businesses as a whole, directly or indirectly, benefitted from the nuclear plant. Because of the good local economy and also the subsidies from the government for having a nuclear plant, the infrastructure of the area was improved and the local people could enjoy good public and cultural facilities. Kainuma states that the local economic dependency on the nuclear plant works like a drug. People know that having nuclear reactors may harm their health, yet once they have them, they cannot help wanting more. Their upgraded livelihood depends on the reactors because there are no major industries other than farming and fishing. They will fall into nuclear reactor addiction. Instead of

---

[102] Japan Nuclear Fuel Limited established a nuclear fuel reprocessing plant in Rokkasho village (六ヶ所村) in Aomori (青森), the northernmost prefecture in Honshu Island of Japan in 1993. The nuclear wastes from reactors all over Japan are gathered in this reprocessing plant in order to extract plutonium and uranium for further usage. However, the plants have had a series of problems and so it has not yet started official operations (as of 2014).

the state/center requesting the peripheries to set up nuclear plants, the peripheries themselves will demand more nuclear plants to be established in their region. This automatic subordination of the peripheries to the center indicates a stabilization of such relationships between the two areas (Kainuma 2011).

A similar subordination pattern can be expected to occur between Hanoi and Ninh Thuận once the nuclear reactor is in operation. The position of Ninh Thuận/Panduranga overlaps with the role that northeastern Japan has played. It has contributed to construct the identity of the center by providing an opposing image as under-developed and backward in comparison with the center which is developed and progressive. By having the nuclear reactors, the periphery will sustain the center's development by supplying energy and human resources which creates and stabilizes the periphery's economic dependency on the center.

Takahashi argues that the nuclear reactor is "the system of sacrifice." He defines this as a system that produces and maintains benefit for a group of people by sacrificing other people's life, health, property, dignity, hope, and so on. Without sacrifices by some, the benefit for others will not be produced or maintained. Such a sacrifice is glorified for the community and therefore is justified. At the nuclear reactor, workers are exposed to the radiation on a daily basis. They work at the price of their health for economic benefit. Once an accident occurs, the local people living around the reactor and its environment will be sacrificed (Takahashi 2012: 27, 37-38, 63-66). The nuclear reactors presuppose such sacrifices though they are never mentioned. Instead, how bright and prosperous the future will be for the region because of the nuclear power plant is highlighted.

The system of sacrifice which divides people into two sides—the people to sacrifice and the people to enjoy the benefits of these sacrifices—can be seen as a kind of colonialism (Takahashi 2012: 27, 74, 198-205). There are some discussions to equate[103] Fukushima's situation to Okinawa (沖縄) where the US base in Japan is concentrated. The Okinawa prefecture, which consists of numerous small islands in the East China Sea and where less than 1% of the Japanese population lives, has to endure having 75% of the

---

[103] It is difficult to compare the Okinawa and Fukushima cases since Okinawa was forced to bear the large US military base without any question, while Fukushima invited the nuclear reactors to the region. The *Asahi* newspaper reported that Japan had abandoned the plan to export its nuclear plant technology to Turkey in December 2018 (*The Asahi Shinbun* 2018). In the following week, it also reported that another nuclear plant technology export to the Unitd Kingdom (UK) will be highly unlikely to be materialized (*The Asahi Shinbun* 2019).

US base presence in Japan. Having the people of Okinawa make a sacrifice for the rest of Japan has been done through the democratic process. Putting the largest and the most dangerous US military bases in Okinawa was approved by the Parliament whose right is granted by the Japanese Constitution. As a small prefecture, Okinawa can only send as many as ten representatives to the Parliament and such a small number can never revert any decisions made by the majority. The democratic principle of majority rule has become a violence of numbers. The same logic can be applied to the case of nuclear power plants. If the establishment of the location of a nuclear plant is made as a "national decision" (the majority's will), the local region has no choice but to accept the "democratic decision" even though it requires their sacrifice. The democratic system based on majority rule is to legitimize internal colonization (Nomura 2005: 224; Takahashi 2012: 206-208). Henmi describes this process as *kimin* (棄民), abandoning citizens. The state does not hesitate to abandon its own people for the attainment of its national policies (Henmi 2012: 272).

Exporting nuclear plants and nuclear technologies implicates Japan by its strategy of exporting the system of sacrifice and the creation of internal colonialism. As I complete the writing of this book, the Vietnamese government has wisely abandoned its plan to import nuclear power plants from Japan as proposed in 2016. I wholeheartedly respect their sensible decision although my own government still continues its shameless attempts to sell its nuclear technology to others. If Vietnam wishes to avoid the same mistakes that Japan has committed, it should seriously review its national energy program. By mobilizing national wisdom and technology, the Vietnamese government can look for clean and sustainable alternative energy, and Japan should work with Vietnam and other countries in their search for clean and environmentally friendly energy. As the first and only country to be exposed to atomic bombs and also causing one of the worst nuclear accidents in the history of mankind, Japan should be the front runner in the search for alternative energy sources and the preacher of the risks involved with nuclear power in the world today.

The Cham are the ethnic minority in Vietnam. As long as their minority status is destined to be sacrificed for the majority, their ethnic identity ends up with some problematic notions: the people of the lost country of Champa, the people of no country, the defeated people, loss of land, loss of culture, and so on. If their ethnic identity will continue to be based on such antagonistic dualism, they may never be fully integrated into the nation of Vietnam.

APPENDIX

Balamon funerals

The Balamon people used to organize funeral ceremonies on auspicious days. For that reason, the body of the deceased was sometimes left for several days. However, the law imposed by the state dictated that the Balamon people must bury the deceased immediately. A few years after the death when the Balamon had saved up enough money to hold a proper funeral, the body of the deceased could be reclaimed and a funeral organized. There are roughly four different kinds of funerals practiced by the Balamon people: *Dan Ram, Dam Mutai Tha Urang Pa Seh, Dam Mutai Twa Urang Pa Seh,* and *Dam Mutai Pa Urang Pa Seh.*

Dam Ram

This is a funeral for a person whose body has been lost for various reasons, such as in the case of war or accident, or for small infants or children whose bodies have been buried for some time and can no longer be found. *Dam Ram* lasts for half a day and it is usually organized for the afternoon. One Balamon priest conducts the ceremony and he reconstructs a deceased body with a coconut shell, rice, and rice powder dyed in five different colors. The reconstructed body is buried and a small mound is made.

Dam Mutai Tha Urang Pa Seh

This is a funeral for a person under 15 years old. A Balamon priest conducts the ceremony, it lasts for two days, and the deceased is buried without cremation. The funeral shows a symbolic association with water. Some binary opposition can be constructed in a comparison between cremation and burial as below.

Cremation	Burial
Adults (above 15 years old)	Children (below 15 years old)
Fire (smoke)	Water
Upward	Downward
Heaven	Underground
Gods	Ancestors

Dam Mutai Twa Urang Pa Seh

This is the most commonly organized funeral. It lasts for four days and usually starts on a Wednesday. Cremation of the deceased then takes place on the Saturday. Two Balamon priests conduct the ceremony. If the deceased died in an accident or due to any kind of violence, the priests conduct extra rituals.

Dam Mutai Pa Urang Pa Seh

This is the most lavish funeral and is organized by particular lineages. The funeral has an almost identical sequence to *Dam Mutai Twa Urang Pa Seh*; however, there are four priests to conduct the ceremonies and several different ceremonial objects are used.

Ceremonies organized after the cremation

Patrip

While a corpse is being cremated, the skull is taken out of the cremation fire, and nine pieces of bone are cut out from a section of the forehead. These nine pieces of bone are called *talang* and are kept in a container called a *klong*. The *klong* is kept hidden by the family for some time, but every year they display the *klong* and organize a ceremony to commemorate the deceased; this ceremony is called *Patrip*. The Balamon people believe that the biological death of a person is a separation of their soul from its body. While the body is temporarily buried until the funeral, the soul of the person remains in the household in the form of a spirit called a *bhut*. A *bhut* can be identified by the deceased person's name and age, the same as for living beings. After the cremation, the soul of the deceased is considered to be going to one of seven levels of heaven and to have become a servant of the supreme god Po Ku. In this stage, the deceased loses his/her individuality. He/she is no longer identified by his/her name or age. The *Patrip* is the ceremony for the temporary unification of the soul and body of the deceased person. The deceased's soul comes back from heaven to stay with their family shortly. The *talang* are the places for the soul to stay while in this world. That is why if *talang* are missing for some reason, the new *talang* must be created out of a certain kind of metal.

Ban Kut

Once one lineage accumulates a certain number of *klong*, they will organize a ceremony called *ban kut* to bury the *talang*. The people who belong to the same lineage bring their *klong* and take out the *talang* to put into a basket. The female *talang* go into the female basket, while the male *talang* go into the male basket, and they are buried under separate tombstones called *kut*. The *talang* of the deceased whose body parts were missing at the time of their death are buried in the back of the *kut* in principle, but some lineages elect a separate *kut* to bury this kind of *talang*. After *ban kut*, the soul of the deceased is considered to join the ancestral spirit *muk kay* and his/her individual identity seems to be totally eradicated.

Ceremonies during *Ramuwan*

Ramuwan is equivalent to Ramadan observed by other Muslim people. It is during the ninth month of the Islamic calendar, and the people who live away come back to their natal homes to celebrate the holy month which involves a series of ceremonies as below:

1. **Four days prior to *Ramuwan***
   For three days, Bani people visit their graveyards to invite ancestral spirits to their homes. This ceremony is called *sah-pan*.

2. **One – three days prior to *Ramuwan***
   Bani people organize ceremonies for their ancestors at home called *bbang amuk kay*. It can be organized by a household on any day within the three days before *Ramuwan*. In this ceremony, the name of a deceased individual is called and the family offers a tray of food to

them. The eldest woman in the household is responsible for remembering the names of the deceased.

3. **First day of *Ramuwan***

    At sunset, the sounds of a drum of each *thang muki* (village mosque) signals *ricauv (richo)* to mark the beginning of *Ramuwan*. Bani priests enter the *thang muki* and every household sends one female representative with a plate of offerings to seek forgiveness for bad deeds that people committed in the previous year. The priests remain in the *thang muki* away from their family for the next 30 days.

4. **First three days of *Ramuwan***

    The priests remain inside of the *thang muki* and do not eat or talk from dawn to sunset. They are only allowed to take some salt during the daytime. While the priests are fasting, Bani lay people are not allowed to enter the *thang muki*, men are not allowed to shave, and women are not allowed to have their hair cut. If there is a death during the first three days of *Ramuwan*, the deceased will be left without being buried.

5. **Fourth day of *Ramuwan***

    The priests end their fasting during the daytime and Bani lay people can enter the *thang muki*. After this day until the end of *Ramuwan*, if a woman is menstruating, she is not allowed to enter the *thang muki*.

6. **First 15 days of *Ramuwan***

    The priests are not allowed to shave during the first 15 days of *Ramuwan*. The Bani lay people do not fast during *Ramuwan* but they are not allowed to eat meat during the first 15 days (fish are allowed).

7. **The 15th day of *Ramuwan***

    A ceremony is held called *Amu Trun*, the advent of Eva (one of the Prophets, equivalent to Eve). Each household sends a plate of offerings to the *thang muki*. From this day, the taboo of meat is lifted.

8. **The 20th day of *Ramuwan***

    A ceremony called *On Trun*, the advent of Adam (one of the Prophets), is held. Each household sends a plate of offerings to the *thang muki*.

9. **The 30th day of *Ramuwan***

    A ceremony called *Kalaih Ramuwan* is held to mark the end of *Ramuwan*. During *Kalaih Ramuwan*, a ceremony for the promotion of priests is held.

10. **Three months after *Ramuwan***
    A ceremony called *Kalaih Waha* is organized.

Ranks of priests

Balamon priests (*Halau Tamunay Ahier*)

Pa She: The lowest rank of Balamon priests.

Po Baik: The second highest rank of Balamon priests. In order to enter the status of *Po Baik*, a Balamon priest must conduct a ceremony called *Mno Cha* over three years. After obtaining the rank of *Po Baik*, the priest should not engage in any physical labor including agriculture. He must spend his days praying and studying religious texts.

Po Dhia (Po Sa): The highest rank of Balamon priests. Each Balamon temple has one *Po Dhia*.

Bani priests (*Halau Tamunay Awal*)

Ong Char (Po Char): The lowest rank of Bani Priests, a rank which has to be held for three years. *Ong Char* wear a white turban without red tassels.

Ong Mu Tinh: *Ong Mu Tinh* are allowed to wear a white turban with red tassels called *khan mu tan tai pi*. They have a duty to perform the call for prayer. The main *Ong Mu Tinh* who calls for prayer is called *Mu Tinh Kal* and his assistant is called *Mu Tinh Kok Kai*.

Ong Katip: After serving as *Mu Tinh Kal*, an *Ong Mu Tinh* becomes *Ong Katip*. The term of this rank is three years. Along with *Ong Imum Tum*, *Ong Katip* plays a leading role in prayers.

Ong Imum Tum: The main priest to conduct ceremonies at the *thang muki*. Their term is three years.

Ong Imum Klak: After serving as *Ong Imum Tum*, a priest becomes *Ong Imum Klak* (Old Imam). Eventually, one of *Ong Imum Klak* will hold the rank of *Ong Guru*. Meanwhile, they take turns in performing the role of *Ong Imum Tum*.

Ong Guru: The highest rank of Bani priests. In each *thang muki* there is one *Ong Guru*. Without *Ong Guru*, significant ceremonies such as funerals cannot be conducted.

Relationships of priests and other religious practitioners

There are various musicians, dancers, and other religious practitioners involved in conducting the Cham rituals. There is a certain rule to regulate their association with Balamon and Bani priests and also among themselves. Some of the main roles are described below.

Muk Pachau

A female assistant to the Balamon priests. Each Balamon temple has one *Muk Pachau*. She opens the temple at *Kate* which is one of the most significant ceremonies of the Cham people. *Muk Pachau* must observe the same taboos as the Balamon priests.

Ong Tamunay

A male caretaker of the Balamon temple. Each Balamon temple has one *Ong Tamunay*. *Ong Tamunay* must observe the same taboos as the Balamon priests).

Ong Kadhar

A male musician who plays a two-stringed instrument called a *kani* which is necessary for conducting funerals and a ceremony at *Kate*. *Ong Kadhar* conducts the ceremony to receive Raglay people who keep the clothing of the deity Po Inu' Nu'gar in preparation for *Kate* rituals. *Ong Kadhar* also conducts the ceremony to sacrifice a buffalo called *Kalng Koi Kubao* with *Muk Pachau*.

Muk Poh

A female assistant to the Bani priests. Each Bani village has one or two *Muk Poh*. *Muk Poh* prepares a ceremonial plate of food for Bani priests and she is the first person to pray at the *thang muki* which signals other people to begin their prayers.

Ong Muton

A male musician who plays a drum called a *paranun* which is the essential instrument for various *Rija* ceremonies. *Ong Muton* conducts the *Rija* ceremonies with *Muk Rija* and *Ong Kaing*. *Ong Muton* must observe the same taboos as the Bani priests. If an *Ong Muton* is from the Balamon group, he also has to observe the taboos of Balamon.

Muk Rija

A female ritual dancer. Each lineage of both Balamon and Bani have one *Muk Rija*. She must observe the same taboos as the Bani priests. If a *Muk Rija* is from the Balamon group, she must also observe the taboos of Balamon.

Ong Kaing

A male ritual dancer who performs at *Rija Nugar*, including fire walking. Each Cham village has one *Ong Kaing*. Despite their close ceremonial association with *Ong Muton*, *Ong Kaing* does not have a ceremonial association with the Bani priests. When a *Rija Nugar* is performed in a Bani village, there is a separate shack built for the Bani priests to observe the ceremony.

We can group the religious practitioners into *ahier* and *awal* groups as below:

Ahier	*Awal*
Muk Pachau	*Muk Poh*
Ong Kadar	*Ong Muton*
Ong Tamunay	*Muk Rija*
	Ong Kaing

The priests and religious practitioners of the *ahier* group cannot have ceremonial associations with those of the *awal* group and vice-versa.

BIBLIOGRAPHY

Adams, Kathleen M. 1997a. Ethnic Tourism and the Renegotiating of Tradition in Tana Toraja. *Ethnology,* Vol. 36, No. 4: 309-320.

Adams, Parveen. 1979. A Note on the Distinction between Sexual Division and Sexual Differences. *M/f,* No. 3: 51-57.

Andaya, Leonard Y. 2010. *Leaves of the Same Tree: Trade and Ethnicity in the Straits of Melaka.* Singapore: NUS Press.

Aoyagi, Yuji (青柳). 1999. Production and Trade of Champa Ceramics in the 15th Century. In Nguyễn Thế Anh & Yoshiaki Ishizawa (eds.), *Trade and Navigation in Southeast Asia (14th–19th centuries),* 91-100. Paris & Montreal: Sophia University.

Aymonier, Étienne F. 1890. Legendes Historiques des Chams. *Excursions et Recounaisance,* Vol. 14, No. 32: 145-206.

Bang Thanh. 1995. Ethnic Kitsch. *Vietnam Investment Review.* December 18-24: 7.

Baudesson, Henry. 1919. *Indo-China and its Primitive People by Captain Henry Baudesson,* translated by E. Appleby Holt. London: Hutchinson & Co.

BBC. 2012. http://www.bbc.co.uk/vietnamese/vietnam/2012/06/120531_xuandien_investigation.shtml (accessed February 3, 2013).

Bedlington, Stanley S. 1978. *Malaysia and Singapore: The Building of New States.* Ithaca and London: Cornell University Press.

Belo, Jane. 1949. *Bali: Rangda and Barong.* Monographs of the American Ethnological Society, No. 16. Seattle & London: University of Washington Press.

Benedict, Paul K. 1941. A Cham Colony on the Island of Hainan. *Harvard Journal of Asiatic Studies,* VI: 129-134.

Blood, Doris. 1981. Aspects of Cham Culture. *Notes from Indochina on Ethnic Minority Cultures.* Summer Institute of Linguistics - Museum of Anthropological Publication, No. 6: 1-34.

Bronson, Bennet. 1977. Exchange at the Upstream and Downstream Ends: Notes Toward a Functional Model of the Coastal State in Southeast Asia.

In K. L. Hutterer (ed.), *Economic Exchange and Social Interaction in Southeast Asia: Perspectives from Prehistory, History and Ethnography*, 39-52. Ann Arbor: Center for South and Southeast Asian Studies, The University of Michigan.

Butterfield, Fox. 1979. Vietnam Refugees Say Attacks on Communists Continue in Highlands. *New York Times*, June 1.

Cabaton, Antoine. 1965. Indochina. In *Encyclopaedia of Islam*. Vol. III: 1208-1212. Leiden, Brill, London: Luzac.

Cao Xuan Pho. 1988. Cham People and Cham Sculpture. In State Committee for Social Sciences of Vietnam & Institute of Southeast Asian Studies (ed.), *Cham Sculpture Album*, 185-217. Hanoi: Social Sciences Publishing House.

Chambert-Loir, Henri. 1994. On the Historical and Literary Relations between Champa and the Malay World. In Huynh Dinh Te (trans.), *Proceedings of the Seminar on Champa,* 87-99. University of Copenhagen: Cordova, CA. (Originally published in French in 1988 as *Actes du seminaire sur le Campa*, Organise a L'Universite de Copenhague, le 23 Mai 1987. Association Centre d'Histoire et Civilisation de la Péninsule Indochinoise: Paris.)

Chanda, Nayan. 1979. Ieng Sary: Unite for Our Country. *Far Eastern Economic Review,* 104, No. 25, June 22: 10-11.

Chanda, Nayan. 1981. The Enemies Within. *Far Eastern Economic Review,* October 30: 9-10.

Chaturachinda, Gwyneth, Krishnamurty, Sunanda & Tabtiang, Pauline, W. 2000. *Dictionary of South and Southeast Asian Art*. Chiang Mai: Silkworm Books.

Cheung, Siu-Woo. 1995. Millenarianism, Christian Movements, and Ethnic Change among the Miao in Southwest China. In S. Harrell (ed.), *Cultural Encounters on China's Ethnic Frontiers*, 217-247. Seattle and London: University of Washington Press.

Chu Thái So'n & Đào Hùng. 1991. *Vietnam A Multicultural Mosaic.* Hanoi: Vietnam Foreign Language Publishing House Hanoi.

Chuengsatiansup, Komatra. 1998. Marginality, Suffering and Community: The Politics of Collective Experience and Empowerment in Thailand. Paper presented to Vietnamese–Thai Collaborative Workshop on Ethnic Communities in Changing Environment. Chiang Mai, Thailand, December.

Coedès, George. 1966. *The Making of South East Asia*, translated by H. M. Wright. Berkeley and Los Angeles: University of California Press. (Originally published in French, 1962, *Les Peuples de la Péninsule*

Indochinoise. Paris: Dunod.)

Coedès, George. 1968. *The Indianized States of Southeast Asia*, Vella, W. F. (ed.), translated by S. Brown Cowing. Hanolulu: University of Hawaii Press. (Originally published in French, 1964, *Les États hindouisés d'Indochine et d'Indonésie*. Paris: E. De Boccard.)

Collins, William A. 1996. The Chams of Cambodia. In *Interdisciplinary Research on Ethnic Groups in Cambodia, final draft reports*, 15-107. Phnom Penh: Center for Advanced Study.

Condominas, George. 1977. *We have Eaten the Forest. First: The Story of a Montagnard Village in the Central Highlands of Vietnam*. (Originally published in French in 1957 as *Nous Avons Mange la Foret de la Pierre-Genie Goo*. English translation by Foulke, A. New York: Hill and Wang.)

Connor, Walker. 1984. *The National Question in Marxist-Leninist Theory and Strategy*. Princeton, New Jersey: Princeton University Press.

Đặng Nghiêm Vạn. 1990. We need an Organization strong enough to carry on tribal work. *Tap chi cong San*, No. 8, August 89: 51-54, JPRS-ATC-90-002, April 2, 1990.

Đặng Nghiêm Vạn, Chu Thái So'n & Lu'u Hùng. 1984. *Ethnic Minorities in Vietnam*. Hanoi: Foreign Languages Publishing House.

Đặng Nghiêm Vạn, Chu Thái So'n & Lu'u Hùng. 1993. *Ethnic Minorities in Vietnam*. Hanoi: The Gioi Publishers.

Dang Quang Trung. 1989. Implementation of Nationalities Policy viewed: first Installment. *Nhan Dan*, July 31: 3, FBIS-EAS – 89-I77.

Dampier, William. 1697. *A New Voyage round the World*, edited by Sir A. Gray. London: Argonaut.

Engels, Friedrich. 1985. *The Origin of the Family, Private Property and the State*, (edition with a new introduction by Michele Barrett), England: Penguin Books. (Originally published in German in 1884. The first English edition was published by Lawrence & Wishart in 1972.)

Eriksen, Thomas Hylland. 1993. *Ethnicity and Nationalism: Anthropological Perspectives*. London, Boulder, CO: Pluto Press.

Evans, Grant. 1985. Vietnamese Communist Anthropology. *Camberra Anthropology*, Vol. 8, No. 1 & 2: 116-147.

Far Eastern Economic Review. 1992. Lost Tribe. *Far Eastern Economic Review*. July 23: 7.

Farouk, Omar. 2008. The re-organization of Islam in Cambodia and Laos. In O. Farouk & H. Yamamoto (eds.), *Islam at the Margins: The Muslims of Indochina*, 70-85. CIAS Discussion Paper No. 3. Kyoto, Japan: Center for Integrated Area Studies, Kyoto University.

Foucault, Michel. 1984. *The Foucault Reader,* edited by P. Rabinow. London: Penguin Books.
Gammelgaard, J. 1990. Ethnic Minorities in Vietnam. Unpublished report on a Mission to Vietnam, 12 November–14 December, FAO Hanoi, Vietnam.
Gladney, Dru. C. 1998. Clashed Civilizations? Muslims and Chinese identities in the PRC. In D. C. Gladney (ed.), *Making Majorities: Constituting the Nation in Japan, Korea, China, Malaysia, Fiji, Turkey, and the United States*, 106-134. Stanford, CA: Stanford University Press.
Gladney, Dru. C. 2003. *Dislocating China: Muslims, Minorities and Other Subaltern Subjects*. London: University of Chicago Press.
Glazer, Nathan & Moyniham, Daniel P. (ed.). 1975. *Ethnicity: Theory and Experience*. Cambridge, Mass.: Harvard University Press.
Glover, Ian & Nguyễn Kim Dung. 2011. Chapter 2: Excavations at Gò Cẩm, Quảng Nam 2000-3: Linyi and the emergence of the Cham kingdoms. In Trần Kỳ Phu'o'ng & B. Lockhard (eds.), *The Cham of Vietnam: History, society and art*, 54-80. Singapore: NUS Press.
Guy, John. 2009. Artistic exchange, regional dialogue and the Cham territories. In A. Hardy, M. Cucarzi & P. Zolese (eds.), *Champa and the Archaeology of Mỹ So'n (Vietnam)*, 127-154. Singapore: NUS Press.
Hall, Daniel. G. E. 1960. Looking at Southeast Asian History. *Journal of Asian Studies*, 19: 243-253.
Hall, Kenneth R. 1985. *Maritime Trade and Early State Development in Southeast Asia*. Honolulu: University of Hawaii Press.
Hardy, Andrew. 2009. Eaglewood and the economic history of Champa and central Vietnam, In A. Hardy, M. Cucarzi & P. Zolese (eds.), *Champa and the Archaeology of Mỹ So'n (Vietnam)*, 107-126. Singapore: NUS Press.
Harrell, Stevan. 1995. Introduction: Civilizing Projects and the Reaction to Them. In S. Harrell (ed.), *Cultural Encounters on China's Ethnic Frontiers*, 3-36. Seattle: University of Washington Press.
Harrell, Stevan. 1996a. Languages Defining Ethnicity in Southwest China. In G. De Vos & L. Romanucci-Ross (eds.), *Ethnic Identity*, 97-114. London, Walnut Creek & New Deli: Altamira Press.
Harrell, Stevan. 1996b. The Nationalities Question and the Prmi Problem. In M. J. Brown (ed.), *Negotiating Ethnicities in China and Taiwan*, 274-296. Berkeley, CA: Institute of East Asian Studies, UC-Berkeley.
Harrell, Stevan. 2001. *Ways of Being Ethnic in Southwest China*. Seattle: University of Washington Press.
Hickey, Gerald C. 1982a. *Sons of the Mountains: Ethnohistory of the*

Vietnamese Central Highlands to 1954. New Haven, Connecticut: Yale University Press.

Hickey, Gerald C. 1982b. *Free in the Forest: Ethnohistory of the Vietnamese Central Highlands, 1954-1976*. New Haven, Connecticut: Yale University Press.

Hickey, Gerald C. 1993. *Shattered World: Adaptation and Survival among Vietnam's Highland People during the Vietnam War*. Philadelphia: University of Pennsylvania Press.

Hoskins, Janet. 1987. Complementarity in this World and the Next: Gender and Agency in Kodi Mortuary Ceremonies. In M. Strathern (ed.), *Dealing with Inequality*, 174-206. Cambridge: Cambridge University Press.

Hy Van Luong. 1992. *Revolution in the Village: Tradition and Transformation in North Vietnam, 1925–1988*. Honolulu, Hawaii: University of Hawaii Press.

Jackson, Larry R. 1969. The Vietnamese Revolution and the Montagnards. *Asian Survey*, 9 (5): 313-330.

Jamieson, Neil L. 1993. *Understanding Vietnam*. Berkeley: University of California Press.

Jamieson, Neil L. 1996. The Evolving Context of Contemporary Vietnamese Painting. In *Cultural Representation in Transition: New Vietnamese Painting*, 14-27. Bangkok: Siam Society.

Jaspan, Mervyn A. 1970. Recent Developments among the Cham of Indo-China: The revival of Champa. *Asian Affairs*, 57, No. 2: 170-176.

Kamarulnizam, Abdullah. 2003. *The Politics of Islam in Contemporary Malaysia*. Bangi: Penerbit Universiti Kebangsaan, Malaysia.

Kennedy, Laurel B. & Williams, Mary R. 2001. The Past Without the Pain: The Manufacture of Nostalgia in Vietnam's Tourism Industry. In Tai Hue-Tam Ho (ed.), *Country of Memory: Remaking the Past in Late Socialist Vietnam*, 135-163. Ewing, NJ: University of California Press.

Keyes, Charles F. 1987. Tribal Peoples and the Nation-State in Mainland Southeast Asia. In B. Anderson et al. (eds.), *Southeast Asian Tribal Groups and Ethnic Minorities, Cultural Survival Report* 22, 19-26. Cambridge, Mass.: Cultural Survival Inc.

Khong Dien. 2002. *Population and Ethno-Demography in Vietnam*. Chiang Mai, Thailand: Silkworm.

Kiernan, Ben. 1988. Orphans of Genocide: The Cham Muslims of Campuchea Under Pol Pot. *Bulletin of Concerned Asian Scholars*, Vol. 20, No. 4.

Kiernan, Ben. 1999. *The Pol Pot Regime: Race, Power and Genocide in*

Cambodia under the Khmer Rouge, 1975–1979. Chaing Mai: Silkworm Books. (First published by Yale University in 1996.)

Kleinen, John. 1999. *Facing the Future, Reviving the Past: A Study of Social Change in a Northern Vietnamese Village.* Singapore: Institute of Southeast Asian Studies.

Kraevskaia, Natasha. 2005. *From Nostalgia towards Exploitation: Essays on Contemporary Art in Vietnam.* Hanoi: Kim Dong Publishing House.

Labrie, Norman C. 1971. FULRO: The History of Political Tension in the South Vietnamese Highland. M.A. Thesis at Department of Government, University of Massachusetts.

Lafont, Pierre B. 1964. Contribution a L' Étude des Structures Cociales des Cham du Viet-Nam. *Buletin l'Ecole Francaise D'extrême Orient,* Tome LII Fasc. 1: 157-171.

Leach, Edmund R. 1964. *Political Systems of Highland Burma: A Study of Kachin Social Structure.* London and Atlantic Highlands, NJ: The Athlone Press.

Leuba, Jeanne. 1915. Les Chams d'autrefois et d'aujour d' hui. *Revue Indochinoise,* Juillet.

Li Tana. 1998. *Nguyễn Cochinchina: Southern Vietnam in the Seventeenth and Eighteenth Centuries.* Ithaca, NY: Cornell Southeast Asia Program Publication.

Lockhart, Bruce M. 2011. Chapter 1 Colonial and post-colonial construction of "Champa". In Trần Kỳ Phuo'o'ng & B. Lockhart (eds.), *The Cham of Vietnam: History, society and art.*, 1-53. Singapore: National University of Singapore Press.

Lục Văn Pao. 1992. Nationalisties Issues Discussed. *Nhan Dan,* February 13: 1, JPRS-SEA-92-009, April 23.

Mạc Đu'ò'ng. 1991. Article on Renovation, Nationalities issue. *Saigon Giai Phong* September 7: 2, JPRS-SEA-91-026.

Macdonald, Sharon. 1993. Identity Complexes in Western Europe: Social Anthropological Perspectives. In S. Macdonald (ed.), *Inside European Identitites: Ethnography in Western Europe,* 1-26. Providence, Oxford: Berg.

Majumdar, Ramesh C. 1985. *Champa: History and culture of an Indian colonial kingdom in the Far East 2nd– 16th century A.D.* Delhi: Gian Publishing House.

Mak Phoen. 1988. The Cham Community in Cambodia from the Fifteenth to the Nineteenth Century. In Huynh Dinh Te (trans.), *Proceedings of the Seminar on Champa,* 76-86. University of Copenhagen: Cordova, CA. (Originally published in French in 1988 as *Actes du seminaire sur le Campa, Organise a L'Universite de Copenhague*, le 23 Mai 1987. Association Centre d'Histoire et Civilisation de la Péninsule Indochinoise: Paris.)

Malarney, Shaun K. 2002. *Culture, Ritual and Revolution in Vietnam.* London: Routledge Curzon.

Manguin, Pierre-Yves. 1985. The Introduction of Islam to Champa. *Journal of the Malaysian Branch of the royal Asiatic Society,* 58.1: 1-28. (Originally published in French in 1979 as *L'introduction de l'Islam au Champa.* In *Bulletin de l'Ecole Francaise d'Extreme-Orient,* LXVI: 255-287.)

Marr, David. 1981. *Vietnamese Tradition on Trial 1920–1945.* Berkeley: University of California Press.

Marxists Internet Archive. 1913. http://www.marxists.org/reference/archive/stalin/works/1913/03.htm (accessed February 11, 2013).

Maspero, Georges. 2002. *The Champa Kingdom: the history of an extinct Vietnamese culture,* translated by W. E. J. Tips. Bangkok: White Lotus. (Originally published as Georges Maspero, Le Royaume de Champa 1928, 2nd rev. ed. Paris & Brussels: Les Editions G. Van Oest.)

McDonald, Maryon. 1989. *We are not French! Language, Culture and Identity in Brittany.* London: Routledge.

McElwee, Pamela. 2011. "Blood Relatives" or Uneasy Neighbors? Kinh Migrant and Ethnic Minority Interactions in the Tru'ờ'ng So'n Mountains. In P. Taylor (ed.), *Minorities at Large: New Approaches to Minority Ethnicity in Vietnam,* 81-116. Singapore: Institute of Southeast Asian Studies.

Moerman, Michael. 1965. Ethnic Identification in a Complex Civilization: Who Are the Lue? *American Anthropologist,* 67: 1215-1230.

Momoki, Shiro 2011. Chapter 5: 'Mandala Champa' see from Chinese sources'. In Trần Kỳ Phu'o'ng & B. Lockhart (ed.), *The Cham of Vietnam: History, Society and Art,* 120-137. Singapore: NUS Press.

Montagnard Foundation Inc. 1998. *Montagnard Longhouse: A Newsletter of the Montagnard Foundation Inc.,* Vol. 10, No. 1: 1-5.

Morris-Suzuki, Tessa. 1996. A Descent into the Past: The Frontier in the Construction of Japanese Identity. In Multicultural Japan: Paleolithic to Postmodern, edited by D. Denoon, M. Hudson, G. McCormack & T. Morris-Suzuki, 81-94. Cambridge, UK: Cambridge University Press.

Moura, Jean. 1883. *Le Royaume du Cambodge,* 2 volumes. Paris: Leroux.

Mukerji, Chandra. 1983. *From Graven Images: Patterns of Modern Materialism.* New York: Columbia University Press.

Mus, Paul. 1975. *India seen from the East: Indian and indigenous cults in Champa*, edited by I. W. Mabbett and D. P. Chandler, translated by I. W. Mabbett. Monash. Cheltenham, Victoria: Centre of Southeast Asian Studies, Monash University. (Originally published in French in 1933 as *Cultes indiens et indigènes au Champa*. In *Bulletin de l'Ecole Francaise d'Extrême Orient*, Vol. xxxiii: 367-410.)

Nagata, Judith. 1986. The Impact of the Islamic Revival (Dakwah) on the Religious Culture of Malaysia. In B. Matthews & J. Nagata (eds.), *Religion, Values and Development in Southeast Asia*, 37-50. Singapore: Institute of Southeast Asian Studies.

Ner, Marcel. 1941. Les Musulmans de l'Indochine Francaise. *Bulletin de l'Ecole Francaise d'Estreme-Orient*, XLI: 151-203.

Ngo Duc Thinh. 1987. The Permeation and Emergence of the New in the Culture of the Ethnic Minorities. Tạp chí Cộng sản, No. 4, April 87: 64-68. JPRS-ATC-87-003.

Nguyễn Khắc Viện. 1987. *Vietnam, a Long History*. Hanoi: Foreign Languages Publishing House.

Nông Đú'c Mạnh. 1992. Army Journal on Nationalities Policy. *Tap Chi Quoc Phong toan Dan*, April: 3-12, JPRS-SEA-92-011, May 29, 1992.

O'Connor, Richard. 1995. Agricultural Change and Ethnic Succession in Southeast Asian States: A Case for Regional Anthropology. *Journal of Asian Studies*, 54(4): 986-996.

Osnos, Peter. 1971. 'Security' a disaster for Montagnards. *Washington Post*. April 25: A1, A3.

Pairaudeau, Natasha. 2009. Indians as French Citizens in Colonial Indochina: 1858–1940. Ph.D. Thesis. Department of History, School of Oriental and African Studies, University of London.

Pang, Keng-Fong. 1996. Being Hui, Huan-nang, and Utsat Simultaneously: Contextualizing History and Identities of the Austronesian-Speaking Hainan Muslims. In M. J. Brown (ed.), *Negotiating Ethnicities in China and Taiwan*, 183-207. Berkeley: Institute of East Asian Studies, University of California, Berkeley & Center for Chinese Studies.

Perkins, Teresa E. 1979. Rethinking Stereotypes. In M. Barrett, P. Corrigan, A. Kuhn & J. Wolff (eds.), *Ideology and Cultural Production*, 135-159. London: Croom Helm.

Phan Ngoc Chien. 1993. Ethnic Identification of the Montagnards in the Central Highlands of Vietnam. M.A. Research competency paper at Department of Anthropology, University Washington, Seattle, USA.

Phan Ngoc Chien. 1997. The "Community of Vietnamese nations": The State's Hegemonic Discourse in the Process of Nation Building. A paper presented at the Third Euroviet Conference in Amsterdam, Netherland, July 25-27.

Po Dharma. 1990. Deux Princes Malais au Champa: leur Role dans la Vie Socio-Politique et Religieuse de ce pays. In *Le Monde Indochinois et La Peninsule Malaise.* Contribution de la Delegation Francaise au Deuxime Congres International sur la Civilisation Malaise, 19-28, Kuala Lumpur.

Po Dharma. 1994. Status of the Latest Research on the date of the Absorption of Champa by Vietnam. In Huynh Dinh Te (trans.), *Proceedings of the Seminar on Champa*, 59-70. University of Copenhagen: Cordova, CA. (Originally published in French in 1988 as *Actes du seminaire sur le Campa, Organise a L'Universite de Copenhague*, le 23 Mai 1987. Association Centre d'Histoire et Civilisation de la Péninsule Indochinoise: Paris.)

Quach-Langlet, Tam. 1994. The Geographical Setting of Old Champa. In Huynh Dinh Te (trans.), *Proceedings of the Seminar on Champa*, 53-64. University of Copenhagen: Cordova, CA. (Originally published in French in 1988 as *Actes du seminaire sur le Campa, Organise a L'Universite de Copenhague*, le 23 Mai 1987. Association Centre d'Histoire et Civilisation de la Péninsule Indochinoise: Paris.)

Quinn-Judge, Paul. 1982. Flushing out FULRO. *Far Eastern Economic Review,* October 8: 14.

Ravaisse, Paul. 1922. Deux Inscriptions Configues du Campa. *Journal Asiatique*, 11 serie, No. 20: 247-289.

Reid, Anthony. 1993. Islamization and Christianization in Southeast Asia: The Critical Phase 1550–1650. In A. Reid (ed.), *Southeast Asia in the Early Modern Era*, 151-179. Ithaca: Cornell University Press.

Reid, Anthony. 1995. Continuity and Change in the Austronesian Tradition to Islam and Christianity. In D. Tryon (ed.), *The Austronesians*, 314-331. Canberra: Australian National University.

Reid, Anthony. 1999. *Charting the Shape of Early Modern Southeast Asia.* Chiang Mai: Silkworm Books.

Robson, Stuart O. 1981. Java at the Crossroads: Aspects of Javanese Cultural History in the 14th and 15th Centuries. *Bijdragen tot de taal, Laude-eu Volkenkunde,* 137: 259-292.

Roff, William R. 1994. *The Origins of Malay Nationalism,* 2nd Edition. Kuala Lumpur, New York, Oxford, Singapore: Oxford University Press.

Said, Edward W. 1978. *Orientalism.* New York: Pantheon Books.

Salemink, Oscar. 1991. Mois and Maquis: The Invention and Appropriation of Vietnam's Montagnards from Sabatier to the CIA. In G. W. Stocking (ed.), *History of Anthropology*, 243-284. Madison: University of

Wisconsin Press.

Salemink, Oscar. 2003. *The Ethnography of Vietnam's Central Highlanders: A historical contextualization, 1850–1900*. London & New York: Routledge Curzon.

Scott, James. 1985. *Weapons of the Weak: Everyday Forms of Peasant Resistance*. New Haven, London: Yale University Press.

Scupin, Raymond. 1980. Islam in Thailand before the Bangkok Period. *Journal of the Siam Society*, Vol. 68, part 1: 55-71.

Scupin, Raymond. 1995. Historical, Ethnographic, and Contemporary Political Analyses of the Muslims of Kampuchea and Vietnam. *Social Issues in Southeast Asia*, Vol. 10, No. 2: 301-328.

Scupin, Raymond. 2000. Cham Muslim in Thailand: A Model of a Moral Community. In I. Alee, H. Madmarn, I. Yusuf, Y. Talek, S. Waehama & M. Narongraksaket (eds.), *Islamic Studies in ASEAN: Presentations of an International Seminar*, Pattani: College of Islamic Studies, Prince of Songkla University.

Shaw, Alison. 1988. *A Pakistani Community in Britain*. Oxford: Basil Blackwell.

Shils, Edward. 1980. *Tradition*. Glencoe Ill.: Free Press.

Smith, Monica L. 1999. Indianizatoin from the Indian point of view: Trade and cultural contacts with Southeast Asia in the early 1st millennium C. E. *Journal of the Economic and Social History of the Orient*, 42, 1: 1-26.

Sollors, Werner. 1989. Introduction: The Invention of Ethnicity. In W. Sollors (ed.), *The Invention of Ethnicity*, ix-xx. New York: Oxford University Press.

Southworth, William A. 2011. River settlement and coastal trade: Towards a specific model of early state development in Champa. In Trần Kỳ Phu'o'ng & B. M. Lockhard (eds.), *The Cham of Vietnam: History, society and art*, 102-119. Singapore: NUS Press.

Stokhof, Malte. 2008. The Baweans of Ho Chi Minh City. In O. Farouk & H. Yamamoto (eds.), *Islam at the Margins: The Muslims of Indochina*, 34-58, CIAS Discussion Paper No. 3. Kyoto, Japan: Center for Integrated Area Studies, Kyoto University.

Taylor, Keith W. 1983. *The Birth of Vietnam*. Berkeley, Los Angeles, Oxford: University of California Press.

Taylor, Nora A. 1989. The Sculpture of the Cham King Po Rame of Panduranga: A Discussion on the Historical and Religious Significance of the Post-Mortem Deification of Kings in the Art of Champa. Unpublished paper for Asian Studies 601, Cornell University.

Taylor, Nora A. 1999. Pho' Phai and Faux Phais: The Market for Fakes in Vietnam and the Appropriation of National Symbol. *Ethnos,* Vol. 64, No. 2: 232-248.

Taylor, Nora A. 2007. Vietnamese anti-Art and anti-Vietnamese Artists: Experimental Performance Culture in Hà Nội's Alternative Exhibition Spaces. *Journal of Vietnamese Studies*, Vol. 2, No. 2: 108-128.

Taylor, Nora A. 2009. Painters in Hanoi: An Ethnography of Vietnamese Art. Singapore: National University of Singapore Press.

Taylor, Philip. 2007. Cham Muslims of the Mekong Delta: Place and Mobility in the Cosmopolitan Periphery. Honolulu: University Hawai'i Press.

The Asahi Shinbun. 2018. Japan Dropping Nuclear Plant Export to Turkey over Rising Costs. December 6. http://www.asahi.com/ajw/articles/AJ201812060029.html (accessed February 2, 2019).

The Asahi Shinbun. 2019. Hitachi Halts British Nuclear Project as Energy Supply Crunch Looms. January 18. http://www.asahi.com/ajw/articles/AJ201901180011.html (accessed February 2, 2019).

Thurgood, Graham. 1999. *From ancient Cham to modern dialects: two thousand years of language contact and change.* Honolulu: University of Hawai'i Press.

Thurgood, Graham. 2007. From Malay to Sinitic: the restructuring of Tsat under intense language contact. *SEALS XII Papers from the 12th Annual Meeting of the Southeast Asian Linguistics Society 2002*, edited by R. Wayland et al., 129-136. Canberra, Australia: Pacific Linguistics, Research School of Pacific and Asian Studies, The Australian National University.

Tonkin, Elizabeth, McDonald, Maryon & Chapman, Malcolm. 1989. *History and Ethnicity, ASA Monographies, 27.* London: Routledge.

Tran Ky Phu'o'ng. 2006. *Cultural Resource and Heritage Issues of Historic Champa States in Vietnam: Champa Origins, Reconfirmed Nomenclatures, and Preservation of States.* Asia Research Institute working paper series, No. 75. Singapore: Asia Research Institute.

Trần Quốc Vượng. 2011. Chapter 10: Việt-Cham cultural contacts. In Trần Kỳ Phu'o'ng & B. Lockhart (eds.), *The Cham of Vietnam: History Society and Art*, 263-276. Singapore: NUS Press.

Truong Van Mon. 2008. *Historical Relations between Champa and the Malay Peninsula during 17th to 19th Century: A Study on Development of Raja Praong Ritual.* M. A. thesis. Department of History, Faculty of

Arts and Social Sciences, University of Malaya, Kuala Lumpur.
Tu Wei-Ming. 1994. Cultural China: The Periphery as the Center. In T. W. Ming (ed.), *The Living Tree: Meaning of Being Chinese Today*, 1-34. Stanford: Stanford University Press. (Originally published in the spring 1991 issue of *Daedalus*, Vol. 120, No. 2, The Proceedings of the American Academy of Arts and Sciences.)
Vickery, Michael. 2009. A Short History of Champa. In A. Hardy, M. Cucarzi & P. Zolese (eds.), *Champa and the Archaeology of Mỹ So'n (Vietnam)*, 45-60. Singapore: NUS Press.
Viet Nam News. 1997. Dang Hung Revives Exotic Cham Dance. September 10.
Viet Nam News. 1998. July 7, July 17, July 18, August.
Volk, Nancy. 1979. A Temporary Community in a Temporary World. Ph. D. Dissertation at Department of Anthropology, University of Washington.
Wade, Geoff. 1993. On the Possible Cham Origin of the Philippine Scripts. *Journal of Southeast Asian Studies*, 24 (1): 44-87.
Wallman, Sandra. 1979. Introduction: The Scope for Ethnicity. In S. Wallman (ed.), *Ethnicity at Work*, 1-16. London: Macmillan.
Weber, Nicolas. 2012. The destruction and assimilation of Campa (1832–35) as seen from Cam sources. *Journal of Southeast Asian Studies,* 43 (1): 158-180.
Williams, Brakette. 1989. A Class Act: Anthropology and the Race to Nation across Ethnic Terrain. *Annual Review of Anthropology,* 18: 401-444.
Wolters, Oliver W. 1999. *History, culture, and religion in Southeast Asian perspectives*. Cornell Ithaca: Southeast Asia Program Publications. (Original edition published in 1982 by the Institute of Southeast Asian Studies, Singapore.)
Wong, Danny Tze-Ken. 2013. The Cham arrivals in Malaysia. *Archipel,* 85: 151-165.
Woodside, Alexander. 1971. *Vietnam and Chinese Model: A Comparative Study of Nguyen and Ch'ing Civil Government in the First Half of the Nineteenth Century*. Cambridge, Mass.: Harvard University Press.
Yamagata, Mariko (山形真理子). 2011. Chapter 3: Trà kiệu during the second and third centuries CE: The foundaiton of Linyi from an archaeological perspective. In Trần Kỳ Phu'o'ng & B. Lockhard (eds.), *The Cham of Vietnam: History, society and art*, 81-101. Singapore: NUS Press.
Ysa, Osman. 2002. *Oukoubah: Justice for the Cham Muslims under the*

Democratic Kampuchea Regime. Phnom Penh: Documentation Center of Cambodia.

Ysa, Osman. 2006. *The Cham rebellion: Survivors' stories from the villages.* Phnom Penh: Documentation Center of Cambodia.

Zain bin Musa, Mohamad. 2008. Dynamics of Faith: Imam Musa in the Revival of Islam Teaching in Cambodia. In O. Farouk & H. Yamamoto (eds.), *Islam at the Margins: The Muslims of Indochina,* 59-69. CIAS Discussion Paper No. 3. Kyoto, Japan: Center for Integrated Area Studies, Kyoto University.

Zain bin Musa, Mohamad. 2011. History of Education among the Cambodian Muslim. *Malaysian Journal of History, Politics, and Strategies Studies,* 38 (1): 81-105.

Vietnamese language

Bảovệtôquốc blog. http://baovetoquoc.blogspot.com.au/2012/06/appealtojapanese (accessed Feburary 3, 2013; site now discontinued).

Đặng Hùng. 1998. *Bu'ó'c Đầu Tìm Hiểu Phục Hồi Múa Cung Đình Chăm (The Steps of Understanding and Reconstructing Cham Court Dance).* Thành Phố Hồ Chí Minh (Ho Chi Minh City): Trung Tăm Văn Hóa Dân Tộc Thành Phố Hồ Chí Minh (The Centre of Ethnic Culture of Ho Chi Minh City).

Dohamide & Dorohiem. 2004. *Bangsa Champa: Tìm về một cội nguồn cánh xa (The Nation of Champa: Searching for a far root).* California: Southeast Asian Culture and Education Foundation & VIET Foundation.

Inrasara. 1993. *Văn Học Chăm (Cham Literature).* Thành Phố Hồ Chí Minh (Ho Chi Minh City): Nhà Xuất Bản Văn Họa Dân Tộc Thành Phố Hồ Chí Minh. (Ho Chi Minh City ethnic culture publishing house).

Mạc Đu'ò'ng. 1978. Chủ nghĩa thụ'c dân mó'i và vấn dân tộc it ghu'ò'i ở' Nam Việt Nam 1954–1975 (*Nhũ'ng vấn đề Dân tộc học ở' miền nam Việt Nam (Several Problems of Ethnology in Southern Vietnam).* Thành phố Hồ Chí Minh (Ho Chi Minh City): Ban Dân tộc, Viện Khoa học Xã hội tại Thành phố Hồ Chí Minh (Office of Ethnic groups, Institute of Social Sciences in Ho Chi Minh City).

Ngôn Vĩnh. 1982. *FULRO?* Nhà Xuất Bản Công An Nhân Dân (The People's Public Security Publishing House).

Nguyễn Hồng Du'o'ng (ed.) 2007. *Một số vấn đề co' bản về Tôn Giáo Tín Ngu'õ'ng của Đôăng Bào Chăm o' Hai tỉnh Bình Thuận Ninh Thuận Hiện Nay (Contemporary problems relating to the religious beliefs among the Cham communities in two provinces of Binh Thuan and Ninh*

Thuan). Hà Nội (Hanoi): Nhà Xuất Bản Khoa Học Xả Hội (Social Science Publishing House).

Nguyễn Kim Loan. 2007. *Họa Sĩ Việt Nam: Chân Dung & Sáng Tạo (Vietnamese Artists: their profile and works)*. Thành Phố Hồ Chí Minh (Ho Chi Minh City): Nhà Xuất Bản Mỹ Thuật (Art Publishing House).

Nguyễn Trắc Dĩ. 1969. *Tìm Hiểu Phong-Trào Tranh – Đấu FULRO (Understanding resistance movement of FULRO)*. Saigon: Bộ Phát Triển Sắc Tộc (Ministry for Development of Ethnic Minority People).

Nguyễn Tuấn Triết. 1989. Phong trào đấu tranh chống đế quốc xâm lu'o'c của đồng bào o' tỉnh Thuận Hải (A Movement of Anti Imperial Invasion among the Cham People in Thuận Hải province). In Phan Xuân Biên et al. (eds.), *Ngu'o'i Châm o' Thuận Hải (Cham People in Thuan Hai Province)*, 325-347. Thành Phố Hồ Chí Minh: So' văn hóa thông tin Thuận Hải.

Nguyễn Văn Luận. 1974. *Ngu'ò'i Chàm Hồi-Giáo Miền Tây Nam-Phần Việt-Nam (Western Muslim Cham of Southern Vietnam)*. Sài Gòn (Saigon): Bộ Văn Hóa Giáo Dục và Thanh Niên (Ministry of Culture, Education and Youth).

Phan An. 1989. Ngu'ò'i Chăm Thuận Hải trong Chặng Đu'ò'ng Đầu Tiên Xây Dụ'ng Chủ Nghĩa Xã Hội (Cham people in Thuan Hai Province in the beginning of the way to establish Socialist society). In Phan Xuân Biên et al. (eds.), *Ngu'o'i Châm o' Thuận Hải (Cham People in Thuan Hai Province)*, 348-364. Thành Phố Hồ Chí Minh: So' văn hóa thông tin Thuận Hải (Office of Culture and Information of Ninh Thuan Province).

Phan Lạc Tuyên. 1993. *Lịch Sử' Bang Giao Việt Nam – Đông Nam Á tru'ó'c Công Nguyên đến thế kỷ XIX (The History of Internatioanl Relations of Vietnam and Southeast Asia: Before Christ to the 19th Century)*. Thành Phố Hồ Chí Minh (Ho Chi Minh City): Thành Phố Hồ Chí Minh' Bố Giáo Dục và Đào Tạo Viện Đào Tạo Mở: Rộng Khoa Đông Nam Á Học.

Phan Thị Yến Tuyết. 1993. *Nhà o' Trang Phục Ăn Uống của các Dân Tộc vùng Đông Bằng Sông Cù'u Long (Housing, clothing and diet of the people of the Mekong Delta)*. Thành Phố Hồ Chí Minh (Ho Chi Minh City): Nhà Xuất Bản Khoa Học Xã Hội (Social Sciences Publishing house).

Phan Văn Dốp & Nguyễn Thị Nhung. 2006. *Cộng Đồng Ngu'ò'i Chăm Hồi Giáo o' Nam Bộ Trong Quan Hệ gió'i và Phát Triển (Gender relationship and development among the Muslim Cham in South)*. Hà Nội (Hanoi): Nhà Xuất Bản Nông Nghiệp (Agriculture Publishing House).

Phan Xuân Biên. 1989. Gia Đình và Hôn Nhấn của Ngu'ò'i Chăm ỏ' Thuận Hải (Family and Marriage of the Cham people in Thuan Hai Province). In Phan Xuân Biên et al. (eds.), *Ngu'o'i Châm o' Thuận Hải (Cham People in Thuận Hải Province)*, 164-200. TP. Hồ Chí Minh (Ho Chi Minh City): So' văn hóa thông tin Thuận Hải (Office of Culture and Information of Ninh Thuan Province).

Thành Phần. 2007. *Danh Mục thu' Tịch chăm ỏ' Việt Nam (The Catalogue of Cham Manuscripts in Vietnam)*. TP. Hồ Chí Minh (Ho Chi Minh City): Nhà Xuất Bản Trẻ (Children's Publishing House).

Trần Quốc Vuợng. 1995. Miền Trung Việt Nam và Văn Hóa Chămpa (Central Vietnam and Culture of Champa). *Nghiện Cú'u Đông Nam Á (Southeast Asian Studies)*, 21: 8-24.

Trần Thị Minh Thu. Khat quát về Hòi giáo và Hòi giáo ỏ' Việt Nam. tgcp.gov.vn/Plus.aspx/vi/News/38/0/162/0/954/KHAT_QUAT_VE_H OI_GIAO_VA_HOI_GIAO_O_VIET_NAM (accessed December 2, 2011).

Tru'o'ng Hũ'u Quỳnh et al. 2002. *Đại Cu'o'ng Lịch Sủ' Việt Nam*. Hà Nội (Hanoi): Nhà Xuất Bản Giáo Dục (Education Publishing House).

Japanese language

Arima Tetsuo (有馬哲夫). 2008. *原発・正力・CIA：機密文書で読む昭和裏面史 (Genpatsu, Shouriki, CIA: Kimitsubunsho de yomuShowa Rimenshi) (Nuclear Power, Shouriki, CIA)*. 東京(Tokyo): 新潮社 (Shinchosha).

Asahi Shinbun (朝日新聞) (Asahi newspaper). 201. 社説 (Shasetsu) (Editorials) ベトナムに原発、国益不明の輸出やめよ(Betonamu ni Genpatsu Kokueki Fumei no Yushutu Yameyo) (Stop Exporting Nuclear Power Plants to Vietnam, whose National Benefits are Unclear). August 24.

Asahi Shinbun Digital (朝日新聞デジタル). 2013 (accessed February 3, 2013).

Asahi Shinbun Tokubetsuhodobu (朝日新聞特別報道部). 2012. *プロメテウスの罠：明かされなかった福島原発事故の事実* (Purometeusu no wana: akasarenakatta Fukushim genpatsujiko no jijitsu）東京 (Tokyo)：朝日新聞社/学研パブリッシング(Asahi Shinbunsha /Gakken publishing).

Chang Hsiang-Yi. 1974. 南宋時代の市舶司貿易に関する一考察 (Nanso jidai no shihakushiboueki nikansuru ichikosatsu) (The Examination of Trade Carried out through the Shih-po-ssu-seen during the Southern Sung Dynasty). In 青山博士古希記念宋代史論集 *(Aoyama Hakushi Koki Kinen Sodaishi Ronshu) (A festschrift for Dr. Aoyma on his 70th birthday – collection of historical studies on Song dynasty)*, 263-294. 東京 (Tokyo): 初心書房 (Shoshin Shobo).

Endo Masayuki（遠藤正之）. 1996. 10-15 世紀チャンパ王国の構造 (10-15 seiki Chanpa oukoku no

kozo) (The Political Structure of the Champa Kingdom between the 10th and the 15th Century). 東洋史学論集 *(Toyoshigaku ronshu) (The Collection of Studies of Eastern History)*, 立教大学大学院 (Rikkyo daigaku daigakuin) (The Graduate School of Rikkyo University), 2: 73-91.

Fukushima Project Iinkai (Fukushima プロジェクト委員会) (The Committee of Fukushima Project). 2012. *Fukushima レポート：原発事故の本質 (Fukushima Repoto: Genpatsujiko no honshitsu) (The Fukushima Report: Realities of Nuclear Reactor Accidents)*. 東京 (Tokyo): 日経 BP コンサルティング(Nikkei BP Consulting).

Gensuikin (原水禁) (Japanese National Congress Against Atomic Hydrogen Bombs). http://www.gensuikin.org/data/genpatuichiran.html (accessed February 2, 2012).

Henmi Yo (辺見庸). 2012. 徹底的な破壊から光 (Tetteitekina hakai kara hikari) (The light after the complete destruction). In 徳間書店出版局編 (Tokushimashoten shuppankyoku hen) (Tokushimashoten shuppankyoku ed.) この国はどこで間違えたのか：沖縄と福島から見えた日本 *(Konokuniha dokode machigaetanoka: Okinawa to Fukushima kara mieta Nihon) (Since when this country has made a mistake: Japan through Okinawa and Fukushima)*. pp:249-291. 東京 (Tokyo): 徳間書店 (Tokumashoten).

Higuchi Hideo (樋口英夫). 1995. *風景のない国・チャンパ王国　遺された末裔を追って (Fukei no nai kuni Chanpa oukoku: Nokosareta matsuei o otte) (A Country Without Landscapes—Kingdom of Cham: visiting its descendents)*. 東京 (Tokyo): 平河出版社 (Hirakawa shuppannsha).

Higuchi Hideo (樋口英夫). 1999. *チャンパ：歴史・末裔・建築 (Chanpa: Rekishi—Matsuei—Kenchiku) (Champa: History—Descendants—Architectures)*. 東京(Tokyo)：めこん (Mekon).

Ito Masako (伊藤正子). 2008. *民族という政治：ベトナム民族分類の政治と現在 (Minzoku toiu Seiji: Betonamu Minzokubunrui no Rekishi to Genzai) (Politics of Ethnic Classi)fication in Vietnam: History of Ethnic classification in Vietnam)*. 東京 (Tokyo): 理想社 (Risosha). (English translation of the book titled *Politics of Ethnic Classification in*

Vietnam published in 2013, translated by Minako Sato, by Kyoto University Press and Trans Pacific Press.)

Ito Masako (伊藤正子). 2009a. 『先住民』を認めることができないベトナム (『Senjumin』o mitumerukotogadekinai Betonamu) (The Vietnamese cannot recognize "indigenous people"). 人権と部落問題 *(Jinken to buraku mondai) (Human rights and Buraku problems)*, 61 (1): 33-41.

Ito Masako (伊藤正子). 2009b. ベトナムの『民族法』の行方－『伝統文化』の保護から少数民族管理へ (Betonamu no "Minzokuho" no yukue – "Dentobunka" no hogo kara Shosuminzoku kanri he) (Future of "Law of Ethnic Groups" – from "protection of tradition" to control of ethnic minority people). 東南アジア－歴史と文化 *(Tonanajia – Rekishi to Bunka) (Southeast Asia – History and Culture)*, 東南アジア学会 (Tonanajia gakkai) (Association of Southeast Asian Studies), No.38: 46-63.

Ito Masako (伊藤正子). 2011. 私の視点 (Watashi no shiten) (My Opinion). *朝日新聞 (Asahi Shinbun)* (Asahi newspaper), October 7.

Ito Masako (伊藤正子). 2012. ここが原発の輸出先だ (Kokoga Genpatu no Yushutsusaki da) (Here is where we export the nuclear plant). 朝日新聞ウィークリー *AERA (Asahi Shinbun Weekly AERA)*, June 4, p. 45.

Ito Masako (伊藤正子) & Yoshi-i, Miwako (吉井美和子) (eds.). 2015. 原発輸出の欺瞞：日本とベトナム、「友好」の舞台裏 *(Genpatsuyushutu no giman: Nihon to Betonamu,「yuko」no butaiura) (The deceit of Japan's export of nuclear program: the backstage of amity between Japan and Vietnam)*. 東京 (Tokyo): 明石書店 (Akashi Shoten).

Kainuma Hiroshi (開沼博). 2011.「フクシマ」論：原子力ムラはなぜうまれたのか (「Fukushima」ron: Genshiryokumura ha naze umaretanoka (The theory of "Fukushima": How was the nuclear village conceived). 東京 (Tokyo)：青土社 (Seidosha).

Loomba, Ania (ルーンバ、アーニャ). 2001. 吉原ゆかり訳 (Yoshino Yukari trans.) ポストコロニアル理論入門 (Posuto koroniaru riron nyumon) 東京 (Tokyo)：松柏社 (Shohakusha) (Originally published in 1998 in English as *Colonialism/Post colonialism*, London: Routledge).

Momoki Shiro (桃木至朗). 1990. 10-15 世紀の南海交易とヴェトナム（10-15 seiki no Nankaikoueki to Vetonamu）(South China Sea Maritime Trade and Vietnam during the 10th–15th Centuries). 東洋史学論集 (Toyoshigaku ronshu) (Collection of theses on East Asian

History) (立教大学大学院) (Rikkyo daigaku daigakuin) (Graduate School, Rikkyo University), 2: 73-91.

Momoki Shiro (桃木至朗). 1994a. 新しいチャンパ史 (Atarashii Chanpashi) (The New History of Champa). In チャンパ王国の遺跡と文化 *(Chanpa oukoku no iseki to bunka)(The Historical Vestiges and Culture of Champa Kingdom).* 東京 (Tokyo): トヨタ財団 (The Toyota Foundation), pp.65-72.

Momoki Shiro (桃木至朗). 1994b. チャム族 (Chamu zoku) (The Cham ethnic group). *季刊民族学 (Kikan Minzokugaku)(Quarterly Anthropology),* No. 67: 20-37.

Momoki Shiro (桃木至朗). 1997. 東南アジア前近代国家研究の現在、チャンパーの場合 (Tonan ajia zenkindai kokka kenkyu no genzai, Chanpa no baai) (Studies of pre-modern states in Southeast Asia: a case of Studies of Champa). *東南アジア史の中の「中央」と「地方」に関する研究成果報告書 (Tonan ajiashi no 「chuo」 to 「chiho」 nikansuru kenkyu seika hokokusho) (The Research Report of Studies of "Center" and "Peripheries"),* 文部省科学研究費補助金 (Monbukagakukenkyuhi hojokin) (The research fund for scientific research by Ministry of Education), 研究課課題番号 (Kenkyuka kadaibango) (The funding number) 06041072.

Momoki Shiro (桃木至朗). 1999. *チャンパ:歴史・末裔・建築 (Chanpa: Rekishi ・ Matsuei ・ Kenchiku) (Champa: History, Descendants & Architecture).* 東京 (Tokyo): めこん (Mekon).

Momoki Shiro (桃木至朗). 2001. 東南アジアの海と陸：チャンパとチャム族のネットワーク(Tonan ajia no umi to riku: Chanpa to Chamu zoku no nettowaaku) (The ocean and the land of Southeast Asia: Champa and the Cham people's network). In 尾本恵市, 濱下武志, 村井吉敬, 家島彦一編 (Omoto Keiichi, Hamashita Takishi, Murai Yoshinori, Yajima Hikoichi, eds.) *海のアジア：島とひとのダイナミズム (Umi no ajia: Shima to hito no dainamizumu)(The Ocean of Asia: The Dynamism of islands and people).* 東京 (Tokyo): 岩波書店 (Iwanami shoten), pp. 61-84.

Nagai Yoshimi (永井義美). 2009. ベトナム社会主義共和国における民族意識の変容—チャンパの文化遺跡保護を中心に *(Betonamu shakaishugikyowakoku niokeru minzokuishiki no henyo – Chanpa no bunkaisekihogo o chushin ni) (Transformation of National Identity of Social Republic of Vietnam: Through Protection of the Champa Cultural Heritage).* 埼玉大学博士論文(Saitama daigaku hakaseronbun) (Ph. D. Dissertation, Saitama University).

Nakamura Rie (中村理恵). 2014. ヴェトナム、ニントゥアン省のチャ

ム族のリネージ調査から (Vetonamu, Nin toan sho no Chamu zoku no rineji chosa kara) (The studies on lineage amongst the Cham people in Ninh Thuan Province in Vietnam). *アジア文化研究所研究年報 (Ajia bunkakenkyjo kenkyunenpo) (Annual Journal of the Asian cultures Research Institute)*, No.49.

Nihon Genshiryoku Sangyo Kyokai (日本原子力産業協会) (Nihon genshiryoku sangyo kyokai) (Japan Atomic Industrial Forum, Inc.) (JAIF). http://www.jaif.or.jp/ja/nuclear_world/data/f0302.html (accessed February, 2012).

Nishimoto Yoichi (西本陽一). 2000. 北タイ・クリスチャン・ラフ族における民族関係の経験と自嘲の語り (Kita Tai・kurisuchan・Rafuzoku niokeru minzokukanke no keiken to jicho no katari) (Northern Thai Christian Lahu Narratives of Inferiority and Experience of Ethnic Power Relations). *民族学研究 (Minzokugaku kenkyu)(The Studies of Ethnology)*, Vol. 64, No. 4: 425-446.

Nomura Hiroya (野村浩也). 2005. *無意識の植民地主義：日本人の米軍基地と沖縄人 (Muishiki no shokuminchishugi: Nihonjin no beigunkichi to Okinawajin) (Unconscious Colonialism: US Military base for Japanese and the People of Okinawa).* 東京 (Tokyo): お茶の水書房 (Ochanomizu shobo).

Sakurai Yumio (桜井由躬雄). 1993. 地域からの世界史 第４巻 東南アジア(Chiiki karano sekaishi dai 4 kan Tonan ajia) (The World History from the Regions). 東京 (Tokyo): 朝日新聞 (Asahi shinbun).

Shige-eda Yutaka (重枝豊). 1994. チャンパ王国の遺跡 (Chanpa oukoku no iseki) (The Historical Vestiges of Champa Kingdom). *チャンパ王国の遺跡と文化 (Champa oukoku no iseki to bunka) (The Historical Vestiges and Culture of Champa Kingdom)*, 9-61. 東京 (Tokyo): トヨタ財団 (The Toyota Foundation).

Shige-eda Yutaka (重枝豊) & Tran Ky Phu'o'ng (チャン・キー・フォン). 1997. チャンパ遺跡：海に向かって立つ (*Chanpa iseki: Umi nimukatte tatsu) (The Champa Vestiges: Standing facing to the Sea).* 東京 (Tokyo): 連合出版 (Rengo Shuppan).

Shimizu Shuji (清水修二). 2012. カネの切れ目は好機 (Kane no kiremeha kouki) (It is a chance when the funding exhausted). In 徳間書店出版局編 (Tokumashoten shuppankyoku hen) (Tokumashoten Publishing office ed.) *この国はどこで間違えたのか：沖縄と福島から見えた日本(Konokuni ha dokode machigaetanoka: Okinawa to Fukushima karamieta Nihon) (Since when this country has made a mistake: Japan through Okinawa and Fukushima)*.東京 (Tokyo): 徳間書店 (Tokumashoten). pp:184-220.

Shin-e Toshihiko (新江俊彦). 1991. チャンパーの滅亡の年代について (Chanpaa no Metsubou no Nendai nitsuite) (About the date of the end of Champa). 白山史学 (Hakusanshigaku) (Hakusan Historical Studies), 27: 46-70.

Shin-e Toshihiko (新江俊彦). 2001a. 現代ベトナム小民族開発政策における国家と慣習法の間の距離：タイン・ファン「南越現代チャム族の慣習法と農村開発」解題 (Gendai Betonamu shousuminzoku kaihatuseisaku niokeru kokka to kanshuho no aidano kyori: Tain Fan 「Nanetu gendai Chamuzoku no kanshuho to nosonkaihatu」 Kaidai) (The distance between customary laws and the nation-state in the developmental policies among the contemporary Cham ethnic group:the annotated bibliography "The distance between the customary laws of the contemporary Cham people in southern Vietnam and development of the agrarian societies" by Tanh Phan). ベトナムの社会と文化 (Betonamu no shakai to bunka) (Vietnamese society and culture) 第3号：224-240.

Shin-e Toshihiko (新江俊彦). 2001b. 資料：現代ベトナムの民族政策文書 チャム人同胞に対する工作に関する中央書記局3号通知訳と解説(Shiryo: Gendai Betonamu no Minzoku Seisakubunsho: Chamujin doho nitaisuru Kousaku ni kansuru Chuou shokikyoku 3go tsuchi yaku to kaisetsu) (Resources: Contemporary Vietnam's official document on their ethnic minority people, The Notice No. 3 of the Central Politburo on policies toward Cham Nationalities, Translation and explanation). ベトナムの社会と文化 (Betonamu no Shakai to Bunka) (Vietnamese Society and Culture), No. 3: 241-251.

Shin-e Toshihiko (新江俊彦). 2007. ベトナムの少数民族定住政策史 (Betonamu no Shosuminzoku Teijuuseisakushi) (The Vietnamese History of Sedentarization Policies of Ethnic Minority people). Tokyo (東京): Fukyosha (風響社).

Shutoken Hangenpatu Rengo (首都圏反原発連合) (Metropolitan Coalition Against Nukes). http://coalitionagainstnukes.jp/ (accessed February 4, 2013).

Sugimoto Naojiro (杉本直次郎). 1956. チアムパの名に探る (Chiamupa no nanisaguru) (A Search of the Name of Champa). 東南アジア史研究 (The Studies of Southeast Asian History), 121-142. 東京 (Tokyo): 日本学術振興会 (Nippon Gakujutsu Shinkokai).

Takahashi Testuya (高橋哲哉). 2012. 犠牲のシステム 福島・沖縄 (Gisei no shisutemu Fukushima・Okinawa) (The system of sacrifice Fukushima・Okinawa). 集英社新書 (Shueisha shinsho) (Shueisha shinsho series). 東京 (Tokyo)：集英社 (Shueisha).

Takezawa Yasuko (竹沢泰子). 1988. アメリカ合衆国におけるステレオタイプとエスニシティ：広告とジョークに見られる民族像のダイナミックス (Amerika gasshukoku niokeru sutereotaipu to esunishiti: Kokoku to joku nimirareru minzokuzou no dainamikkusu) (Ethnic stereotypes in the USA: the Dynamics of images of the ethnic groups in advertisement and jokes). 民俗学研究 *(The Studies of Anthropology)*, Vol. 52, No. 4: 363-390.

Tasaka Kodo (田坂興道). 1952. 占城回教史序説：東南アジア回教史序説の一部として」(Chanpa kaikyo shi josetsu: Tonan ajia kaikyoushi josetsu no ichibu toshite) (A Brief History of Islam in Champa: A contribution to the History of Islam in Southeast Asia), 東方学 *(Eastern Studies)*, Vol. 4: 52-60.

Tokyo Shinbun （東京新聞） (Tokyo newspaper). http://www.tokyo-np.co.jp/article/politics/news/CK2013011702000105.html, (accessed February 2, 2013).

Trần Kỳ Phu'o'ng (チャン・キー・フォン). 1994. チャンパの彫刻芸術 (Chanpa no chokoku geijutsu) (The Art of Champa's Sculptures). チャンパ王国の遺跡と文化 *(Chanpa oukoku no iseki to bunka) (The Historical Vestiges and Culture of Champa Kingdom)*. 東京 (Tokyo): トヨタ財団 (The Toyota Foundation). pp101-108.

Yamamoto Nobuo (山本信夫), Hasebe Gakuji (長谷部楽爾), Aoyagi Yoji (青柳洋治), Ogawa Hidefumi (小川英文). 1993. ベトナム陶磁の編年的研究とチャンパ古窯の発掘調査：ゴーサイン古窯址群の発掘調査 (Betonamu Touji no Hennenteki kenkyu to Champa Koyo no Hakkutsu Chosa) (Studies of Vietnamese porcelain and ceramics in chronological order and the excavation of old Champa kiln). 上智アジア学 *(Jochi Ajia Gaku)*, 11: 163-180.

Yamamoto Tatsuro (山本達郎). 1975. ベトナム中国関係史 *(Betonamu Chugoku kankeishi) (History of Vietnamese Relationship to China)*. 東京 (Tokyo): 山川出版 (Yamakawa Shuppan).

Yao Takao (八尾隆生). 1995. 林邑、平成6-8年度文部省科学研究費補助金（国際学術研究）研究成果報告書 *(Rinyu, Heisei 6-8 nendo Monbushoukagakukenkyuuhi hojokin – Kokusaigakujutu kenky – Kenkyuseika hokokusho) (Linyi, The Report of the Research funded by Scientific Research Grant of Ministry of Education, 1994–1995)*. 大阪外国語大学 (Osaka gaikokugo daigaku) (Osaka foreign language University), 1: 1-28.

Yokokura Masayuki (横倉雅幸). 1993. ドンソンとサーフィン (Donson to Saafin) (Đông So'n and Sa Hùynh). 東南アジア：歴史と文化 *(Southeast Asia: History and Culture)*, No. 22: 152-172.

Yoshimoto Yasuko (吉本康子). 2010. イスラーム性とエスニック要素をめぐる交渉過程についての一考察:ベトナムにおけるチャム系ムスリムの事例を中心に (Isuramu sei to Esunikku yoso o meguru koshokatei nituiteno ichi kosatsu: Betonamu niokeru Chamu kei Musurimu no jirei o chushin ni) (A Study of Negotiating Process over Islamness and Ethnic Elements: a case of Cham Muslim in Vietnam). In (篠原啓方 編) (Shinohara Yirotaka ed.) *文化交渉による変容の諸相 (Bunkakosho niyoru Henyo no Shoso) (Various Acculturation through Cultural Exchange)*, 223-247. Osaka (大阪): Kansaidaigaku bunkakoshogaku kyoikukenkyu kyoten (関西大学文化交渉学教育研究拠点) (Institue for Cultural Interaction Studies, Kansai University).

Yoshioka Hitoshi (吉岡斉). 2011. *新版原子力の社会史:その日本的展開 (Shinban Genshiryoku no shakaishi: Sono Nihonteki Tenkai) (The New Edition Social History of Nuclear Power: Its Japanese Development)*. 東京 (Tokyo): 朝日新聞出版 (Asahi Shinbun Shuppann).

Yoshizawa Minami (吉沢南). 1982. *ベトナム現代史の中の諸民族 (Betonamu gendaishinonakano shominzok) (Ethnic Groups in the Modern Vietnamese History)*. 東京 (Tokyo): 朝日出版社(Asahi shuppansha).

Index

Abdul Latif Moulawi, 101
abstract painting, 162
Abu, 27
accident, 8, 9, 11, 119, 121, 149, 187
acculturation, 4
Acehnese, 35
Adams, Kathleen, 138
Adhan, 111
administrative autonomy, 64
agricultural technique, 41
agriculture, 47, 99, 173
Agroville, 48
ahier, 2, 13, 68, 80, 81, 84, 86, 89, 90, 91, 92, 95, 96, 97, 98, 100, 105, 176, 177
Aisah, 4, 5, 63, 113, 117, 118, 119, 120, 121, 139, 140, 141, 142, 152
akafir, 92, 95, 96
akhar thrah, 69, 70, 71, 104, 105, 106, 109
Al-Dimashqi, 27
Ali, 27
alienation, 13, 155, 158
Allah, 2, 74, 103, 117, 121, 133
aloeswood, 24
Âm Nhân, 168
amanta, 20
Amaravati, 17
American, 50, 51, 180, 186
An Giang, 1, 3, 4, 5, 63, 64, 65, 104, 106, 108, 110, 113, 117
An Nho'n, 68, 95, 101, 168
ancient kingdom, 1, 37
Angkor, 108, 110
animism, 21

annexation of Champa, 36
anthropologist, 27, 35, 47, 70, 79, 171, 186, 187
anti-government movement, 48
áo sida, 108
Aomori, 188
Aoyagi Yuji, 32
Apsara dance, 139, 143, 144, 146, 158, 159
Arab, 26, 27, 28, 29, 33, 80, 92, 95, 104, 106, 109, 111
Arabia,, 29
Arabic inscription, 28
Arabic script, 92, 109, 111, 121
archaeological research, 43
archaeological site, 16, 43
archaeology, 7
architecture, 31
aristocrat, 40, 116, 144
army, 32, 33, 38, 123, 150
Art College (*Cao Đẳng Mỹ Thuật*), 174
art gallery, 163, 171
art market, 161, 163, 171, 182
artisan, 28
artwork, 13, 162, 177
Asahi newspaper, 10, 12, 189
Asahi Shinbun Weekly AERA, 12
ASEAN, 10, 152
assimilation, 33, 34, 42, 44, 47, 48, 50, 66, 79
Association of Ethnologists, 60
Association of Malays of Cochinchina, 124
atomic bomb, 190
attaché of the cabinet of the Prime Minister's Office, 127

Australia, 2
Austroasiatic, 6
Austronesian, 86
Austronesiatic, 1, 6
authenticity, 138
autonomous zone, 51, 54
autonomy, 28, 34, 42, 46, 47, 51, 54
awal, 13, 68, 75, 80, 81, 84, 86, 87, 89, 90, 91, 92, 93, 95, 96, 97, 98, 100, 105, 176, 177
Aymonier, Étienne, 25, 71
Ayutthaya, 27, 35
azmat., 121
Ba Cum, 128
Bách Khoa, 128
backward, 39, 40, 56, 79, 104, 138, 147, 180, 185, 188, 189
Bahnar, 4, 48, 50
Bajaraka movement, 48, 51
baju kurung, 108, 141
Balamon, 2, 21, 72, 73, 74, 75, 77, 78, 79, 80, 81, 82, 84, 86, 87, 89, 90, 92, 95, 96, 97, 98, 99, 100, 105, 109, 120, 134, 171, 175, 180, 181
Balinese, 82, 86
Ban Cao Nguyên, 126
Ban Krua, 35
Bangkok, 35, 131
Bangsa Champa, 134, 135
bánh xèo, 112
Bani, 2, 21, 27, 66, 72, 74, 75, 76, 77, 79, 80, 81, 82, 83, 86, 88, 89, 92, 93, 95, 96, 97, 98, 99, 100, 101, 102, 103, 104, 105, 120, 121, 134, 168
Bani scholar, 92
Bảo Đại, 46
Bassac river, 130
Bàu Trúc, 165, 171, 173
Baudesson, Henry, 39
Bawean, 114, 115
Bay of Bengal, 21

Bay of Tonkin, 31
Beijing, 52
Belo, Jane, 82, 86
Bến Tre, 165
Benedict, Paul, 35, 186
Bengal, 19
bhut, 119
bimong, 72, 74
bingun, 80
Bình Định, 14, 17, 32, 43, 143
Bình Nghĩa, 79
Bình Thuận, 2, 3, 17, 24, 32, 101, 106, 150, 174
black magic, 122
Black Thai, 186
blogger, 12
Blood, Doris, 70, 81
Bo Tri-tri,, 32
Bombay, 116
bone, 75, 79, 91
Brahman, 75
bride price, 30
British colonial government, 130
British Malaya, 115, 130
Bronson, Bennet, 22, 23
Buddhism, 20, 26, 75
Buddhist, 20, 26, 31, 95, 121
buffalo sacrifice, 56
buffer, 41
Bùi Xuân Phái, 164
bun bat, 118, 119
Buổi sáng, 126
Buôn Ma Thuột, 45, 53
Bureau of Highland Affairs, 49
bureaucratic maze, 66
burial, 56, 74
Burmese, 35
Cabaton, Antoine, 26, 30, 71
Caliph Usman III, 27
Cambodia, 2, 4, 24, 27, 29, 30, 33, 35, 36, 49, 52, 58, 108, 109, 111, 112, 119, 120, 121, 131, 134, 144, 157

Cambodian Cham, 24
Can Sen So, 48
Cần Thơ', 101
Canada, 2
canton, 46
cao nguyên, 44
Cao Thị Đu'ọ'c, 165, 167, 172
capital, 2, 5, 11, 16, 25, 27, 31, 32, 35, 38, 108, 171
Catholic, 45, 62, 129
Center for Vietnamese and Southeast Asian Studies, 61, 62, 63
Central Committee, 56, 57, 59, 173
Central Highland minority people, 42, 47
Central Highlands, 10, 24, 44, 45, 46, 47, 48, 53, 59, 60, 108, 128, 147, 150, 154, 155
Central Intelligence Agency (CIA), 51
Central Vietnam, 2, 17, 26, 31, 37
Chà Bàn (Trà Bàn), 38
Cham ambassador, 27
Cham artist, 13, 155, 167, 171
Cham book, 70, 71
Cham cultural center, 50, 59, 62, 65, 179
Cham culture, 31, 33, 58, 63, 70, 71, 103, 105, 137, 139, 142, 143, 144, 145, 146, 154, 155, 169, 177, 180, 181, 182
Cham dance, 134, 140, 142, 143, 145, 159, 171, 180
Cham Day, 1
Cham diaspora, 29, 187
Cham ethnic group, 4, 7, 95, 100, 111, 113, 165
Cham ethnic minority, 12, 62, 123, 154, 165, 171, 173
Cham harat, 75
Cham Hroi, 4
Cham jat, 75

Cham language, 25, 35, 58, 70, 71, 111, 114, 186
Cham Language Editing Committee (BBSSCC), 58, 61, 63, 64, 70, 150
Cham migration, 35
Cham music, 142
Cham official, 59
Cham painter, 146, 167, 171
Cham royal court dance, 143, 144, 145, 146, 159
Cham royal treasure, 25
Cham scholar, 27, 52, 65, 70, 71, 75, 106
Cham script, 14, 17, 58, 70, 71, 99, 153
Cham Sea, 26
Cham society, 5
Cham tradition, 34, 103, 104, 139, 145, 153, 171, 177, 180
Cham unit, 179
Cham village, 21, 46, 49, 58, 64, 65, 68, 69, 70, 75, 77, 79, 81, 106, 107, 111, 129, 165, 167, 171, 173, 174, 176, 180
Cham weaving, 156, 158
Chambert-Loir, Henri, 29
Champa, 1, 2, 4, 7, 12, 13, 14, 16, 17, 18, 19, 20, 21, 22, 23, 24, 25, 26, 27, 28, 29, 30, 31, 32, 33, 34, 35, 36, 37, 38, 39, 40, 41, 42, 43, 51, 71, 72, 73, 79, 89, 99, 100, 104, 105, 106, 108, 109, 110, 114, 115, 125, 126, 133, 137, 139, 142, 143, 144, 151, 152, 154, 159, 165, 168, 173, 177, 180, 182, 186, 187, 190
Champa art, 171
Champa ceramics, 32
Champa-Highlands Liberation Front, 51
Champasak, 51

Chanda, Nayan, 52
Châu Đốc, 4, 5, 49, 101, 106, 110, 121, 126, 130, 150
Châu Giang, 107, 109, 111, 118, 119, 121, 150
Châu Phong, 131
Chế Bồng Nga, 31
Chế Mân, 30
Chế Thị Kim Trung, 167, 169, 172, 177, 178
Chef de Canton, 46
Chef des Malais, 130
Chiêm Thành, 23, 110
chieu pang, 97, 98
childbirth, 91
China, 6, 14, 16, 17, 20, 21, 22, 23, 26, 27, 30, 31, 32, 35, 41, 110, 136, 139, 186
Chinese, 6, 16, 20, 22, 27, 28, 32, 35, 41, 47, 80, 81, 86, 110, 113, 122, 128, 145, 185, 186
Chinese ethnic group, 113
Chinese influence, 20
Chinese model, 21
Chinese Muslim, 28
Chinese trader, 46
Chợ Lớn, 122, 128
Christian, 27, 29, 75, 134, 151
Christian civilizing project, 55
Chu Ru, 25, 45
Chuengsatiansup, 67
Chvea, 111, 112, 134
citizen, 11, 136, 152, 179, 190
civilizing project, 55, 56, 144, 145, 146, 147, 152
class struggle, 37, 38, 40
Coedès, George, 2, 19, 20, 29
Cold War, 9
collectivization, 56
Collins, William, 24, 28, 29, 52, 109, 112, 134
colonial, 45, 46, 101, 159
colonialism, 187, 189, 190

colony of India, 19
commercialization, 157
Committee for Ethnic Minorities and Mountainous Areas, 59, 60
Committee of Highlands, 126
commodification of minority, 161
Communist civilizing project, 55, 56, 144
Communist Party, 47, 50, 53, 56, 57, 59, 66, 123, 162, 168, 173
complementarity, 84, 86
complementary dualism, 87
Condominas, George, 47
confederation of principalities, 17
Confucian, 40, 55, 81, 145
Confucian civilizing project, 55
Confucian-based tradition, 145
conscription, 127, 128
conversion, 28, 29, 30, 75, 112
convert, 28, 29, 75, 101, 102, 103, 104, 112, 113, 128
Cornell University, 50
Coromandel, 116
corvée, 23, 24, 45, 46
cosmology, 68, 80, 81, 84
Council of Hakim, 130, 132
coup d'etat, 48, 49
cousin, 5, 107, 139
cremation, 25, 74, 75, 79, 90, 99, 175, 180
cross-cousin marriage, 107
Cù lao Chàm, 27
Cù Mông Pass, 32, 38
cultural agent, 154, 159, 160
cultural antiquity, 151
cultural diversities, 7
cultural exchange, 36, 37, 41, 42
cultural marker, 142, 158
culture, 12, 13, 34, 42, 47, 57, 79, 104, 122, 134, 137, 138, 145, 155, 181
cultureless, 106
curse, 30, 121

custom, 5, 28, 30, 34, 50, 56, 57, 59, 60, 65, 77, 79, 103, 115, 137, 138, 180
Đà Lạt, 10, 70, 155, 156
Đà Nẵng, 2, 26, 116, 159
Đa Phu'ó'c, 131
Đại Việt, 14, 31, 139, 144
Đắk Lắk, 23
Dam Klan, 46
Dam San, 173
Dampier, William, 33
dân tộc, 6, 7, 13, 136, 137, 142, 145, 147, 151, 152, 185
Dân tộc Chàm Lu'ọ'c sủ', 109, 126
dance, 13, 31, 62, 92, 134, 138, 139, 140, 141, 142, 160, 168
Đặng Hùng, 141, 143, 144
Đàng Năng Thọ', 146, 171, 172, 173, 174, 176, 177, 179, 180, 182, 183
Đặng Nghiêm Vạn, 38, 39, 59
Đang Quang Trung, 56
Danh Mal, 124
dark skin, 147
Darlac, 45, 46
definition, 6
DEGA-Cham, 51
Dekkan, 20
Demak's War, 29
Democratic Republic of Vietnam, 54
democratic system, 190
descendants, 1, 35, 73, 111, 115, 133, 186
diaspora, 6
dichotomy, 75, 100, 151
Dictionaire de l'ethnologie et de l'anthropologie, 186
Điên Biên Phú', 158
Dinh Ngoc Thang, 163
Directive 214, 56
Directive 68, 57
Director of Logistics, 127

discourse, 13, 123, 148
Dohamide, 42, 49, 75, 117, 124, 125, 126, 127, 128, 129, 130, 132, 134
đổi mó'i, 13, 56, 103, 152, 153, 155, 162, 180, 183
Domaine de la Couronne du Pays, 46
Đông Du mosque, 116
Đông Du street, 101
Đông Du'o'ng, 26
Đồng Khỏ'i street, 101, 163
Đông So'n, 16
Dorohiem, 42, 124, 125, 128, 130
downstream, 22
dry-rice horticulture, 45
Du'o'ng Bích Hạnh, 186
dualism, 13, 105, 176, 177, 190
dualistic, 75, 81
Dutch Indonesia, 115
dysentery, 48
eaglewood, 24
earth spirit, 21
earthquake, 8, 9, 38, 187
East Asia, 26
East China Sea, 189
Eastern Han, 16
École Française d'Extrême-Orient, 1, 7, 25, 52
economic, 6, 10, 17, 22, 24, 29, 34, 39, 44, 47, 55, 56, 57, 59, 60, 107, 124, 152, 153, 155, 187, 189
economic assistance, 10
Ede, 4, 24, 45, 49, 173
Egypt, 32
electricity, 8, 11
emic, 9, 12, 38, 177
Emiko Stock, 27
Emishi, 188
Endo Masayuki, 17
endogamy, 108
Engels, Friedrich, 39

English, 4, 18, 38, 45, 50, 103, 155, 180
English subjects, 116
entrepôt, 31, 32
Eriksen, Thomas, 186
eroticization, 145
esoteric Buddhism, 26
ethnic classification, 6, 7, 136, 184, 185
ethnic conflict, 59
Ethnic Council, 60
ethnic group, 5, 6, 7, 24, 36, 44, 48, 49, 54, 57, 59, 60, 65, 66, 75, 79, 100, 114, 123, 136, 137, 138, 145, 147, 149, 152, 173, 185, 186, 187
ethnic identity, 6, 13, 14, 35, 104, 105, 106, 110, 113, 114, 117, 123, 132, 133, 134, 136, 137, 138, 142, 146, 151, 182, 184, 187, 190
ethnic information, 65
ethnic minority, 7, 12, 13, 38, 42, 44, 48, 49, 50, 53, 54, 56, 57, 60, 65, 66, 67, 113, 123, 124, 126, 128, 133, 137, 138, 145, 147, 148, 149, 152, 153, 154, 155, 156, 158, 159, 160, 161, 162, 163, 165, 167, 168, 173, 174, 182, 183, 190
ethnic minority culture, 160, 171, 182
ethnic minority policy, 44, 53, 66, 133
ethnic reality, 7
ethnic vocabularies, 177
ethnicity, 6
ethnologist, 6
ethno-nationalism, 51
ethno-nationalist movement, 47, 54, 126
evolution scheme, 79, 148
exogamy, 103, 107
exorcism, 121
Fajr, 111
fall of Champa, 33, 36, 37, 38, 39, 40, 41, 46, 186
family evolution, 39
fan dance, 139, 141
Farouk, Omar, 36
Fatimi, 26
fertility, 80
festival, 1, 52, 61, 138, 154, 168, 169, 170, 180
fetching water dance, 139, 140, 141
feudal, 38, 39, 40
fiancé, 5
field research, 7, 35, 38, 44, 57, 59, 61, 62, 63, 64, 65, 66, 69, 73, 106, 109, 137, 145, 147, 186
final solution, 13
First Indochina War, 21, 26, 46
folk dance, 141, 144
folk song, 99, 107
folk tale, 58
food taboo, 74
foreign Muslim, 28, 103, 116
foreign scholar, 62, 65
foreign tourist, 156, 157, 163
foreigner, 4, 28, 46, 50, 77, 103, 109, 124, 152, 162
fortune teller, 124
fortune-telling, 129
Foucault, Michel, 186
France, 1, 2, 45, 46, 156, 186
Franc-Rhade school, 45
French, 21, 46, 50, 51, 54, 70, 108, 124, 126
French anthropology, 186
French colonial administration, 45, 46, 47, 116, 127
French colonial appointment, 130
French colonial government, 115
French colonial Orientalist, 19
French colonial period, 2, 45, 129, 132

French colonialist, 39, 46
French control, 45, 46
French governor, 101
French Indochina, 109
French influence, 47
French missionary, 46, 50
French Orientalist, 71
French period, 150
French plantation, 45
French priest, 179
French protection, 46
French scholar, 2, 26, 71, 75
Front for the Liberation of Champa, 48
Front for the Liberation of Northern Cambodia, 48
Front for the Liberation of the Champa Highlands, 49
Front for the Liberation of the South Vietnamese Highlands, 49
Front for the Struggle of the Cham, 49
Fukushima, 8, 9, 10, 11, 187, 188, 189
Fukushima disaster, 8
Fukushima nuclear reactor, 8, 9
Fukushima plant, 9
funeral, 56, 77, 78, 79, 89, 90, 91, 93, 99, 173
Ganga Raja, 19
Ganges region, 19
Ganges valley, 20
Garde Indigene Moi, 45
gaze, 163, 168, 171
gender attribute, 82, 92, 95, 96
General Commissariat for Land Development, 47
Geneva Agreements, 47
genuine culture, 138
Geoff Wade, 14
Germany, 156
ghost, 119, 120
Gia Long, 34

Giran, 46
Gladney, Dru, 182, 185
Glover, Ian, 16
Gò Cầm, 16
god Siva, 143, 168
godparents, 91
grape, 68
grassroots organization, 67
Guangzhou, 31
guarantor, 128
Gulf of Siam, 33
Gupta dynasty, 20, 26
Guru, 120, 121, 129
Guru Urang, 97, 120
Guy, John, 22
ha kleh., 119
Hai, 148, 149
Hải Phòng, 116
Hải Vân Pass, 30
Hainan, 31, 35, 186
Hainques, 30
Haja Amina, 109
Haji Ayob, 131
Haji Hosen, 131
Haji Mamod, 124
Hakim, 4, 101, 120, 129, 132
Hakim Idress, 131
hala kapu, 89
hala tam tara, 89
halal, 92, 108, 116
Halau Tamunay ahier, 74
Halau Tamunay awal, 74
Hall, Daniel, 28
Hall, Kenneth, 22
Hàm Nghi, 45
Han, 11, 16, 19, 56, 145
handicraft, 155, 156, 157
Hanoi, 11, 52, 55, 58, 62, 116, 139, 143, 146, 153, 157, 164, 167, 173, 174, 182, 186, 189
Harrell, Stevan, 55, 56, 79, 144, 145, 184
harvest feast, 56

Henmi Yo, 190
Henri Parmentier, 26
heritage, 7, 13, 43, 44, 58, 65, 104, 105, 108, 109, 112, 126, 134, 151, 153, 168, 180
Hickey, Gerald, 49, 51
Hiệp hội Chàm Hồi giáo Việt Nam, 13, 101, 106, 122, 123, 124, 125, 126, 127, 128, 129, 130, 131, 132, 133
High Commission of Peace and Pacification, 126
highland, 23, 24, 25, 37, 42, 44, 45, 46, 47, 48, 51, 53, 163
highland custom, 45
highland ethnic group, 24, 31, 42
highland ethnic minority people, 24, 53
highland minorities, 1, 49, 51, 54, 148, 157
highland minority people, 46, 48, 49
highland minority policy, 49, 55
Highlander, 25, 45, 46, 47, 48, 49, 50, 51, 55
Higuchi Hideo, 36
Hindu Cham, 1, 29
Hindu culture, 2
Hindu heritage, 144
Hindu religion, 19, 21, 26
Hindu tradition, 42, 99
Hinduinization, 19
Hinduism, 1, 2, 20, 21, 26, 72
Hinduist, 29
historicization, 145
Ho Chi Minh City, 4, 38, 53, 56, 57, 61, 62, 63, 65, 66, 70, 71, 108, 110, 113, 114, 116, 118, 119, 128, 131, 139, 146, 153, 156, 157, 160, 163, 165, 174
Ho Chi Minh City Fine Arts University, 165, 168
Ho Chi Minh City Museum of Fine Arts, 168

Ho Chi Minh National Academy of Politics, 60
Hoa, 113, 128, 180
Hoà Hư'ng, 128
Hội An, 27, 32, 159
Hội Đồng Giáo Cả, 130
Hội Mỹ Thật, 162
hon kan, 84, 85, 177
Hong Kong, 6, 108
horticulture, 47
Hosen, 101
Hoskins, Janet, 86
House of Councillors, 12
House of Representatives, 12
Hũ'u Dú'c, 25, 73
Huanwang, 23
Huế, 17, 25, 30, 34, 49, 73, 126, 158
Hui people, 185, 186
husband, 5
huyen, 46
hybrid culture, 37, 41
hygiene, 77, 78, 147
hypothesis, 30
idolater, 27, 33
Ieng Sary, 52
ilimo, 70
image, 7, 17, 41, 46, 124, 138, 144, 154, 162, 164, 165, 166, 167, 168, 171, 172, 173, 182, 183, 189
Imam, 101, 103, 113
Imam Yusof, 131
immigrant, 2, 19, 34
India, 16, 20, 21, 28, 33, 115, 174, 182
Indian, 28, 114, 116
Indian businessman, 101
Indian civilization, 19, 20
Indian colonies, 19
Indian cultural influence, 22
Indian culture, 16, 20, 21
Indian descent, 116
Indian food, 116

Indian history, 20
Indian influence, 20
Indian masjid, 101
Indian merchant, 26
Indian migrant, 19
Indian model, 21
Indian Muslim, 101, 116
Indian political techniques, 20
Indian techniques, 16
Indian-descended Muslim, 116
Indianized countries, 19
Indian-style dance, 139
Indianzation, 19
indigenized Islam, 1
Indochina, 16, 19, 20, 21, 27, 36, 44, 52, 55, 111, 116, 131
Indochinese Peninsula, 16, 41
Indonesia, 11, 21, 112, 115, 152
Indrapura, 17, 30, 35, 73
infrastructure, 10, 16, 45, 47, 108, 188
Inrasara, 98, 168
inscription, 2, 16, 17, 19, 20, 26, 27, 29, 71
Institute of Administration, 126
Institute of Social Sciences, 38
integration, 14, 154, 162
International Islamic Conference of Southeast Asia and the Far East, 129
international Muslim communities, 127, 129, 133
international port, 42
International Voluntary Service, 50
International Women's Club, 157
invented tradition, 13
Irregular Defense Groups (CIDG), 51
irrigation, 176
Ishibashi, 8
Islam, 2, 4, 13, 26, 27, 28, 29, 30, 42, 74, 75, 89, 92, 98, 100, 104, 106, 109, 111, 112, 113, 114, 116, 121, 122, 123, 127, 128, 132, 133, 134, 135, 139, 142, 152, 185
Islam-based Cham ethnicity, 133
Islamic attires, 108
Islamic Center, 4, 110
Islamic ceramic, 27
Islamic education, 126
Islamic *jin*, 119
Islamic law, 130
Islamic tomb stones, 28
Islamization, 29, 30, 90
Ito Masako, 6, 11, 12, 57, 59, 60, 154
Ja Tin, 90
Jacob, 131
Jahnavi, 19
jama'ah Azhar, 110, 111, 129, 132
jama'ah Mubarak, 111, 130
jama'ah Rahim, 115
Jamia al Musulman, 101
Japan, 8, 9, 10, 11, 12, 27, 32, 62, 95, 108, 110, 139, 157, 187, 189, 190
Japan Nuclear Fuel Limited, 188
Japan's Peace Constitution, 9
Japanese, 8, 10, 11, 27, 32, 36, 43, 62, 70, 95, 110, 136, 159, 187, 189
Japanese government, 9, 11, 12
Jarai, 46, 48, 53
Jaspan, Mervyn, 51
Java, 29, 115
Java Kur, 111, 124, 130, 131, 132, 133
jawi, 106
jin, 119
Johor, 33
joke, 147, 149, 152
Jva, 111
Jveas, 27
Jyasmine Tham, 134
Kafir, 95, 150

Kagoshima University, 12
Kainuma Kenji, 188
kajan, 77
kalaih Ramuwan, 94
Kalon, 24
Kampuchea Krom, 48, 51
Kampuchea Krom (KKK), 48
Kampuchea Nord, 51
kampulan qasidah, 139, 142, 152
Kanchi, 20
Kánh Hoa district, 101
Karah, 93
Katambong, 126, 127
Katan, 92
Kate, 25, 154, 168, 169, 170, 171, 180
Kauthara, 17, 32
Kennedy, Laurel, 166
khan djram, 82, 83
Khánh Hòa, 16, 17, 32
Khmer, 36, 47, 48, 49, 50, 51, 57, 64, 108, 110, 111, 128, 134, 143, 185
Khmer Islam, 112, 134
Khmer Krom, 49, 50, 51
Khmer language, 111
Khmer Rouge, 36, 52, 58
Kiernan, Ben, 52
King Narai, 33
King Taksin, 35
Kinh, 13, 30, 31, 36, 37, 38, 39, 40, 41, 42, 46, 47, 50, 51, 55, 56, 59, 63, 64, 68, 70, 71, 73, 79, 106, 112, 113, 114, 121, 128, 129, 136, 137, 138, 145, 147, 148, 149, 150, 151, 152, 154, 155, 156, 157, 158, 159, 165, 167, 168, 170, 171, 172, 180, 182
Kinh artist, 165, 167
Kinh culture, 45, 79, 138, 158
Kinh ethnic group, 79, 112
Kinh majority, 13, 45, 47, 171, 185

Kinh Muslim, 128
Kinh painter, 170
Kinh scholar, 71
klam, 80
Klang Kôi Kubao, 57
klong, 91
Kobe University, 8
Kodi, 86
Koho, 25, 48, 155, 156
Korea, 108
Krek tree, 24
Kuala Lumpur, 7
kut, 76
Kyoto University, 11, 12
Labrie, Norman, 47, 51, 54
Lafont, Pierre, 75
Lafu people, 151
land ownership, 49
language, 1, 6, 35, 44, 47, 49, 58, 60, 61, 71, 77, 79, 87, 104, 111, 115, 134, 136, 141, 145, 155, 177, 184
language class, 125
Laos, 36, 51, 144
law court, 45, 47, 49
Law of Ethnic Groups, 59, 60
Lê dynasty, 32, 37, 139
Lê Hồng Phong High School, 126
Lê Thánh Tông, 32, 38
Lê Văn Khôi, 34
Leach, Edmund, 6
Leclère, 29
Legafashion, 157
legend, 24, 69, 73, 80, 81, 174
Leopold Sabatier, 45
Les Kosem, 49
Li Tana, 31, 185
Liangshan, 79
Liberal Democratic Party (LDP), 10
Lieutenant Colonel, 49
life cycle, 91
lineage, 24, 69, 76, 92, 103, 107, 173, 177

Lingling-o, 14
Linyi, 16, 17, 23
Linyu gaku, 139
literature, 17, 70
local scholar, 21, 68, 70, 71, 73, 81
Lockhart, Bruce, 36, 37, 38, 41
Lon Nol, 49
Lon Non, 49
Long An, 127
Long Xuyên, 63
loom, 157
Lower Diet, 8, 10
lowland, 1, 23, 46, 47, 54, 55
lowland Cham, 1, 25
Lý Nhân Tông, 139
Lý Thái Tông, 139
lycée, 49, 70
lyric poetry, 98
Ma Delta, 40
Mã Thành Lâm, 101
Madras, 116
madrasah, 129
magic, 61, 81, 120, 121, 131
Mahamad Ally, 101
Mahayana Buddhism, 26
Mahot, 30
Maideen, 101
majority, 13, 42, 47, 50, 59, 64, 109, 115, 116, 125, 137, 138, 144, 145, 147, 152, 154, 155, 162, 165, 168, 171, 172, 182, 190
majority Kinh, 13, 42, 152
Majumdar, Ramesh Chandra, 19
Mak Phoen, 35
Makassar, 33
Malacca, 30, 33
malaria, 48
Malay, 30, 108, 111, 112, 115, 124, 130, 134, 140, 152
Malay colonies, 30
Malay immigration, 26
Malay Muslim, 29, 131
Malay Peninsula, 90

Malay people, 33, 124
Malay world, 27, 29, 90
Malay-Indonesian-descended Muslim, 116
Malayo-Polynesian, 1, 25, 45
Malaysia, 4, 7, 11, 32, 36, 108, 109, 110, 115, 123, 129, 131, 132, 134, 142
mandala, 16, 17, 18, 19, 21, 23, 42
mandala overlord, 17, 21
Mandarin system, 40
March 11, 2011, 7, 8
maritime trade, 24, 31, 32, 33, 42
Marr, David, 37
marriage, 5, 39, 41, 42, 56, 75, 77, 81, 112, 113, 114, 121, 131, 168
Marxist, 6, 38, 39, 80, 162
masjid, 4, 92, 111, 119, 124, 131
Masjid Azhar, 109
Masjid Catinat, 101, 116
Masjid Jamia Al Muslimin, 116
masjid Musulman Jamia Al Muslimin, 131
Masjidir Rahim, 114, 115
Maspero, Georges, 16, 28
matay ea, 118
matriarchal, 39
matrilineal, 1, 39, 69, 75, 107, 114, 176, 185
matrilocal, 39, 69, 107, 185
Mayavaram, 116
McElwee, Pamela, 66
Mecca, 4, 29, 56, 57, 109, 129, 154, 187
Meiji period, 136
Mekong Delta, 1, 4, 5, 13, 32, 40, 42, 48, 61, 63, 100, 101, 102, 104, 105, 106, 107, 108, 109, 110, 111, 112, 114, 115, 117, 120, 121, 122, 124, 126, 130, 132, 133, 134, 137, 139, 142, 150, 151, 157, 165
meltdown, 8, 9, 10

Metropolitan Coalition against Nukes, 11
Miao, 134
Michigan State University, 127
Middle East, 26, 29, 142
migration, 38, 42, 134, 154
military service, 23, 127, 128
Minh Mạng, 34
Minh Mỹ, 101
Ministry of Culture, Sports and Tourism, 60, 173, 180
Ministry of Defense, 49, 54
Ministry of Development of Ethnic Minorities (MDEM), 50, 51, 53, 54, 123, 128
Ministry of Education, 60
Ministry of Finance, 126
Ministry of Foreign Affairs, 62
Ministry of Health, 60
Ministry of Interior, 54, 60, 62, 63, 126
Ministry of Open Arms and Revolutionary Development, 54
minority culture, 56, 59, 137, 138, 153, 154, 160, 161
minority language, 58
minority policy, 13, 44, 47, 54, 55, 56, 57, 59, 66, 71
minority weaving, 156, 158
minzoku, 136
Mnong, 49
Mnong Gar, 47
Moerman, Michael, 6
Momoki Shiro, 16, 30, 33
money exchange, 116
Mongol invasion, 37, 41
Mon-Khmer, 44
monolithic, 7
monopoly, 65
Monsoon culture, 21
Montagnard Foundation, Inc, 52
Moor, 30
Morgan, Lewis, 39

Moura, Jean, 28
Mousa Misky, 132
Moussay, Gérard, 50, 179
Mr. Ty, 70
Mubarak, 111, 130, 131
muda, 130, 131, 132
Mufti, 101, 109, 130, 132
Mufti Umar Aly, 101
muk kay, 103
Muk Poh, 93, 95
Muk Rija, 177
Mukerji, Chandra, 154
multi-cropping garden farmer, 31
Mus, Paul, 21
music, 31, 37, 62, 139, 140
music band, 140
musician, 90, 97, 139, 168, 170, 171, 177
Muslim, 4, 13, 26, 27, 28, 29, 33, 35, 36, 49, 52, 57, 95, 100, 101, 102, 108, 109, 111, 112, 113, 114, 115, 116, 117, 119, 122, 127, 128, 130, 131, 132, 133, 134, 141, 142, 146, 186
Muslim Cham, 5, 13, 29, 35, 49, 56, 100, 101, 102, 104, 106, 108, 109, 110, 113, 117, 119, 121, 122, 123, 124, 126, 127, 128, 130, 131, 132, 134, 142, 146, 150, 154, 179, 186
Muslim community, 27, 28, 57, 109, 115, 116, 122, 129, 130, 132, 133
Muslim merchant, 27, 28, 33, 111, 115, 116
Muslim minority, 182
Mỹ Nghiệp, 156, 157, 165
Mỹ So'n, 7, 158
myth, 9, 136, 187
Nancy, 124, 125, 126
Nara period, 139
National Assembly, 59, 144
national defense, 162, 163

national ethnic group, 37, 60
National Liberation Front (NLF), 47
national library, 126
national museum, 167
national security, 9, 10
national unity, 41, 50, 162
nationalities, 6
nation-state, 7, 13, 17, 136
Nay Luett, 53
Nepal, 26
Ner, Marcel, 116, 128
New Life Hamlet, 48
Ngô Đình Diệm, 47, 48, 123, 129
Ngô Đình Diệm, 124
Ngôn Vĩnh, 50
Nguyễn Cao Kỳ, 127
Nguyễn Công Văn, 170, 171
Nguyễn Hồng Du'o'ng, 124, 130, 131
Nguyễn Khắc Viện, 37, 40, 41
Nguyễn Khánh, 49
Nguyễn lord, 31, 32, 34
Nguyễn Phúc Ánh, 34
Nguyễn Tấn Dũng, 10
Nguyễn Thị Minh Khai street, 113
Nguyễn Vân Đài, 68
Nguyễn Văn Linh, 153
Nguyễn Văn Luận, 123, 125, 129, 130, 132
Nguyễn Văn Thiệu, 53
Nguyễn Xuân Diện, 11
Nha Trang, 116
Nho Lâm, 101
Ninh Thuận, 2, 3, 4, 5, 10, 12, 13, 17, 21, 53, 56, 57, 58, 61, 62, 64, 65, 66, 68, 69, 70, 77, 79, 89, 99, 100, 101, 102, 103, 104, 106, 108, 120, 121, 155, 165, 168, 170, 173, 174, 176, 180, 189
Nishimoto Yoichi, 151
Nishimura Masanari, 43
non-Islamic belief, 122, 133
non-Islamic *jin*, 119, 120
non-Islamic religious practice, 114
non-Orthodox Islamic belief, 117
North Carolina, 25, 52
North Korea, 143
northeast India, 26
northern highland ethnic minority refugee, 50
Northern Sung dynasty, 28
Notice No. 3 of the Central Politburo on policies toward the Cham ethnic group, 57, 59, 153, 154
nuclear accident, 190
nuclear bomb, 9
nuclear businesses, 11
nuclear energy, 9, 10, 11, 187
nuclear plant technology, 189
nuclear power, 9, 10, 11, 12, 189, 190
nuclear reactor, 8, 9, 10, 187, 188, 189
nuclear reactor addiction, 188
nuclear technology, 9, 11, 190
nuclear village, 188
nuclear waste, 11, 188
nuclear weapon, 9
Nugyễn court, 24
O'Connor, Richard, 31
offering, 77, 78, 81, 89, 93, 176, 180
Office for Scientific Research and International Cooperation, 63
Office of Culture and Information, 57, 59, 62, 64, 65, 66
Office of Religion, 66
Okinawa, 189
Onagawa nuclear plant, 8
Ông Bài Mốt, 124
Ong Guru, 93, 94
Ong Kaing, 168, 170
Ong Kathar, 169, 170, 175
Ong Muthon, 177

oral tradition, 70, 89
Orientalist, 70
Orthodox Islam, 66, 100, 101, 102, 103, 104, 117, 122, 134
Orthodox Muslim, 100, 102, 103, 104
Ou Lien, 16
padang, 97, 98
Pakistan, 115
Palei Bingu, 21, 73
Palei Rio, 21, 73
Panduranga, 2, 17, 27, 29, 32, 34, 35, 73, 189
Pang, Keng-Fong, 35, 186
Paris Foreign Missions Society, 30
patri, 19, 117, 118
patrimonial bureaucracy, 19
Paul Nur, 50
Pays Montagnard du Sud, 46, 128
People's Committee, 40, 61, 63, 66, 137
People's Republic of China (PRC), 36, 52, 55, 79, 134, 143, 144, 182, 185
Perkins, Teresa, 147
Persian, 26, 27, 28
petition, 4, 12
Petrus Ký high school, 126
Phan Đăng Nhật, 173, 174
Phan Lạc Tuyên, 40
Phan Rang, 5, 10, 25, 27, 35, 38, 40, 50, 53, 59, 61, 69, 109, 110, 121, 149, 168, 171, 180
Phan Ri, 38, 101
Phan Thị Yến Tuyết, 107, 139
Phan Xuân Biên, 39
Philippines, 11, 14, 16, 32
Phnom Penh, 49, 52
photo journalist, 36
Phú Nhuận, 4, 77, 101
Phú Yên, 4, 32, 138
Phu'ó'c Đồng, 90

Phu'óc Nho'n, 69, 74, 76, 94, 101, 102, 103
Phum Soai, 49
pilgrimage, 4, 29, 56, 109, 129, 153, 154, 187
pillar, 106, 117, 118
piracy, 22, 109, 123
Pleiku, 49, 50
plutonium, 9, 188
Po Alwah, 74, 89, 92, 96, 97, 99, 100, 150
Po Alwah Hu, 99, 100
Po Dharma, 1, 7, 17, 33, 34, 53, 89, 90
Po Gelong Gahoul, 25
Po Inu Nugar, 25, 74, 90, 99, 100
Po Klong Garai, 74, 78, 84, 134, 143, 167, 170, 173, 180
Po Klong High School, 53, 56, 173, 179
Po Klong Khuan, 38
Po Ku, 99, 100
Po Nubi, 80, 89, 97
Po Nubi Atam, 89
Po Nubi Eta, 89
Po Nubi Ichbrahim, 81
Po Nubi Mohamat, 80, 90, 99, 100
Po Nubi Mota, 89
Po Rame, 24, 29, 74, 175
Po Yang, 72, 74
Poix Sea, 27
Pol Pot, 36, 52, 120
police, 53, 128
Politburo of the Communist Party, 60
Politburo Resolution Five, 153
polyandry, 39
polygamy, 129
Pompeii, 43
Pondicherry, 116
population, 2
port-city, 16
Portuguese, 29

pre-Chamic, 2
pre-reunification, 10, 44
Prime Minister Naoto Kan, 10
Prime Minister Yasuhiko Noda, 10
privacy, 12
pro-American Highlander, 51
propaganda, 54
Prophet, 27, 131
Prophet Mohammed's birthday, 110
proselytization, 56, 101, 103
proselytizing Islam, 101
proto-Chamic, 35
psychological composition, 56
Pu, 27
pura, 17, 20, 22, 23, 73
pure culture, 70
Python God movement, 46
Quảng Bình, 17, 30
Quảng Nam-Đà Nẵng, 17
Quảng Ngãi, 17, 32
Quảng Trị, 17, 30, 126
Queen Bia Thanh Chi, 175
Quinn-Judge, Paul, 52
Qur'an, 4, 56, 57, 81, 104, 109, 111, 115, 119, 120, 121, 122, 129
Qur'an reading competitions, 4, 129
race, 75, 136, 186
radiation, 187, 189
Raglay, 25
rain, 175, 176
rakat, 131
Ramadan, 92, 104
Ramuwan, 92, 93
rap, 90
rapport, 12
Ravaisse, Paul, 27, 28
rebellion, 16, 22
rebirth, 90, 91
Red River, 31, 40
red seal ships, 32
refugee, 1, 29, 30, 35, 36, 47, 135
Reid, Anthony, 28
relay port, 2

religious belief, 41
religious dance, 144
religious group, 1, 105
religious leader, 4, 20, 28, 30, 120, 121, 127, 129, 131, 132
religious pantheon, 89
relocation, 48
Republic of Vietnam, 47
research, 5
resettlement, 48
reunification, 2, 44, 52, 55, 103, 152, 154, 180
Rhade, 24, 48
rice, 32, 91, 93, 99, 161, 176
rice cultivation, 14
rice field, 24, 56, 68, 180
ridicul, 147, 148, 149, 151, 152
Rih Nan, 16
Rija prong, 89, 177, 178, 179
ritual dancer, 173
ritual musician, 97, 175
riverine center, 22
riverine exchange, 22
riverine system, 22, 23
river-mouth urban centers, 22
Rokkasho village, 188
Royal Chronicles of Champa, 17
royal court dance, 139, 143, 144, 159
Royal Khmer Army, 49
rubber, 46
Rue Catinat, 101
Russian, 10
Sa Hùynh, 14, 16
sacrifice, 12, 57, 99, 162, 187, 189, 190
Sài Gòn Giải Phóng, 52
Said, Edward, 70
Saigon, 42, 47, 49, 51, 54, 55, 101, 102, 114, 115, 122, 123, 124, 126, 127, 128, 132, 173, 179
Sakurai, Yumio, 16
Salemink, Oscar, 51

salmonella, 48
Sanskrit, 16, 69
Sarazin, 30
sati, 99
Saudi Arabia, 129
Sayid Mustafa, 109
Saykhol Islam, 129, 130
Scarborough, Jay, 50
Scott, James, 148, 151
sculpture, 31, 144, 159, 165, 175
Scupin, Raymond, 26, 27, 35
sea-oriented, 1, 14
Seattle, 1
secession, 54
Second Indochina War, 47, 122
second-hand clothing, 108
secular education, 133
Seih es-Sug, 28
self-conscious identity, 136
self-determination, 44
self-empowerment, 125, 126, 133
self-identity, 6
Sendai plain, 8
shaman, 81, 97, 99, 110, 120
Shi'ia, 27
Shils, Edward, 184
Shin-e Toshihiko, 2, 10, 24, 33, 53
Shinzo Abe, 10
shuinsen, 32
Siam, 45
Siamese, 45
SIDA, 108
signifier, 168
Sihanouk, Norodom, 134
Sinhapura, 27
Sino-Tibetan, 6
Siva dance, 143
Siva statue, 143
Siva-worshipping, 143
slash-and-burn, 45, 47
Smith, Monica, 20
socialism, 44, 55, 57
socialist, 44, 55, 56, 79, 179

socialist culture, 57
Socialist Realism, 162
Socialist Republic of Vietnam, 14, 55, 180
solidarity, 40, 41, 47, 50, 51, 57, 67, 132, 163, 168
sorcery, 121, 129
South China Sea, 2, 14, 26, 30, 31
South Vietnam, 10, 13, 42, 44, 47, 49, 50, 51, 53, 54, 115, 127, 129, 150, 173, 184
South Vietnam's premier's office, 126
south-central coast area, 2, 5, 13, 29, 68, 69, 101, 105, 106, 107, 110, 114, 119, 120, 121, 133, 137, 141, 142, 152, 157
Southeast Asia, 2, 11, 16, 17, 18, 19, 20, 26, 27, 28, 29, 30, 31, 33, 35, 40, 41, 66, 86, 141, 144
Southeast Asian archipelago, 16
Southeast Asian Studies, 12, 63
southern India, 20, 116
southward expansion (*nam tiến*), 14, 30, 31, 36, 38, 185
Southworth, William, 22
Spanish navy, 33
spirit, 19, 21, 97, 117, 120, 125, 131
Spivak, Gayatri, 183
Sre, 45
Sri Mara, 16
Srivijaya, 2
Stalin, Joseph, 6, 136
Standing Committee of the National Assembly, 60
state discourse, 184
state vocabularies, 183
stereotypes, 147, 148, 151, 152
Strategic Hamlet, 48
sub-group, 4, 111, 133, 137
Sufi mystic, 28
Sufism, 28, 117
sugar cane, 43, 73

Sugimoto Naojiro, 19, 20
suicide, 119
Sulawesi, 138
Sumatra, 2, 35
Sunni Islam, 75, 101, 102, 103
Sunni Muslim, 1, 4, 106
superstition, 59, 79, 104, 117, 120, 180
survival, 13, 40
survival tale, 150
swing, 177
Sỹ Hoang, 165
syariah, 130
symbolic vocabularies, 13, 155
symbolism, 86, 96, 173, 176, 177
sympathizer, 102
Syndic, 28
Taiwan, 6, 14, 108, 185
Takahashi Tetsuya, 189
talang, 91
talisman, 121
Tamil Nadu, 20, 116
tana, 120
Tang dynasty, 27, 31, 41
Tăng Khạo Mat, 129
tanuh riya, 80
Tarawat prayer, 131
Tasaka Kodo, 27, 186
tax, 24, 45, 46
taxation, 23, 45
Tây Ninh, 4, 48
Tây So'n, 34, 39
Taylor, Keith, 185
technology, 11, 190
telecom, 108
terracotta sculpture, 171, 172, 174
territory, 6
textile, 108, 116, 154, 155, 156, 157, 158, 159, 171, 180
Thailand, 11, 27, 33, 35, 36, 109, 131, 144, 151
Thăng Long,, 31
thang muki, 74, 75, 92, 93, 150

Thành Cha, 43
Thanh Hóa, 40
Thành Phần, 70
the 6th Congress, 57
the 7th Congress, 57
the Central Highlands minority people's revolts, 53
The General History of Vietnam, 38
Thế Giới, 126
The Highlander Issue in Vietnam, 49
Thò'i Trang, 158
three non-nuclear principles, 9
Thủ hiến Nam Việt, 126
Thừa Thiên Huế, 17
Thuận Hải, 2, 38, 174
Thuận Thành, 34
Thurgood, Graham, 35, 186
Tibet, 6, 26
Tohoku Electric Power Company, 8
Tokyo Electric Power Company (TEPCO), 8
tomb, 75
Tổng Hội Hồi Giáo Việt Nam, 128
Toraja, 138
tourist, 7
tourist industries, 182
Trà Kiệu, 2, 15, 27
Trà Toàn, 38
Trà Vinh, 51
trade, 2, 10, 19, 20, 22, 27, 28, 29, 30, 32, 33
trading port, 32
tradition, 28, 34, 45, 57, 59, 60, 68, 77, 79, 96, 97, 98, 103, 105, 115, 122, 139, 155, 158, 169, 181
Trần Kỳ Phu'o'ng,, 171
Trân Quang Tấu, 126
Trần Quốc Vượng, 31
Trengganu, 130
tributary relationship, 23
Tru'ò'ng So'n mountains, 17

Truong Van Mon, 177
tsunami, 8, 9, 187
Tu Wei-Ming, 6
Tù' Công Xuân, 101, 128
tua, 130, 131, 132
tualak, 118, 119
tudung, 108
Tuon Haji Umar Ali, 109
turban, 1, 82, 84, 181
Turkey, 189
two realms, 81
ulama, 130
Umar Aly, 101, 129, 130
Umayyads, 27
UNESCO, 7
UNICEF, 40
Union of Soviet Socialist Republics (USSR), 10, 59, 143
Unitd Kingdom (UK), 189
United Arab Emirates, 32
United Nations (UN), 52, 108
United States of America (USA), 1, 2, 9, 10, 52, 108, 123, 127, 134
United Struggle Front for the Oppressed Races (FULRO), 25, 44, 48, 49, 50, 51, 52, 53, 58, 126, 156
unity, 5
University of Chicago, 127
University of Fine Arts, 163, 174
University of Ho Chi Minh City, 61
University of Kansas, 127
University of Malaya, 7, 27
University of Washington,, 1
upland Cham, 1
uprising, 52, 60, 154
upstream, 22, 23, 24
uranium, 9, 188
US military base, 189, 190
Utsat, 35, 186
Vajrayana, 26
Văn Lâm, 21, 101, 102, 103, 128

văn nghệ, 137, 138, 139, 143, 145, 146, 147
vassal, 17, 19, 21
Vedic Hindu tradition, 20
vestige, 2, 7, 23, 39, 134, 144, 151, 154, 180
Vickery, Michael, 17
Viet Minh, 21, 37, 47
Vietnamese Annals, 33
Vietnamese art, 162, 163, 168
Vietnamese Communist, 12, 58
Vietnamese Communist Party, 51, 58
Vietnamese culture, 31, 71, 79, 160
Vietnamese history, 12, 37, 151, 154
Vietnamese language, 61, 115, 125, 142
Vietnamese Muslim, 115, 116
Vietnamese princess, 24, 30
Vietnamese scholar, 36, 39, 139
Vijaya, 17, 28, 29, 32, 33, 35, 37, 38
Võ Cạnh, 16
vocalist, 139
Volk, Nancy, 55
walai, 102
warrior, 29
wedding, 21, 62, 80, 89, 107
welfare, 12, 66
wet-rice, 31, 45, 68, 73, 108
White Thai, 186
Williams, Brakette, 7
Williams, Mary, 166
witchcraft, 121
Wolters, Oliver, 17, 19, 22, 23
World War I, 9, 46
World War II, 9
writing system, 58, 60, 105, 106
Xiang Li, 16
Yamagata Mariko, 16
Yamato, 188
yang, 81, 86
Yang Prong, 23
Yi people, 79

yin, 73, 81, 86
yin-yang, 81
Yokokura Masayuki, 16

Zain bin Musa, 111, 131, 134
Zhancheng, 17, 23